KINAALDÁ

KINAALDÁ

A Study of the Navaho Girl's

Puberty Ceremony

By

CHARLOTTE JOHNSON FRISBIE

University of Utah Press
Salt Lake City

Published 1967 Wesleyan University Press
Rights now held by author
Preface to 1993 edition © copyright 1993 University of Utah Press
All rights reserved

Printed on acid-free paper

Library of Congress Cataloging-in-Publication Data

Frisbie, Charlotte Johnson.
    Kinaaldá : a study of the Navaho girl's puberty ceremony /
Charlotte Johnson Frisbie.
        p.   cm.
    Originally published: Middletown, Conn. : Wesleyan University
Press, 1967. With new pref.
    Revision of master's thesis—Wesleyan University.
    Includes bibliographical references (p.   ) and index.
    ISBN 0-87480-422-1 (pbk. : acid-free paper)
    1. Kinaaldá (Navajo rite) 2. Navajo Indians—Women. 3. Navajo
Indians—Rites and ceremonies. 4. Puberty rites—Southwest, New.
I. Title.
E99.N3F84   1993
299'.74—dc20   93-3341
                                                     CIP

To my parents,
whose love and understanding
made all things possible

Contents

Illustrations

CHARTS

Preface

THIS report is based on field studies conducted during the summers of 1963 and 1964 on the Navaho Reservation in Arizona. The project, an investigation of the Navaho Girl's Puberty Ceremony, or the Kinaaldá, was supported by a National Science Foundation grant, GS-144, as part of a study of Navaho ceremonialism under the direction of Dr. David P. McAllester of Wesleyan University, Middletown, Connecticut.

The study is based on my own field notes, those of Dr. David McAllester, Anne Brown Keith (an anthropology major in the class of 1964 at Radcliffe), and the following workers of the Ramah Project: Flora Bailey, Clyde Kluckhohn, Alexander Leighton, Dorothea Leighton, Robert Rapoport, Janine Chappat Rosenzweig, and Evon Z. Vogt. I am indebted to Dr. McAllester and Anne Keith for access to their unpublished field notes and tapes and for permission to include some of their material in this work. I am also grateful to Dr. McAllester for access to other collections in the Laboratory of Ethnomusicology at Wesleyan University. I wish to thank Dr. Benjamin Colby, of the Laboratory of Anthropology, Santa Fe, New Mexico, for access to the notes of the Ramah Project. Thanks are also due Dr. Evon Z. Vogt, of Harvard University, for permission to quote from these notes.

I am also grateful to the late Dr. Kenneth Foster, of the Museum of Navajo Ceremonial Art in Santa Fe, New Mexico, for use of the Museum's research facilities and permission to include a transcription done by Dr. George Herzog of a Kinaaldá Racing Song. Thanks are also due Dr. J. O. Brew of Harvard University, for permission to use Haile and Wheelwright materials from the Museum's files.

I also wish to thank Dr. Francis Cancian, of Stanford University, for permission to quote from his unpublished B.A. thesis. To the following publishers and foundations I am indebted for permission to quote copyrighted material: Harvard University Press, Bollingen Foundation, J. J. Augustin, Inc., Franciscan Fathers of St. Michaels Press, Free Press of Glencoe, The Macmillan Company, and Faber and Faber, Ltd.

To the many Navaho who helped me with this project, I wish to include a special word of thanks. Particular mention should be made of my chief informant, Frank Mitchell, his family, my interpreter, Albert ("Chic") Sandoval, his wife, and some of the many singers with whom I worked—Blue Mule, Charlie Watchman, Walter Davis, and Totsoni Mark.

To the numerous faculty members of Wesleyan University, the University of New Mexico, and elsewhere who gave me their support and confidence through the years while this project was being completed I offer sincere thanks: to Professor Richard Winslow, of Wesleyan, for his encouragement; to Dr. Leland Wyman, of Boston University, for his advice; to Dr. Willard Rhodes, of Columbia University, for his interest and sensitive evaluation; and to Dr. W. W. Hill, Dr. Stanley Newman, and Dr. Harry Basehart, of the University of New Mexico, for their time, interest, helpful criticisms, and numerous suggestions. To Mrs. William Langer of Wesleyan University, who typed the manuscript when it was in its Master's thesis stage, I am also deeply indebted.

My greatest thanks go to Dr. David McAllester, who for two years deeply stimulated my interest in the American Indian and unselfishly gave of his time to train me in Navaho studies. It is he who gave me the opportunity to do this research, and it is he who with patience, humor, and true perception gave me the support necessary for the completion of this project.

Finally, I wish to thank my husband, Ted, who shared much of the work involved in transforming *Kinaaldá* from a Master's thesis into its current form. He was a source of constant encouragement and, at many times, my best critic. Many of his suggestions have been incorporated into the revisions which have been made.

CHARLOTTE JOHNSON FRISBIE

University of New Mexico
September 1, 1966

Preface to the 1993 Edition

ALMOST thirty years have passed since I began my study of the Navajo girl's puberty ceremony, or Kinaaldá, which resulted in the original edition of this work. Since then, I have continued to study Navajo culture, returning to the Southwest as often as teaching and other responsibilities in Illinois permitted. During these years, I have had the good fortune to receive invitations to participate in a number of Kinaaldá in a variety of reservation communities; these opportunities have allowed me at least to stay in touch with the ceremony. On the basis of these personal experiences and observations, I can now say that my earlier predictions (see p. 392) of a healthy future for the ceremony have proven correct. Moreover, Navajos themselves have also commented on the continuing vitality and importance of the ceremony; see, for example, R. Roessel (1981), Begay (1983), and M. Roessel (1991).

If I had the opportunity to do a study of Kinaaldá today for the first time, the end results would undoubtedly be different. Sensitivities have changed, as have political issues, self-determination concerns, and a number of other matters. I, too, have changed as an anthropologist; I am much more interested in action anthropology and in facilitating, enhancing, or otherwise increasing the sound of native peoples' voices speaking for themselves about issues that concern them. Self-determination includes telling one's own stories, as well as the choice of sharing them. If Frank Mitchell (1978) were alive today, I suspect he would still want his ceremonial knowledge recorded and this study published as one of the ways to address his concerns about preserving that knowledge. His children have had time to discuss the idea of a new edition, and are supportive of making available once again a work that has been out of print for over twenty years. But how some Navajos would react to such a study, if published for the first time today, is not clear; in some places there exist strong sentiments against publishing anything associated with ceremonial beliefs and practices. For this and other reasons, approval for reprinting the volume was obtained from the Navajo Nation's Historic Preservation Department, which is now responsible for evaluating all applications for ethnographic and archaeological research on the reservation and issuing permits for accepted projects. So, my thanks go to Jeff Grathwohl of the University of Utah Press and a number of other individuals, both Navajos and non-Navajos, for making a reprint edition possible.

Since reprinting is essentially that, only minimal changes can be made beyond the insertion of a new Preface. Two changes I would choose to make are not possible: a conversion of the orthography into the now-standard Young and Morgan system and a correction in the spelling of "Navajo" in accordance with tribal preference announced in an April 1969 Tribal Council resolution.

Additional literature about Kinaaldá and issues related to the ceremony has appeared since the 1967 study. Of major importance are some Navajo-authored works, published through the Rough Rock Demonstration School, which expand the number of versions of the Kinaaldá texts available in print, while sometimes also contributing to published discussions of the ceremony. For example, Shirley M. Begay's (1983) *Kinaaldá: A Navajo Puberty Ceremony* is a richly illustrated, bilingual account which includes both text (pp. 1–9) and personal experience (pp. 41–169). Another version of the Kinaaldá texts (pp. 22–25, 66–68) is available in Roger Hathale's (1986) bilingual *Hózhǫ́ǫ́jí Hane' (Blessingway)*. Ruth Roessel's (1981) *Women in Navajo Society* includes comments on the ceremony as well as a photographic presentation (pp. 83–99) of her oldest daughter's Kinaaldá.

Several other Navajo-authored works should also be mentioned. Puberty ceremonies continue to interest readers of more popular publications, such as *New Mexico Magazine* and *Native Peoples*. The Navajo Kinaaldá and its equivalent among various groups of Apaches still attract photographers, and the photo of a girl undergoing a puberty ceremony often appears on the cover of a magazine that has an accompanying article with more photographs. For example, Monty Roessel, a Navajo, contributed an article with photographs on Kinaaldá to the Native American issue of *New Mexico Magazine* in August 1991. The Mescalero Apache ceremony was featured earlier in the same magazine in an article coauthored by anthropologist Claire Farrer and the late Bernard Second (1989), a Mescalero Apache singer. The White Mountain Apache equivalent was described, with photographs, by Anna Early Goseyun, a White Mountain Apache tribal juvenile judge, in the summer 1991 issue of *Native Peoples*.

In addition to writing popular articles, Navajos have also contributed, since 1967, to discussions of some of the questions long addressed by outsider anthropologists, especially those concerned with classifications of Navajo ceremonies and explanations of their development. Here, the colored charts designed by Eddie Tso and Lloyd Thompson (1984, 1985) deserve mention, as do the ideas of Harry Walters (1990). Based on work with elders and ceremonialists, Walters (1990:48) explicated the development of Blessingway and suggested four versions of the ceremony which emerged at different times in Navajo history. The girl's puberty ceremony, or Kinaaldá, is the first one in his scheme and is considered the "original Blessingway."

Supplemental information published by non-Navajos relevant to understanding Kinaaldá has also emerged since 1967. Wyman's (1970) *Blessingway* provides a basic source for texts and practices of the Blessingway and its derivative ceremonies, such as Kinaaldá. Community studies, namely those by Shepardson and Hammond (1970) and Lamphere (1977), include data on Kinaaldá. The ethnomusicological literature contains discussions of several issues I raised in the original study, such as vocables (see also Frisbie 1980) and Corn Grinding songs, which are now viewed as popular, traditional songs that are sung outside the Kinaaldá context and are available on commercial recordings (see Frisbie 1977). For those interested in Native American foods, recipes (see this volume, pp. 411-12) for *'alkaan,* the cake baked in the ground during the final night of a Kinaaldá, are now available in Navajo cookbooks (see Navajo Curriculum Center 1986:9).

The literature on Navajo women has also grown since 1967. While this has been most dramatic in the areas of ethnicity and gender, some more traditional, biographical work continues to be published; the life history of Irene Stewart (1980), and the biographical information on Annie Dodge Wauneka, both in the Hoffman and Johnson (1970:292-307) collection and in Nelson (1972) are examples. Griffen's current work as editor of the Leighton and Leighton collection hopefully will lead to the emergence of the women's life histories included in the collection; *Lucky, the Navajo Singer* (Leighton and Leighton 1992) is the first of the men's documents to emerge from that source. My work on the life history of Tall Woman, Rose Mitchell, is also in progress.

Other information on Navajo women reflective of current research trends can now be found in a variety of places. In addition to R. Roessel (1981) and Begay (1983) mentioned above, there are the dissertations by Edith Harrison (1973), Christine Conte (1984), and Karen Ritts (1989), works by Lamphere (1974) and Wright (1981), and the nine articles (Frisbie 1982, D. Leighton 1982, Wright 1982, Metcalf 1982, Griffen 1982, Conte 1982, Parezo 1982, Shepardson 1982, and Joe 1982) derived from a session on "Women in Conti-

nuity and Change: The Navajo Example'' at the 1981 American Anthropological Association meetings and published in *American Indian Quarterly* 6 (1 &
2), 1982. There are also papers on the Navajo family by Joe (1988) and
Hauswald (1988), Lamphere's work (1989) on Navajo women's roles, my
work (1989) on the relationship of gender and Navajo music, Harris's work
(1990) on ethnicity and gender, and Hedlund's ongoing (1985) work with
Navajo grandmothers. Then, too, a description of a Navajo medicine woman is
included in the Native American medicine women's section of Perrone,
Stockel, and Krueger (1989:29–44), and a discussion of women and men in
Navajo ceremonialism is included in Faris and Walters (1990:4–6).

On the reservation, women's issues and concerns have led to the development of interest groups, task forces, and public symposia. R. Roessel
(1981:133) mentions the Navajo Women's Association and its concerns; at
present, as publicized in the *Navajo Times* (see Benson 1992), the Navajo
Women's Commission (initiated in 1983 and recently reactivated) is sponsor-
ing public hearings where people discuss abuse, domestic violence, crime,
sexual harassment, incest, rape, and many other issues of concern to today's
women.

Since no ceremonial beliefs and practices are static or exist in a vacuum,
so, too, the Kinaaldá has continued to change, in response to wagework eco-
nomics and other factors. Unlike some ceremonies, however, whose goals
have been subsumed under, fused with, or replaced by practices/beliefs of
outside mainstream religions, the Native American Church, the Church of
Jesus Christ of Latter-day Saints, or one or more of the versions of evangeli-
cal Protestantism (see Frisbie 1992), I have yet to see the vitality of Kinaaldá
threatened. Despite the multiple religious options available to today's Navajos and the characteristic multiple religious affiliations, I know of no mainline
or expanding religions on the reservation that have developed an alternative
way of celebrating a Navajo girl's puberty. Perhaps an explanation lies in the
basic cultural perceptions of female pubescence and its worth, and perhaps
this attitudinal difference, itself, actually protects the ceremony and helps
ensure its enduring viability.

As noted in the original study reprinted here, the changes that I have continued to witness in Kinaaldá over time are more procedural than functional.
Some of these concern length. Most of the Kinaaldá I have witnessed or participated in since the middle 1970s were scheduled so that the *bijí*, or all-night
sing, was held on a Saturday night. Weekends, now, are the times when many
people are not at work and thus available to help with the labor involved in
ceremonies and are able to participate and, therefore, receive the blessings of
the ceremony. If a Kinaaldá occurs in the summertime, care is usually taken to

schedule it so as not to conflict with other local ceremonies, especially Ene-
myways, which are apt to attract large crowds.

Apparently, in some places, the ceremony has been shortened from the
original four days to two days, in response to girls' school schedules (M.
Roessel 1991:90). Earlier (this volume, p. 83, 385), I noted that school
attendance could cause postponement of the ceremony in some areas, and I
also included an example of one ceremony shortened to three days because of
school.

It is not uncommon now, at least in certain parts of the reservation, for the
singer to arrive near sundown on the *biji̧*, rather than on the first day, to sing
appropriate songs during the initial combing, dressing, and racing. While the
role of the "ideal woman" remains essentially the same, it is now possible, at
least according to some, for a non-Navajo to be asked to serve in this role, if
that's what the sponsors want to do. The respect for individualism has not
lessened and details continue to be "up to her," "up to him," "up to them."
Female ceremonial practitioners, or medicine women, are more apparent
now, at least in my observations. Women do get hired to lead Kinaaldá; as in
the past, other women may come specifically to contribute Spinning Songs,
Weaving Songs, and any others that the girl or her family have requested.

While the instructions to the girl have remained intact, my observations
indicate that, at least in some locales, two more have become common. Both
are associated with the ceremonial racing which continues to involve either
two or three daily races as in the past. Today's Kinaaldá is often reminded to
be careful of the traffic while doing her ceremonial running. There is much
more of a chance now, even on dirt roads, that runners will be hit by speeding
cars and pickups. The other concern is care of the jewelry worn during the
race, especially beads, pins, and earrings. "Watch your jewelry while you
run," "don't lose any of your jewelry during your race" are frequent warn-
ings before each of the races. The loss of jewelry or a turquoise from a piece
of jewelry during the running causes much concern and many will help retrace
the route until the missing item is found.

Recently, I have noticed more tokenism expressed toward the need to
grind corn for the *'alkaan* with a metate and mano. Today, such grinding is
frequently minimal and often restricted to the third day or, in shortened ceremonies, to the night before or the morning of the day the cake is prepared.
While other options, such as the use of metal grinders at home, or commercial
grinding at mills in Gallup and elsewhere were noted earlier (see p. 385),
today it is common for most, though not all, of the corn to be ground by these
alternative methods (see also M. Roessel 1991:90). As in the past in some
areas (this volume, 78, 80, 82, 84, 86–87), the practice continues of substitut-

ing a giveaway of canned goods and other items for the traditional 'alkaan if the girl or her family decide, for whatever reasons, not to make the Kinaaldá cake. My observations indicate that although the use of substitutes remains an option it has not increased in frequency.

In closing, let me add that both of the girls featured in the original work are currently employed in health care professions and both have become grand-mothers. In addition, both continue to display the industriousness and other qualities deemed desirable in Navajo women and highlighted and underscored by the Kinaaldá ceremony.

Charlotte J. Frisbie
November 1, 1992

Bibliography

Begay, Shirley M.
    1983 *Kinaaldá: A Navajo Puberty Ceremony.* 2d rev. ed. Bilingual. Rough Rock, Ariz.: Rough Rock Demonstration School, Navajo Curriculum Center.
Benson, Michael
    1992 Women Voice Concerns, Share Ideas at Shiprock Hearing. *Navajo Times,* August 13, pp. 1, 12.
Conte, Christine
    1982 Ladies, Livestock, Land, and Lucre: Women's Networks and Social Status on the Western Navajo Reservation. *American Indian Quarterly* 6 (1 & 2):105–24.
    1984 The Navajo Sex-Gender System. Ph.D. diss. New School of Social Research, NY.
Faris, James C., and Harry Walters
    1990 Navajo History: Some Implications of Contrasts of Navajo Ceremonial Discourse. *History and Anthropology* 5:1–18.
Farrer, Claire R., and Bernard Second
    1989 Coming of Age: Mescalero Maidens Graduate to Womanhood. *New Mexico Magazine* 67(7):50–59.
Frisbie, Charlotte J.
    1977 Review of Navajo Corn Grinding & Shoe Game Songs. IH 1507. *Ethnomusicology* 21 (2):355–56.
    1980 Vocables in Navajo Ceremonial Music. *Ethnomusicology* 24 (3):347–92.
    1982 Traditional Navajo Women: Ethnographic and Life History Portrayals. *American Indian Quarterly* 6 (1 & 2):11–33.
    1989 Gender and Navajo Music: Unanswered Questions. In *Women in North American Indian Music: Six Essays,* edited by Richard Keeling, 21–38. Bloomington, Indiana: Society for Ethnomusicology, Special Series 6.
    1992 Temporal Change in Navajo Religion, 1868–1990. *Journal of the Southwest* 34 (4):457–514.
Goseyun, Anna Early
    1991 Carla's Sunrise. *Native Peoples* 4 (4):8–16.

Griffen, Joyce
  1982 Life Is Harder Here: The Case of the Urban Navajo Woman. *American Indian Quarterly* 6 (1 & 2):90–104. [Also guest editor of this issue of the journal.]
Harris, Betty J.
  1990 Ethnicity and Gender in the Global Periphery: A Comparison of Basotho and Navajo Women. *American Indian Culture and Research Journal* 14 (4):15–38.
Harrison, Edith S.
  1973 Women in Navajo Myth: A Study in the Symbolism of Matriliny. Ph.D. diss., Univ. of Massachusetts.
Hathale, Roger
  1986 *Hózhǫ́ǫ́jí Hane'*, *Blessingway*. Rough Rock, Ariz. Rough Rock Demonstration School, Navajo Mental Health Program.
Hauswald, Lizabeth
  1988 Child Abuse and Child Neglect: Navajo Families in Crisis. *Diné Be'iina'* 1 (2):37–53.
Hedlund, Ann Lane
  1985 Give and Take: Contributions to Household Economies by Elderly Navajo and Pueblo Women. Paper presented at annual meeting, American Anthropological Association, Washington, D.C., December.
Hoffman, Virginia, and Broderick Johnson
  1970 *Navajo Biographies*. Chinle, Ariz. Rough Rock Demonstration School.
Joe, Jennie R.
  1982 Cultural Influences on Navajo Mothers with Disabled Children. *American Indian Quarterly* 6 (1 & 2):170–90.
  1988 Breaking the Navajo Family: Governmental Interference and Forced Relocation. *Diné Be'iina'* 1 (2):1–21.
Lamphere, Louise
  1974 Strategies, Cooperation, and Conflict among Women in Domestic Groups. In *Woman, Culture and Society*, edited by Michelle Rosaldo and Louise Lamphere, 97–112. Stanford: Stanford University Press.
  1977 *To Run after Them: The Cultural and Social Bases of Cooperation in a Navajo Community*. Tucson: University of Arizona Press.
  1989 Historical and Regional Variability in Navajo Women's Roles. *Journal of Anthropological Research* 45 (4):431–56. [Also guest editor of this special issue on Navajo Ethnology.]
Leighton, Alexander H., and Dorothea C. Leighton
  1992 *Lucky, the Navajo Singer*. Edited and annotated by Joyce J. Griffen. Albuquerque: University of New Mexico Press.
Leighton, Dorothea C.
  1982 As I Knew Them: Navajo Women in 1940. *American Indian Quarterly* 6 (1 & 2):43–51.
Metcalf, Ann
  1982 Navajo Women in the City: Lessons from a Quarter-Century of Relocation. *American Indian Quarterly* 6 (1 & 2):71–89.
Mitchell, Frank
  1978 *Navajo Blessingway Singer: The Autobiography of Frank Mitchell,*

1881-1967, edited by Charlotte J. Frisbie and David P. McAllester. Tucson: University of Arizona Press.

Navajo Curriculum Center
1986 *Cookbook, Ch'iyáán 'ííł'íní binaaltsoos.* Chinle, Ariz.: Rough Rock Demonstration School.

Nelson, Mary Carroll
1972 *Annie Wauneka.* Minneapolis: Dillon Press, Inc.

Parezo, Nancy J.
1982 Navajo Sandpaintings: The Importance of Sex Roles in Craft Production. *American Indian Quarterly* 6 (1 & 2):125–48.

Perrone, Bobette, H. Henrietta Stockel, and Victoria Krueger
1989 *Medicine Women, Curanderas, and Women Doctors.* Norman: University of Oklahoma Press.

Ritts, Karen Rose
1989 Turnings: From Life History to Group Biography—Four Generations of Change in a Navajo Family. Ph.D diss., Anthropology Department, Northwestern University.

Roessel, Monty
1991 Navajo Puberty Rites. *New Mexico Magazine* 69 (8):86–95.

Roessel, Ruth
1981 *Women in Navajo Society.* Chinle, Ariz. Rough Rock Demonstration School.

Shepardson, Mary
1982 The Status of Navajo Women. *American Indian Quarterly* 6 (1 & 2):149–69.

Shepardson, Mary, and Blodwen Hammond
1970 *The Navajo Mountain Community: Social Organization and Kinship Terminology.* Berkeley: University of California Press.

Stewart, Irene
1980 *A Voice in Her Tribe: A Navajo Woman's Own Story,* edited by Doris Dawdy, Anthropological Papers 17. Socorro, NM: Ballena Press.

Tso, Eddie, and Lloyd Thompson
1984 Traditional Navajo Ceremonies. Multicolored chart available from the authors.
1985 Wholistic Navajo. Multicolored chart available from the authors.

Walters, Harry
1990 A New Perspective on Navajo History. Senior Study Paper, Goddard College, Plainfield, Vermont, January. Ms. available from author.

Wright, Anne
1981 Attitudes toward Childbearing and Menstruation among the Navajo. In *Anthropology of Human Birth,* edited by Margarita Kay, 377–94. Philadelphia: F. A. Davis.
1982 An Ethnography of the Navajo Reproductive Cycle. *American Indian Quarterly* 6 (1 & 2): 52–70.

Wyman, Leland C.
1970 *Blessingway,* with three versions of the myth recorded and translated from the Navajo by Father Bernard Haile, O.F.M. Tucson: University of Arizona Press.

KINAALDÁ

Introduction

THE aim of this study is to present a detailed account of the Navaho Kinaaldá,[1] or the Girl's Puberty Ceremony. Although forty-two accounts of this ceremony are available, only one of these, that of Wyman and Bailey,[2] attempts to describe the ceremony in its entirety. The author was interested in supplementing the mythological material connected with the ceremony, investigating regional differences in procedure, and documenting the music used during the ceremony. While Kinaaldá songs had been recorded by Wheelwright, Herzog, and Keith, none had been published. Since the entire last night *(biji)* of this ceremony and, in some regions, part of the first day as well are spent in song, it seemed important to determine what happens musically. The author was particularly interested in seeing if the songs could be distinguished from one another, if they were similar to songs from other ceremonies, if they exemplified Navaho chant style, and if their texts were concerned with puberty per se. One final

---

[1]Navaho words are spelled according to the government system of transcription, as delineated in Robert Young, "The Navaho Language," *The Navaho Yearbook*, Report VI, Fiscal Year 1957 (Window Rock, Ariz.: Navaho Agency, 1957), pp. 153–184. The word "kinaaldá" will be used both as a singular and plural form, as in Navaho. The context will indicate the number. Since "Kinaaldá," "hogan" (house), and "belagáana" (American) are Navaho words that have come over into English usage, they are not considered "foreign" and therefore are not italicized when used in this work.

[2]Leland Wyman and Flora Bailey, "Navaho Girl's Puberty Rite," *New Mexico Anthropologist*, XXV, No. 1 (January–March, 1943), pp. 3–12.

concern of the study was to view the Kinaaldá in its cultural context: to see how it expressed the over-all value system of the
Navaho and how it had been affected by acculturation.

The author's field work was conducted during the summers
of 1963 and 1964 in two areas of the reservation, Chinle and
Lukachukai, Arizona. Ten Kinaaldá were known to have been given
in this region during the summer of 1963. Presumably this represented only a small proportion of those which were held. Of
the five performed in Chinle, two were recorded and studied and
portions of a third were observed. The fourth was closed to
"non-Navaho," and the fifth took place while the researcher was
attending a Blessing Way Ceremony in another area. Work in
Lukachukai was restricted because of the particular attitudes of
the dozen families visited. An attempt was made to observe and
record five Kinaaldá. However, permission was given to observe
only parts of two.

The participant-observer method was employed throughout
the field work. Photographs were taken and recordings made of
solo and ceremonial singing whenever possible. The data from
the ceremonies were supplemented by controlled interviews with
singers, their wives, various adolescent girls, and their mothers.
Singers were asked to tell what they could of the myth connected
with the ceremony, to discuss the procedures and the songs involved in present-day Kinaaldá, and to perform representative examples of the latter. Female informants were asked to talk about
their own Kinaaldá and, if they were mothers, to discuss those of
their children, both the ceremonies that had already occurred and
those that might be held in the future. Each girl and woman was
also asked direct questions covering items on an organized check
list. In most cases, notes were made as the informant talked;
sometimes, however, they were written down from memory directly after the interview. Several of the interviews were recorded. In Chinle, fifteen informants were contacted: five chanters, four girls, three women, and three men who knew Kinaaldá

songs but were not official practitioners. In Lukachukai, seven informants were contacted: five chanters, one man who had much ceremonial knowledge, and his wife.

The author's data were supplemented by observations, notes, and musical materials of other field workers whenever these were available and pertinent. In this way, information from thirty-five informants was added to that gathered from the author's twenty-two informants. The additional data were derived from the following: Lukachukai: one chanter; Pinedale: seventeen informants (twelve girls, three chanters, and two of their wives); Two Wells: three informants (two men, one of whom knew some songs, and one woman); Ramah: thirteen informants (seven men and six women); and Nava: one chanter.

The music is from solo recordings[3] made in Lukachukai and from ceremonial as well as solo ones made in Chinle. The tapes of the author have been augmented by ceremonial recordings taken by Anne Keith at Pinedale, ceremonial recordings from Chinle and solo ones from Red Rock made by Dr. McAllester, and Mary Wheelwright's solo recordings from Nava, New Mexico.

---

[3]Solo recordings refer to singing done specifically for recording purposes, rather than in conjunction with actual ceremonies.

CHAPTER ONE

The Kinaaldá and Its Myth

Attitude toward Pubescence

IN many societies, puberty is an event surrounded by what Cancian has termed "a hygienic silence."[1] Although implicit in "debutante balls and religious confirmation in some churches,"[2] puberty generally remains unmentioned and uncelebrated within American culture.

In contrast to our attitude toward this life crisis, many of the Indian tribes living within the United States surround pubescence with elaborate rituals. Among our largest Indian group, the Navaho, a girl's puberty is celebrated by a public ceremony. As Frank Mitchell (FM)[3] said: "We believe that when a girl has her first period there is nothing wrong with that. It is something sacred to us."[4]

Prepubescent Navaho girls are often prepared by their mothers for the onset of menstruation.[5] Around the age of ten a girl learns of the great power she will possess and of the

---

[1]Francis Cancian, "A Photo-Ethnography of the White Mountain Apaches" (unpublished thesis for Bachelor of Arts Degree with Distinction in Anthropology, Wesleyan University, Middletown, Connecticut, 1956), p. 76.

[2]Dorothea Leighton and Clyde Kluckhohn, *Children of the People* (Cambridge, Mass.: Harvard University Press, 1947), p. 87.

[3]Informants will be identified by initials; a key to these appears in Appendix A.

[4]David McAllester, Field Notes, July 19–20, 1961, p. 7b. For the location of all field notes and other MSS, please see the Bibliography.

[5]Anne Keith, however, found that many girls in the Pinedale, New Mexico, area are not told anything about menstruation by anyone until it happens.

restrictions she must obey during her periods to avoid harming others. For instance, she must not enter a ceremonial hogan, see sand paintings, attend a sing, join in any dancing, go into the fields, have contact with livestock or children, carry water, use the sudatory, urinate in places with which others might have contact, or visit persons who are sick. Violation of these taboos may result in injury to others in the form of general illness, impotency, and various types of crippling, including kyphosis.

The menstrual blood of the first two periods is not particularly feared. It is believed that dangers from menstrual blood increase with age, and the Blessing Way Songs sung for the girl on those two occasions are seen as being capable of counteracting any danger that may be present.[6]

The onset of menstruation is regarded by the Navaho as a time for rejoicing. The fact is announced to the whole community in a dramatic four-night ceremony. This is held immediately or as soon as possible after menstruation begins, and it progresses right through the girl's period. Formerly, the girl was considered ready for adult life after her first menstruation;[7] she became a tribal symbol of fecundity. Leighton and Kluckhohn report that according to earlier marriage customs, most Navaho girls were married within a year after puberty, if not before; present-day Navaho still say that "a girl's first bleeding is an order from the Holy People to marry."[8] If a girl marries before puberty, the Kinaaldá is held at her first menses. If there is only one period before a child is born, the second ceremony, if given, takes place at the child's birth. In this case, the girl observes all the ceremonial restrictions, but is not required to make the ceremonial run.[9]

---

[6]See Flora Bailey, "Some Sex Beliefs and Practices in a Navaho Community," *Papers of the Peabody Museum of American Archaeology and Ethnology*, Harvard University, Vol. XL, No. 2 (1950), p. 10.

[7]Leighton and Kluckhohn, p. 76. FM, however, said this was not true until after the second menstrual period.

[8]Leighton and Kluckhohn, p. 76.

[9]See Leland Wyman and Flora Bailey, "Navaho Girl's Puberty Rite," *New Mexico Anthropologist*, XXV, No. 1 (January–March, 1943), p. 3, and Gladys Reichard, *Social Life of the Navajo Indians*, Columbia University Contributions to Anthropology, VII (New York: Columbia University Press, 1928), p. 136. In the notes in the files of the Laboratory of Anthropology in Santa Fe, New Mexico, there is one reference to a Kinaaldá given for a married woman.

Meaning of the Word "Kinaaldá"

The term for the puberty ceremony is "kinaaldá" or "ki-
naaldááh." Most Navaho use this word to refer to the first menses,
alluding to the ceremonial rather than the physiological event.
Frank Mitchell, Edward Sapir, and Father Berard Haile, however,
do not agree with this usage. According to Frank, the term
"kinaaldá" refers to the girl and to the house in which she was
formerly isolated during that period. Other informants used the
term in the manner Frank suggested, namely, as a synonym for
"pubescent girl." One of Sapir's informants, Albert G. ("Chic")
Sandoval (CS), said that Sapir had told him that "kinaaldá" was an
Athabascan term which, in Chic's words, was "used in Alaska
where the people live in ice houses."[10] Chic also said: "*Sidá*
means 'sitting alone,' i.e., isolated in the ice house. There a girl
is isolated from the family when she gets in that way. The form
of the word used in Alaska is *kin ya shidáh*. This has been cor-
rupted to 'kinaaldá' by the Navaho."[11] Wyman and Bailey[12] say
that the Navaho cannot agree on an exact translation of the term,
explaining it as "sliding off the house" or as "house sitting," as
Father Berard Haile does: *kin*, "house"; *naaldá* (verb), "to sit."[13]
Haile's translation is probably a reference to the segregation hut
formerly used during menstruation.

Classification of the Ceremony

The Kinaaldá is typical of the Navaho ceremonial pattern in
its use of songs, prayers, taboos, purification rites, and a final
night of singing. Sand paintings and masks, however, are not

---

[10]McAllester, Field Notes, July 19–20, 1961, p. 10a.
[11]Charlotte Johnson, Field Notes, July 1, 1963.
[12]Wyman and Bailey, p. 3.
[13]Father Berard Haile, *A Stem Vocabulary of the Navaho Language* (St. Michaels, Ariz.:
St. Michaels Press, 1950), I, 78, 209.

used,[14] probably because Changing Woman, the chief deity associated with the ceremony, is never represented in these ways. Prayer sticks, rattles, and drums are also absent, as are the purification rites of the sweat bath and emetics associated with larger ceremonials.

The Kinaaldá is classified by Wyman and Kluckhohn[15] as one special "rite"[16] in the 1A category of the common, general Blessing Way Ceremonial. It is viewed as part of the Blessing Way Ceremony by singers and nonchanters alike. When discussing the term "kinaaldá," Frank Mitchell said that Kinaaldá is not the name of the ceremony; Hózhǫ́ǫ́jí (Blessing Way) is. In giving his version of the Kinaaldá myth, Frank said, "One of the main things that we Navaho have is the Blessing Way Ceremony in which the Kinaaldá is included." Later he stated that the Kinaaldá is, for him, the most important Navaho ceremony. Other singers have said that the Blessing Way actually began with the Kinaaldá.[17]

Being part of the Blessing Way complex, the Kinaaldá is prophylactic, rather than curative; it ushers the girl into society, invokes positive blessing on her, insures her health, prosperity, and well-being, and protects her from potential misfortune. As in the Seed Blessing, Wedding, and House Blessing—other ceremonies which comprise subtypes in this general classification—the Kinaaldá is built on procedures that derive from the common, general 1A Blessing Way Ceremonial (of Wyman and Kluckhohn). For example, all its songs are Hózhǫ́ǫ́jí, or Blessing Way songs.

---

[14]David Villaseñor, in *Tapestries in Sand* (Healdsburg, Calif.: Naturegraph Company, 1963), p. 30, claims that a sand painting entitled "The Seed Blessing Way Chant" (pictured on p. 40 of the same work) is used during a girl's puberty rites. There is no reliable evidence for a sand painting in this ceremony.

[15]Leland Wyman and Clyde Kluckhohn, "Navaho Classification of Their Song Ceremonials," *Memoirs of the American Anthropological Assoc.* L (1938), 18−19.

[16]In the present book, "ceremony" means a collection of ritual acts which have a name and an origin legend and are performed according to codified procedures. The word "rite" is being used to indicate "a ceremonial act," following *Webster's Collegiate Dictionary* (Springfield, Mass.: G. and C. Merriam Co., 1937), p. 861. This is a departure from the usage in Wyman and Kluckhohn, p. 4, n. 6.

[17]See Father Berard Haile, "Creation and Emergence Myth of the Navajo" (MS), pp. 241, 254, 270, and Haile, "Origin Legend of the Navaho Enemy Way," *Yale University Publications in Anthropology*, XVII (1938), 87, 91, and 251.

There are, however, important differences between *Hózhǫ́ǫ́jí*
and Kinaaldá. The ceremonies differ in length, bathing ritual, type
of prayers, manner of applying corn pollen, racing, making a
corncake, manner of obtaining the yucca root, ritual of orienting
the ceremonial basket, ownership of property which may be displayed, and the goods with which the singer is paid.

The Myth

Like all Navaho ceremonies, the Kinaaldá is rationalized
by myths which present the legendary origin of the ritual and its
transmission to mankind. The myth mentioning the origin of the
puberty ceremony is usually included in the Creation Story. Ten
versions of the story of the first Kinaaldá, Changing Woman's
Puberty Ceremony, have been published. These are by the following authors: Curtis, Wheelwright, Reichard, Matthews, The Franciscan Fathers, Haile (three), Wyman and Bailey, and Goddard.[18]
Seven others are included here; these were collected by David
McAllester, Alexander Leighton, Dorothea Leighton, Anne Keith,
and the author (three). The myth collected from Frank Mitchell
by the author during the summer of 1963 is given in the following
section. The other six previously unavailable myths appear in
Appendix B.

The Kinaaldá myth collected from Frank Mitchell in 1963
was recorded on tape in Navaho without interruption. It consists
of a description of three Kinaaldá: the original ceremony done for
Changing Woman and the two puberty ceremonies of the first girl
born to the Navaho after their creation by Changing Woman. This
myth was later translated by Chic Sandoval.

---

[18] The complete reference for these myths are found in Appendix B.

Frank Mitchell's Kinaaldá Myth (1963)[19]

I am going to tell the story I know about the beginning of the
Kinaaldá ceremony, its purpose, and why such things were laid
down for the people.

Kinaaldá of Changing Woman

It was a long time ago that Changing Woman had her Kinaaldá.
She made herself become kinaaldá. This happened after the creation of the Earth People. The ceremony was started so women
would be able to have children and the human race would be able
to multiply. To do this, women had to have relations with men.
The Kinaaldá was created to make it holy and effective, as the
Holy People wanted it to be. They called many meetings to discuss how they should do this ceremony.

In the beginning, there was fog at the top of Blanca Peak. After
four days, the fog covered everything down to the base. Coyote, of
course, went there to find out what was happening. When he went
running over there, he saw a baby floating on the lake which was at
the top of Blanca Peak. He wanted to pick up the baby and bring it
back, but he was not able to. So he came back and reported it to
Hashch'éhooghan (Hogan God). Hashch'éhooghan went over there
and could not get it either. Then Talking God went there, got the
baby out of the lake, and brought it to the top of Gobernador Knob.

The one who was picked up as a new baby was 'Esdzáánádleehé
(Changing Woman). She was taken home to be raised. In four days
she grew up and became kinaaldá. When this happened, they decided to have a ceremony for her.

At this time, the Holy People were living on the earth. They
came to her ceremony, and many of them sang songs for her. They
did this so that she would be holy and so she could have children
who would be human beings with enough sense to think for themselves and a language with which to understand each other.

The first Kinaaldá took place at the rim of the Emergence
Place in the First Woman's home. All kinds of Holy People were
there. The first time that Changing Woman had it, they used the
original Chief Hogan Songs. The second time, they used the Hogan
Songs which belonged to Talking God.

The first ceremony took place at Ch'óol'į'í (Gobernador Knob);

---

[19]In presenting data from my informants and those of other field workers, the language
and sometimes the order have been edited for the sake of clarity. The personal philosophy found
interspersed with the mythological data in the present account is irrelevant for current purposes
and has been eliminated.

this is a place that is now on the Jicarilla Apache Reservation. When Changing Woman became kinaaldá, Salt Woman, who was the first White Shell Woman, gave her her own name, "White Shell Woman." She dressed her in white shell clothes. Changing Woman was also painted with white shell; that is why she was called "White Shell Woman."

The Kinaaldá started when White Shell Woman first menstruated. It is still done the same way today. At her first ceremony, White Shell Woman ran around the turquoise that was in the east. That is why the kinaaldá today wears turquoise. During her second ceremony, she started from the west, where there was white shell. The second menstruation was connected with white shell.

Nine days after that, Changing Woman gave birth to Naaghéé' neezgháni (Monster Slayer) and Tó bájíshchíní (Born for Water), twin boys. These two were put on earth so that all the monsters which were eating the human beings would be killed. They rid the earth of all these monsters; that is why they were called Holy People. As soon as they had done this, their mother, Changing Woman, who was then living at Gobernador Knob, left and went to her home in the west, where she lives today.

After she moved to her home in the west, she created the Navaho people. When she had done this, she told these human beings to go to their original home, which was the Navaho country. Before they left, she said, "After this, all the girls born to you will have periods at certain times when they become women. When the time comes, you must set a day and fix the girl up to be kinaaldá; you must have these songs sung and do whatever else needs to be done at that time. After this period, a girl is a woman and will start having children."

She also told the people to make a round cake representing Mother Earth during the Kinaaldá. She said that this cake should be given to the singers who helped with the singing during the ceremony. She told the people how to make the cake; one of the things that she mentioned was that the cornhusks were to be placed in the east, south, west, north (in the four directions) and in the center of the pit.

That is what 'Esdzáánádleehé told the people she made in the west. She told them to go to their own country and do this.

When 'Esdzáánádleehé created the people in the west, she made four groups. These were the four original clans of the Navaho people: Tó díchi'íini, Bitter Water Clan; Kiiya'áani, Tall House Clan; Tó'áhání, Short Distance to Water Clan; and Hashtł'ishni, Mud Clan. They were told to go to their own country.

When the four clans were created by 'Esdzáánádleehé, pairs, male and female, were made in each clan. They were ordered to be man and wife so there would be more children. The first child that was born was a girl.

When the people were ready to leave, 'Esdzą́ą́nádleehé said, "You must go right back to my first home (Gobernador Knob), There is a cornfield there by the name of Dá'ák'eh jigishí (Where One Gazes on a Cornfield). That field is mine; when you go back, you are to settle there and let it be yours."

The First Kinaaldá of the First Girl Born on Earth

These people did what 'Esdzą́ą́nádleehé told them to do; they went to Gobernador Knob to the cornfield and settled there. They were living there when the first-born girl became kinaaldá. That was where the first Kinaaldá, which was directed by 'Esdzą́ą́nádleehé, took place. She came there supernaturally and directed the making of the cake.

The only songs that have come down to this day from the first ceremony over that girl without being changed are the Hogan Songs which were sung by the Holy People who were there. After these songs, the Holy People sang others about fabrics,[20] jewels, journeys, mountains, and other things they happened to have in their possession.

When this girl was being prepared for her Kinaaldá, 'Esdzą́ą́nádleehé directed how she was to be fixed. Of course, 'Esdzą́ą́nádleehé had gone through the same things when she had hers for the first time, and she did the same things for the first-born girl. She combed her hair, fixed it in a pony tail, and dressed her in her ceremonial clothes.

After these things had been done, the girl lay on her stomach, and she was molded and pressed so she would have a good figure. When she got up, she ran to the east for her first run. At that time, just as now, anyone could run with her.

When she returned from her first run, she started grinding corn for the cake. The people were told to shell the corn, winnow it, bring it in, and start grinding. 'Esdzą́ą́nádleehé said, "For two full days, the girl shall do this grinding." The first-born girl spent all her time grinding.

On the third day, they started preparing the mush for the cake. The first thing they were told to do was to dig a pit, build a fire in it, and let it get hot. They kept the fire going all day long, so the pit was hot when the mush was ready. Dry corn meal was stirred into the hot water. Then they rubbed the mixture between their

---

[20]Two expressions, yódi'iltas'éí (various fabrics) and ńtł'iz'iltas'éí (various jewels), appear frequently in the song texts. Yódí is "a collective term for fabrics like robes, buckskin or cloths." Haile, A Stem Vocabulary, p. 196. Ńtł'iz is "a collective term to designate jewel stones." Ibid., p. 158.

hands to get the lumps out of the mush. Late in the afternoon, at
sundown, all of the mush was ready to be taken out to the pit.

They cleaned all the ashes and charcoal from the pit. The four
cornhusks were put down to the east, south, west, and north. A
middle piece was then put on. After this had been done, they
started to pour the mush in. Cornhusks were put down at the same
time so that no mush would get on the bare earth. They started
from the center and worked out to the edges of the pit; then they
went up the sides, busily putting husks down all the time. When all
the mush had been poured in, the girl stood with a basket of corn
meal in the east and tossed a pinch of corn meal to the east, to the
west, and back to the east, and then to the south, to the north, and
back to the south. Then she took a handful of corn meal and
sprinkled it in a circle around the pit.

After she had done these things, anyone who wanted to was allowed to take a pinch of corn meal and do what she had done, while
praying for good luck, plenty, good vegetation, and no hunger, hardships, or suffering. When this had been done, husks were placed,
starting from the edge of the pit and going into the center. Then
the gap was closed and husks were put in the center as had been
done earlier. The pit was covered with more husks and then with
dirt. That is the way they were told to do it in the beginning, and
that is how they have been doing it since.

The cake was covered with a thin layer of dirt because the mush
was too soft to have any weight put on it in the beginning; twigs and
little pieces of wood were used until the mush had settled and hardened. Then more dirt was put on, and a big fire was built. The fire
was kept going all night so the cake would cook.

In the evening, the original Chief Hogan Songs were sung; then
the singing was turned over to the people. After all these songs, at
that time, the Twelve Word Songs were not sung.

The cake was cut up and given to the singers. The last thing
that the people did after cutting the cake was to take four pinches
of the cake from the four directions, east, south, west, and north.
These pinches were buried in the center of the pit where the cake
had been baked. They offered these to Mother Earth, who produces
vegetation and makes it possible to grow corn. This was done to
say thanks to the Earth. It is done today. After this, the people
ate. Lots of prayers were offered for good luck and good life.

That is what happened at the first ceremony. From then on,
these things have been carried on by the Navaho. When a girl has
her period, she becomes kinaaldá and has the ceremony.

In the days when the first girl born on earth had her ceremony,
the Holy People were still on the earth. Sometimes they would
come around and check on the Earth People to see if they were

following the rules laid down for them. As time passed, they realized that the Earth People were getting careless about these things. When this happened, 'Esdzą́ą́nádleehé decided to take two young boys of the Tó'áhání Clan, the original clan made by Esdzą́ą́nádleehé in the west, to her home in the west. There she taught them about everything in the past, present, and future.

The boys were given the power to make Blessing Way Songs. They became good at doing this. It was at this time that the Blessing Way Ceremony was started. The Blessing Way Ceremony concerns everything good for the people to live by.

The Second Kinaaldá of the First Girl Born on Earth

The next time they had Kinaaldá, after the first one, they only made a few changes in what they had done before. Because it was the second Kinaaldá, the Hogan Songs of Talking God were sung. When evening came, Talking God came there for a special reason: to sing his Hogan Songs. He sang twelve songs in the first group, twelve in the second, and then one long one. After he sang his songs, he turned the singing over to the rest of the people. During that ceremony, when dawn appeared in the east, the two boys, who by that time had returned to the earth, sang the Dawn Songs for the first time. Since then, these songs have always been sung at dawn. At dawn the girl ran to the east again, as she had done the first time. Four songs were sung for the racing. The people also added the Twelve Word Songs at this time.

After that ceremony, the Holy People and Earth People talked. The Holy People told the Earth People that they would now go away. The Holy People said that some of them would go into the mountains, the rocks, the water, the mountain ranges, and all the sacred places. They said, "But that does not mean that we will not see what is going on with you, because we will. You will be in our sight every day. If you keep the things holy that you have been told about, you will have a long, good life on earth. If you do not, then hardships and evil will come to you, and it will be your own fault for not following these things. We Holy People will not see each other again because we are going to different places to live, out of your sight."

One of the things we are to observe is the Blessing Way Ceremony. The Kinaaldá is included in this. We keep it the way it was when it was started in the beginning so that it will always be sacred and holy.

You asked me for the story of the Kinaaldá. This is it. I have told you what I know and what I have learned from others. I cannot tell you anything that I do not know.

As columns 14–16 of Chart 1 illustrate, variation is evident within Frank's 1963 myth. There are differences in each of the three episodes he related within the framework of the total myth. As columns 12–18 of the same chart demonstrate, there are obvious differences among the four versions collected from Mitchell over a period of thirty-two years. In spite of these variations, Frank insisted that there was only one version of both the Kinaaldá myth and the ceremonial procedure, namely, the initial version established for Changing Woman.

The 1932, 1961, 1963, and 1964 versions of the Kinaaldá myth from Mitchell suggest that a given singer may tell the story differently at every repetition. A comparative study of the thirteen other Kinaaldá myths shown in Chart 1 leads to the hypothesis that no two singer's renditions are ever identical. All but one of the mythological accounts mention that the first ceremony was conducted for Changing Woman. Themes such as the ceremonial dressing, molding, racing, singing, use of a specific number of songs, notifying the Gods for the original ceremony, and the relation between Kinaaldá and Blessing Way are mentioned in more than half of the myths. Other themes are not included as often

Field data show that the medicine men recognize variation in myth-telling and openly discuss it. For example, in the course of Marie Shirley's (MS) Kinaaldá, Frank Mitchell, who was serving as the principal singer, said to Diné łbáhí (Gray Man) (DB), another singer:

> I hear that some say Ch'óol'į'í (Gobernador Knob) first and that you tell it that way too. According to my story, I mention Sisnaajiní (Blanca Peak) first. . . . That's the way my story goes.
> . . . No one is alive now who witnessed that at that time. We disagree with one another on where Changing Woman was picked up as a baby. This is my father's story that I am telling. My father told me, and that's the reason I mention Blanca Peak first and then Gobernador Knob in the song. Of course, you mention it the other way around; I'm not criticizing you; I'm just telling you my way.

There are several possible explanations for the existence of this variation in a culture where ceremonial activity is known to be strictly ordered and formalized. A comparison of the Mitchell myths suggests that the field worker's approach affects the extensiveness of the myth given by the informant. For example, in 1961, when a myth was not specifically requested, Frank included only a few mythological references in his explanation of ceremonial procedure. When the request was made in 1963, however, he distinguished between the myth and the details of present-day procedure and gave a full, separate account of both.

The element of rationalization must also be considered. Myths are commonly viewed as developing after ceremonial practices, serving as rationalizations for them. Thus myths are usually adjusted to the performance procedure and told in such a way as to correspond to the ceremonial practices of particular medicine men.

The oral tradition itself is inevitably responsible for many of the differences which exist in the Kinaaldá myths. So is the Navaho belief that anything in excess is dangerous and to be avoided. Custom prevents a singer from recounting all that he knows; were he not to hold back a bit each time, he would lose his power.[21]

Ladd's "principle of many reasons"[22] may also be a valid explanation for some of the existing variation. Those acquainted with the Navaho are aware that there are alternatives in ritual behavior and that any number of reasons can be used to justify these variations. There is no one way of telling the Kinaaldá myth or singing the Kinaaldá songs.

Perhaps the basic explanation is that Navaho formalism in itself is not totally restrictive. Rules and regulated procedures are numerous, but within certain areas of the ritual, individual variation is permissible. The sand paintings of the larger ceremonials are an illustration. The symbols and figures must

---

[21]Clyde Kluckhohn and Dorothea Leighton, *The Navaho* (Cambridge, Mass.: Harvard University Press, 1948), p. 226.

[22]John Ladd, *The Structure of a Moral Code* (Cambridge, Mass.: Harvard University Press, 1957), p. 223.

Chart I

Authors (columns):

1. Curtis
2. Franciscan Fathers
3. Wyman and Bailey
4. Reichard
5. Wheelwright
6. Matthews
7. Haile
8. Goddard
9. A. Leighton (DS)
10. D. Leighton (TS)
11. Keith (AM, 1963)
12. Haile (FM, 1932)
13. McAllester (FM, 1961)
14. Johnson (FM, 1963) *Changing Woman's Story*
15. Johnson (FM, 1963) *Story of the first earth girl's first Kinaaldá*
16. Johnson (FM, 1963) *Story of the first earth girl's second Kinaaldá*
17. Johnson (FM, 1964)
18. Johnson (TM, 1964)
19. Haile (SC) 1932

Theme Mentioned	1	2	3	4	5	6	7	8	9	10	11	12	13	14	15	16	17	18	19
Kinaaldá as part of the Blessing Way			×		×		×		×			×	×				×		×
Kinaaldá as part of the Emergence Myth		×	×																
Ceremony originated by Changing Woman					×							×	×	×				×	×
Instigated by First Man and First Woman	×		×	×	×	×	×	×			×		×	×					
Given for Changing Woman	×		×			×	×	×		×	×	×	×	×			×	×	×
Conducted on Changing Woman's trip to the west		×		×															
Given for White Shell Woman							×												
Not given for the mother of Enemy Slayer																			
Related to conception			×							×									×
Related to birth of future generations							×			×	×		×	×			×	×	×
Given to benefit the Sun and Moon				×			×							×			×		
Correlated with the disappearance of the gods						×		×							×	×			
Required on this earth													×	×		×	×		
Specific time of occurrence		×	×	×	×			×		×	×	×	×	×				×	
Given at the time of coming of age 14																			
Gods notified of events	×				×		×	×				×		×	×	×			×

Chart I (cont'd)

Theme Mentioned \ Author	1 Curtis	2 Franciscan Fathers	3 Wyman and Bailey	4 Reichard	5 Wheelwright	6 Matthews	7 Haile	8 Goddard	9 A. Leighton (DS)	10 D. Leighton (TS)	11 Keith (AM, 1963)	12 Haile (FM, 1932)	13 McAllester (FM, 1961)	14 Johnson (FM, 1963) Changing Woman's Story	15 Johnson (FM, 1963) Story of the first earth girl's first Kinaaldá	16 Johnson (FM, 1963) Story of the first earth girl's second Kinaaldá	17 Johnson (FM, 1964)	18 Johnson (TM, 1964)	19 Haile (SC) 1932
Ceremony held four days after notification	×																		
Blessing in the hogan							×	×				×					×	×	
Combing of the hair	×			×	×		×	×		×		×			×				×
Dressing the girl	×			×	×	×	×	×		×		×			×	×	×		×
Molding					×			×				×			×	×	×		×
Lamb held at breast while molded														×					
Return goods after molding	×				×					×									×
Girl gives out presents										×									
Receive blanket as a gift	×																		
Naming involved					×		×							×					
Animals involved					×		×	×			×	×							
Race	×			×	×							×		×	×	×	×		×
People follow the girl in the race	×														×	×			
Racing Songs	×									×					×	×		×	
Grinding										×					×	×			
Corncake				×			×			×	×			×	×	×			

Chart I (cont'd)

Author key:
1. Curtis
2. Franciscan Fathers
3. Wyman and Bailey
4. Reichard
5. Wheelwright
6. Matthews
7. Haile
8. Goddard
9. A. Leighton (DS)
10. D. Leighton (TS)
11. Keith (AM, 1963)
12. Haile (FM, 1932)
13. McAllester (FM, 1961)
14. Johnson (FM, 1963) *Changing Woman's Story*
15. Johnson (FM, 1963) *Story of the first earth girl's first Kinaaldá*
16. Johnson (FM, 1963) *Story of the first earth girl's second Kinaaldá*
17. Johnson (FM, 1964)
18. Johnson (TM, 1964)
19. Haile (SC) 1932

Theme Mentioned	1	2	3	4	5	6	7	8	9	10	11	12	13	14	15	16	17	18	19
Music	×	×	×		×		×	×		×		×		×	×	×	×		
Blessing Way songs		×					×			×		×			×	×	×		
Specific number of songs							×	×		×		×			×	×	×	×	×
Song texts given					×			×										×	
Hair washed	×							×											
Jewelry washed	×									×									
Painting					×									×					×
Lifting					×			×											
Specific length of menstrual flow				×		×		×		×									
Second ceremony given							×			×				×					
Musical difference between the first and second Kinaaldá							×								×	×	×	×	×
Difference in type of Hogan Songs used for two ceremonies																×		×	×
Dawn Songs added to Second Kinaaldá																×		×	×
Twelve Word Songs added to Second Kinaaldá																×	×		
Difference in corn used for two ceremonies																	×		
Difference in jewels used for two ceremonies														×					

correspond to rigid specifications. However, in decorating bodies composed of triangles as well as the kilts and sashes worn by the Holy People, the sand painter is free to vary his design.[23] It is a *balance* between formalism and individual variation rather than *formalism per se* that is exemplified in the Kinaaldá myths and in many other aspects of Navaho culture.

---

[23] See Franc Newcomb and Gladys Reichard, *Sandpaintings of the Navajo Shooting Chant* (New York: J. J. Augustin, 1937), p. 86.

CHAPTER TWO

The Ceremony

THE two Kinaaldá observed and recorded in full were held at the Mitchells' in Chinle. Two of Frank's granddaughters,[1] Marie and Lena Shirley, celebrated their pubescence during the summer. Fifteen-year-old Marie had her second Kinaaldá, and thirteen-year-old Lena, her first. Therefore, both types of puberty ceremonies were represented.

To obtain data which could later be used for comparisons, Frank was asked, prior to the ceremony, to describe the ideal Kinaaldá procedure. He ordered the ceremonial activities as follows:

Events for a First Kinaaldá

First Day

> Announce event and discuss start of ceremony.
> Comb hair.
> Dress girl.
> Mold girl inside hogan.
> Girl runs to east; races are run at dawn, noon, and sunset; on the first day the number of races depends on the starting time of the ceremony.
> Grind corn.

---

[1]Refer to Appendix C for the Mitchell genealogy.

Second Day

>Run three times.
>Grind corn.

Third Day

>Run three times.
>Grind corn.
>Dig pit; make fire in it.
>Make batter for *'alkaan*[2] (corncake).
>Put batter in pit; bless it.
>Cover up cake.

Third Night

>Bring goods into hogan.
>Bless hogan.
>Pass corn pollen to people.
>Sing fourteen Chief Hogan Songs.
>Girl leaves and returns.
>Open singing of *Hózhǫ́ǫ́jí* songs.
>Corn pollen after each set of songs.

Fourth Day

>Dawn Song.
>Wash hair and jewelry—four songs.
>Girl runs—sing four songs while she is gone.
>One Twelve Word Song.
>Pass corn pollen.
>People go out of hogan and uncover cake.
>Girl goes out.
>Cut cake.
>Offering.
>Distribute cake to singers and rest of people.
>Feed people.
>Comb girl's hair—two songs.
>Paint girl with white clay—two songs.
>Mold girl outside.
>Return blankets and so forth to owners.
>Distribute any remaining cake.

---

[2]Refer to Appendix D for explanations of Navaho terminology.

Events for a Second Kinaaldá

The procedures are the same as above except that twenty-five Hogan Songs belonging to Talking God are used. If possible, the main singer and the woman attending the girl should be the same for the first and second ceremonies.

The procedural outline obtained by Dr. McAllester in 1961[3] from the same source is almost identical. Frank Mitchell mentioned eight more events in 1961 than in 1963. They included:

First Day

> Put pot of wheat near outdoor cooking fire (after the molding).

Third Day

> Spread wheat in sun to dry (after digging the pit).
> Soak cornhusks (while working on the batter).

Third Night

> Gather soapweed root and white clay for morning (during the singing).

Fourth Day

> Prepare white-clay basket (during the Racing Songs).
> Lift children (after the molding).
> Girl goes back into hogan (after returning goods).
> Retie girl's hair.

The ideal procedure was compared with that set forth in the myth. The fullest account of the three Kinaaldá included in Frank's myth mentions many of the events above, ordered in the same manner.

Mythological Ordering of Events

First Day

> Comb.
> Dress.

---

[3]David McAllester, Field Notes, July 19−20, 1961, pp. 4a−7b.

Mold.
Run.
Grind corn.

Second Day

Run.
Grind corn.

Third Day

Run.
Grind corn.
Dig pit; build fire.
Make mush.
Put batter in pit; bless it.
Cover pit.

Third Night

Sing fourteen Chief Hogan Songs or twenty-five Talking God Hogan
   Songs.
"Free singing."[4]

Fourth Day

Dawn.
Run to the east while four songs are sung.
One Twelve Word Song, unless the ceremony is the first Kinaaldá,
   when this song is omitted.
Cut cake.
Make offering to Mother Earth.

However, some marked discrepancies exist between the
ideal procedure and the mythological one. In the latter, events of
the last day are condensed. There is no mention of washing the
girl's hair at dawn. The ceremony ends with the burial of the offering after the cake has been cut, thus excluding the subsequent
feast, combing, painting, and final molding. Another discrepancy
between mythological and ideal procedures is in the differences
given as the distinguishing factors between the first and second

---

[4]As will be explained in Chapter III, songs used in Kinaaldá are divided into two categories, "fixed songs" and "free songs." Fixed songs must be sung at specific points in the ceremony and by a specific singer; they may or may not accompany rites. Free songs are sung after
the main singer has "turned the singing over to the people." Free songs never accompany rites.

Kinaaldá. According to Frank Mitchell's myth, the addition of the Dawn Songs and the Twelve Word Songs to the second Kinaaldá distinguishes the ceremonies. Thus, while procedural reports are consistent, the mythological order of events does not reflect the one set forth in the procedures in several important instances.

It must now be determined whether or not the actual performance differs from the procedural outline.

The first puberty ceremony witnessed was that of Marie Shirley. The ceremony, which was a *second* Kinaaldá, took place from June 19 through June 23, 1963. It was ordered thus:

Procedural Outline

First Day: June 19, 1963

> Ceremony begins in afternoon.
> Comb girl's hair.
> Tie it with hair string.
> Dress girl.
> Mold girl inside hogan.
> Marie lifts people.
> Marie and others run.
> Marie and others run again at sunset.
> Grind corn after dark.
> Marie sleeps in the northwest part of the hogan, having put jewelry in ceremonial basket.

Second Day: June 20, 1963

> Marie and others run at dawn.
> Milk goats; grind corn.
> Noon race by Marie and others.
> Others grind; Marie sleeps.
> Sunset race by Marie and others.

Third Day: June 21, 1963

> Running at dawn and noon.
> Marie irons, grinds corn, and cleans hogan.
> Marie and others run at sunset.

Fourth Day: June 22, 1963, Bijį́ (Special Day)

Dawn race.
Chop wood; boil water.
Rose Mitchell (RM) digs pit.
Butcher sheep.
Start fire.
Everyone changes clothes.
Breakfast.
Boil water.
Noon race.
Mix mirage powder and corn pollen into flour.
Mix mush and sugar.
Men chop wood.
Lunch.
Many people arrive.
Load of firewood comes.
Mix mush batter.
Tearing of soaked cornhusks.
Pour batter into pit; bless it.
Cover batter.
Evening race by Marie and others.
Timmy Shirley sent after soapweed root.
Supper.

Fourth Night

Bring in pile of sand and water pail.
Feed people.
Bring goods to be blessed into hogan.
Hogan blessed.
Girl circles fire.
Corn pollen passed to people.

Fixed Songs

Twenty-five Hogan Songs. 11:00 P.M.−12:50 A.M.
Corn pollen passed during last song.
Girl leaves and returns.

Free songs

Eight Songs Pertaining to the Pairs. 12:50−1:15 A.M.
Two Songs of Old Age. 1:20−1:28 A.M.
Two Songs Pertaining to the Pairs. 1:31−1:35 A.M.
Eight Songs for Administering the Pollen. 1:36−2:10 A.M.
(Food break here.)

One Twelve Word Song. 2:10 – 2:14 A.M. (This is a fixed song which is interjected into the free singing.)

Corn pollen passed.

One Placing of the Earth Song. 2:15 – 2:28 A.M.

Five Songs of the Picking up of Changing Woman. 2:30 – 3:05 A.M.

Five Corn Beetle Songs. 3:07 – 3:27 A.M.

One Horse Song. 3:30 – 3:34 A.M.

Fifth Day: June 23, 1963[5]

Fixed Songs.

Marie's hair is washed.

> Four Washing Songs. 3:35 – 3:55 A.M. (No. 3 is called Song of the Birth of Dawn.)

Marie runs to the east for the last time.

> Four Racing Songs. 3:55 – 4:35 A.M.

Woman begins to prepare *dleesh* (white clay).

One Twelve Word Song. 4:37 – 4:45 A.M.

Corn pollen passed.

Cake removed from pit but only partially distributed because it has not cooled and hardened properly.

Meal served.

Girl's hair is combed.

> Two Combing Songs are sung. 6:40 – 6:45 A.M.

Marie is painted.

> One Song, a White Clay Song, is sung. 6:47 – 6:50 A.M.

Paint others.

Marie is molded outside the hogan.

Marie returns blankets and other goods.

Marie returns to hogan, and the public part of the ceremony is completed. The Kinaaldá itself actually continues for another four days. Marie remains partially secluded, sleeping in the ceremonial hogan and refraining from regular chores. She is supposed to remain quiet and thoughtful. She may change from ceremonial to regular dress.

---

[5]The Navaho express the length of their ceremonies by the number of nights involved in them; the Kinaaldá is a four-night ceremony, according to most Navaho. New days begin at dawn.

Detailed Account of Marie Shirley's Kinaaldá[6]

The Situation

Frank had been contacted about the fact that the author was interested in studying Kinaaldá before she arrived and had been looking for a patient within his own family. At first, he wanted Geneva Kee to be the kinaaldá, but his wife, Rose, said this would not be right since Geneva had already had two Kinaaldá. Marie Shirley, another of Frank's granddaughters, was then chosen, against her will. She had had her first Kinaaldá the summer before, but had not told anyone when she menstruated the second time and thus had "escaped" a second ceremony until now. As Marie said:

> A lot of the women around the place asked me if I had had it again, and I said no. This summer they asked me again, and I told them that I had been menstruating all the time, but I did not want to be kinaaldá. I moved to Shiprock [New Mexico] to baby-sit for my aunt, and you guys came running after me. I do not like being kinaaldá; I get tired of the beads, the running, and having to sit up all night.

The time of the ceremony was set to accommodate the American Indian Films Group from the University of California at Berkeley, who wished to film it after completing photography of a Red Ant Way Ceremonial near Valley Store, Arizona. Five days elapsed between the start of negotiations and the beginning of the ceremony. Since Marie's menstrual periods lasted for only two days, her second Kinaaldá did not coincide with the actual physiological event any more than did the first ceremony, where there had also been a delay.

Preliminary Preparations

During the five days, various preparations were made for the ceremony. Corn was shelled and some preliminary winnowing

---

[6]All verbatim conversations reported in the detailed account are translated from tapes made during the ceremony.

and grinding were done by Rose Mitchell. During the day before the ceremony was to begin, the hogan was cleaned, groceries were purchased, and the Mitchells were given some ground corn meal by a neighbor. Corn was ground at night in the hogan.

The First Day of the Ceremony: Wednesday, June 19, 1963

In the morning, a sheep was butchered, and Rose Mitchell softened the otter-hair tie to be used in the ceremony, working it in dampened sand with her hands. The jewelry to be worn by Marie Shirley was collected and placed in a ceremonial basket in the hogan. Good blankets were taken from storage and spread around the hogan. During the morning, visitors began to congregate.

Hair-Combing

The ceremony was to begin at 2:00 P.M., but due to complications with film equipment, it started at 2:50 P.M. Marie, dressed in a dark-green cotton skirt, black velvet blouse with silver buttons, a ceremonial sash, white ankle socks, and loafers, made a circuit around the fire and sat on the blanket in the west of the hogan, with her feet extended in front.

May Holtsoh (Yikadesbah Holtsoh), an "aunt" of Marie's, came from the back of the hogan; she removed the bobby pins and rubber bands which had been holding Marie's hair in a pony tail. Then, with a *bé'ezhóó'* (old-fashioned hairbrush), she brushed Marie's hair, down in back and outward on the sides by her ears. The rubber bands were replaced and the pony tail brushed again; next the otter tie was placed over the rubber band and knotted once; another string was tied around this to secure it.

Dressing

The ceremonial articles were taken from the sacred basket and placed on Marie. First, the ceremonial sash, *sis lá chii'*, belonging to Isabell Mitchell (Is.M) was put around her waist by May. Then a concho belt belonging to Frank was put on top of the sash.

Fig. 1. Hair brushing, using the Navaho brush.

Two strings of turquoise beads, one of Geneva's and one of Isabelle's, were put around Marie's neck and fastened with a safety pin. After this, four bracelets were placed on her right arm and three on her left, starting from the elbow in each instance. One belonged to Marie; two each were, respectively, from Augusta Sandoval (Aug. S), Mary Davis, and Rose Mitchell. Marie was already wearing two of her own rings.

Molding

Additional blankets were spread in Marie's ceremonial place in the west. From the bottom to the top, they were piled in the following order: a quilt, Pendleton blanket, plaid wool one, another Pendleton, a third Pendleton, and finally Marie's own Pendleton. Marie lay on top of them on her stomach, with her head to the west and her arms extended in "spread eagle" fashion. May pressed her right and left shoulders, waist, right and left arms, head, and her right and left legs, respectively. Then she pulled her hair. Marie rose and reversed her blanket. Next, she picked it up, folded it, and then returned it to the pile.   Then she picked it up again and folded it around her.   Standing facing the east, she returned the blankets to their owners, Dr. McAllester, Isabelle Mitchell, and Frank Mitchell.   The original blanket was left in place.

Lifting the People

Marie stood in the center of the blanket, facing east.   Spectators circled the fire and formed a line in front of her.   In succession, each one turned his back toward her.   She placed her hands on the back of his neck under the ears and lifted upward.   In the case of Geneva and Isabelle, the motion was downward.

Race Number One

When the lifting was completed, Marie circled the fire and dashed from the hogan for her first run.   Ten people accompanied her; Rose and Frank were the only ones left inside the hogan.   The runners yelled while running, giving falsetto cries that started high and had a strong downward glissando.   After about five minutes, all returned breathless.   Marie sat on the blanket in the west.   All left the hogan after they had recovered their breath.

Race Number Two

6:45 P.M.   The second race took place as the sun began to set.   Marie started from the rear of the hogan, first circling the fire.   The distance covered was greater than in the first race. When she returned, she again circled the fire and then fell exhausted on a mattress now in the hogan.

Nighttime Activities

After dinner, several visitors arrived. Marie, Rose, Geneva, Lena Shirley (LS), Isabelle, Ruth Yazzie, and the author ground corn for several hours in the hogan by the light of a kerosene lantern. Finally the metates (*tsé daashjiń*) and manos (*tsé daash-jéé'*) were swept with brushes (*tsé bee názhó*) and everything put

Fig. 2. Ceremonial dressing.

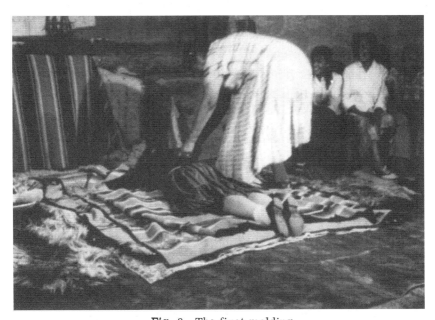

Fig. 3. The first molding.

Fig. 4. Nighttime corn-grinding, using the metate and mano.

away. Marie removed her concho belt and her jewelry (except her own rings), placing these in a ceremonial basket. Then she rolled herself in two blankets, with her own next to her body, and went to sleep in her place in the northwest of the hogan, lying on a mattress covered by a sheepskin.

The Second Day of the Ceremony: Thursday, June 20, 1963

    Race Number One

Rose awakened Marie at 4:30 A.M. and went to Geneva, who aroused Cecilia Sandoval. Marie rose, put on her belt and jewelry, and went outside. She ran, accompanied by five girls. As yesterday, the runners increased their speed as they neared the hogan on their return. Everyone ran into the hogan, circled the fire, and sat down. Marie went again to her ceremonial place. The race had consumed fifteen minutes, and the distance had been increased.

Fig. 5. A race at dawn.

Morning Activities

After the girls had rested, the bedding was removed from the hogan, and Geneva and Marie went to milk the goats.

Jimmy Begay arrived in his truck, and after Frank had donned his jewelry and jacket, they ate and at 5:30 A.M. departed for Gallup, New Mexico, to buy sheep. They returned at 11:30 A.M. with two sheep which had cost thirteen dollars apiece.

Race Number Two

The second race of the day was run at noon and consumed twenty minutes. Marie was accompanied by all the children.

Afternoon Activities

In the afternoon, some corn-grinding was filmed by the American Indian Films Group. The grinding was done according to procedures used in earlier days in order that a record might be made of them. Marie, Geneva, and Isabelle knelt, facing east, behind three metates which were resting on goat- and sheepskins. Marie started the grinding, passing the grist to Isabelle in a ceremonial basket.   After she had ground it to a finer powder, she passed it in the same manner to Geneva.   While the women were grinding, Chic Sandoval sang three of the old Grinding Songs. Much hilarity ensued, especially during the "exchange of compliments" when the singer and the women sprinkled each other with a bit of ground meal.[7]

Race Number Three

Marie ran her third race of the day between 7:00 P.M. and 7:25 P.M. Once again, the distance was increased. Following this, she and Geneva discussed Kinaaldá with the author until dark.

According to Dr. McAllester, Lena Shirley reported that children often play Kinaaldá. They make bracelets of wire and belts from rope; then they race. Dr. McAllester observed some children using comae from cottonwood trees as jewelry. They pinned them to their clothes.

There were no guests present on the second day.

The Third Day of the Ceremony: Friday, June 21, 1963

Races Numbers One and Two

Marie ran from 4:30 A.M. to 5:00 A.M. and again from 11:00 A.M. to 11:35 A.M.

Afternoon Activities

During the afternoon, Geneva and Rose cleaned the place, swept the hogan, tidied the "cook shack," and burned the trash. Marie ironed all afternoon. Several women ground corn, filling three flour sacks with corn meal by evening. The Mitchells said that no more would be needed. The children played at grinding all afternoon, using assorted bricks and stones for implements.

---

[7]See Charlotte Johnson, "Navaho Corn Grinding Songs," *Journal of the Society for Ethnomusicology,* VIII, No. 2 (May, 1964), pp. 101-120.

During the afternoon, there was much discussion about the blowing sand. Isabelle kept saying that with the wind so strong, it was hard for the cake to cook, since the earth did not heat properly.

Another discussion also ensued between Frank and Marie concerning the length of the ceremony. He remained firm in his order that she remain in Chinle until four days after the completion of the public part of the ceremony.

Jimmy Begay and his wife came to dinner; there were no other visitors.

Race Number Three

The third race started at 7:00 P.M. and was forty minutes in length. Again the distance was increased. Marie had wanted to run earlier, but Frank insisted that she wait until sundown. Fifteen people accompanied her at the start, but only ten returned with her. Four smaller children came back earlier and waited by the main gate so as to run to the hogan with Marie. While they waited, "Tiny" Sandoval, the only girl in this group, played at racing. Geneva returned after all had gone to the hogan.

Nighttime

After the race, Marie and the author were alone in the hogan. She complained about being kinaaldá because she was fatigued. "I just ache all over and I am so tired. I am using Bengué now on my aches to get ready to run tomorrow. My legs hurt, and I have been tired all day. I think that I am just too lazy to run tomorrow."

Before going to bed, Marie removed her jewelry as usual. This time, however, the ceremonial baskets were full, and she started to place it in a china dish. Rose entered, said, "No, do not do that," and slapped her hands. Rose then rummaged in a trunk and removed a buckskin bag. She instructed Marie to place her jewelry in that for the night.

The Fourth Day of the Ceremony: June 22, 1963. Saturday. Biji̧.

Race Number One

Marie was awakened by Rose at 4:30 A.M. She dressed and roused Geneva, Lena, Ivonne Shirley, and Cecilia. All ran with her. The race was only fifteen minutes in length. Rose and the author folded blankets and sheepskins and tidied the hogan while Marie was gone.

Morning Activities

The author took Isabelle to Rose's sister's hogan to request assistance, which was not forthcoming. We stopped at one more hogan to find another woman who knew the procedures involved in making the baking pit. The door at the second place was locked.

Jimmy Begay was filling water tanks when we returned. At breakfast he said that the fire should have been started long ago; the Mitchells, however, were awaiting the arrival of the film crew.

Frank and Rose changed their clothes and put on their jewelry.

Making the Pit, Butchering, Wood-Chopping

Large kettles of water were placed on an outdoor fire to boil.

At 6:45 A.M., Rose took a pickax and, after first cleaning the area with a rake, outlined a hole about three feet in diameter southeast of the hogan door. Next she softened the area inside the circle with the ax. Dr. McAllester and the author offered to help. but Rose stopped McAllester, since he was a *jaashzhini* (Black Ears). (He had previously been thrown in the mud at a Squaw Dance.) Chic Sandoval said: "These people [*jaashzhini*], those building fires at Squaw Dances, and the fire dancers who carry torches in the Mountain Chant cannot come near the fire pit or help with the digging. If they do, the cake may not cook; it may stay all mushy."

Having awakened, Frank arrived and began to pound the

earth with the ax. Rose hoed and shoveled the dirt away. Frank soon sat down, saying his back hurt. The author joined Rose in working on the pit with a shovel, pick, and hoe. Frank said that the earth should be arranged in a circle around the pit. Rose said no and directed that it be piled on the north side.

Next a sheep was butchered, and the horses were rounded up. The hole was scraped and the diameter measured with a shovel. It still was not wide enough.

The pit was enlarged and scraped and then swept to remove the loose, caked mud. Wilson brought a carpenter's level and checked the bottom of the pit to see if it were *kehasdon* (straight). At 8:05 A.M., the diameter of the pit was equivalent to the length of the shovel; thus it was finished.

Wilson Yazzie (WY) and Timmy Shirley harnessed the team and went to get a load of wood. When they returned, Wilson and Bobby Mitchell, a relative, began chopping it. Mary and Rose knelt to examine the hole. They decided to deepen the pit by an additional two inches to accommodate the three sacks of meal that were to be used. Frank came out and offered to help. Rose told him no, as he picked up a hoe, and he laughed, saying, "The foreman has fired me already." When the pit was completed, it was 1 foot deep, 56 inches in diameter, and had been dug 85 feet southeast of the hogan door.

A group of children left in the wagon to get water.

8:30 A.M. A match was used to ignite the wood chips which had been placed in the pit. As the fire burned, cedar bark was added.

Clothes Changed

Marie changed her clothes, donning a pink silk skirt and a rust-colored velvet blouse with a silver-trimmed collar. Other girls changed into their "Sunday best."

Fig. 6. Measuring the pit to be used in baking the 'alkaan.

Other Morning Activities

Frank remained at the pit, tending the fire. This act was filmed by the American Indian Films Group. He jokingly said he should stir it with a shovel or a hoe, or he would get dizzy and fall into the fire. However, he continued to use a short stick.

At 9:30 A.M. mutton and tea were served. Then some of the children took the sheep out for herding and led the horses away. The wind started to blow, and the fire burned poorly for a while. There was a general lull in the events.

Race Number Two

Marie ran at 10:45 A.M., returning at 11:25 A.M. Fourteen ran with her. While she was gone, Frank began to worry that some of the people who would normally come to help with the singing would stay away because of the belagáanas.[8]

[8]When the word "belagáana" is used in an English sentence by a Navaho, it is given a plural form, "belagáanas," when the English context requires one, even though in Navaho the form "belagáana" is used as both singular and plural.

Mirage Powder and Corn Pollen Mixed into the Flour

After the race, the author took Isabelle and some others to the trading post to get raisins for the cake. While we were gone, Dr. McAllester observed the following:

Rose entered the hogan, carrying a sheet, which she spread on the floor in the west. Three bags of corn meal were emptied on the sheet. Rose removed a bundle from a chest. Then she knelt beside the meal, facing south, and rubbed powdered aragonite (symbolizing mirage) on the mano. Next she added corn pollen from a jar. She then handed the mano to Marie and instructed her to mix the flour from the east, south, west, and north. She did this. Then she worked the flour with her hands until Rose told her to stop. Chic said that this was done to make the cake rise. The mano was then cleaned with the *tsé bee názhó*; Marie also cleaned her jewelry, using a few of the brush straws.

The pit was cleaned for the first time, and the ashes were emptied from it on the north side.

Mixing the Batter

12:45 P.M. When we returned from the trading post, Isabelle took a basket of corn meal and emptied it on the pile. Marie knelt and, facing west, mixed all the flour, pausing once to remove one of her rings from the pile. On her left hand she was now wearing three new turquoise rings that Louise Davis had given her earlier in the morning. After the mixing, Marie returned to her seat in the northwest and stayed there until the boiling water was brought in. Five large pans were placed near the door of the hogan. On top of three of them were bundles of stirring sticks known as *'adístsiin*. These were lengths of greasewood (*dóghóz-hii*) which had been cleaned and the bark removed. They were tied together with wet rags.

At 1:00 P.M., Rose brought the boiling water and set it in front of the sheet which held the mixed flour. Marie took some flour, put it in the boiling water, using two hands, and began to stir the mixture with a bundle of sticks. Geneva brought in

Fig. 7. Preparing the batter, using the greasewood stirring sticks.

another pail of hot water. Rose began to work with that one. Isabelle entered, carrying a pan full of hot brown liquid, which was
identified as white sugar. One small pan of this was added to
each pail as both Marie and Rose knelt to stir. Geneva said the
sugar should have been yellow, but for some reason it had changed
color. Marie removed her rings to stir; Geneva put them on.

More buckets were carried in, and soon six women were
mixing. A bit of ground wheat was also added to the batter.[9]

Afternoon Activities

At 1:30 P.M., lunch was served. Eleven people arrived.
Some people were fed as others continued the stirring. A friend
of the Mitchells arrived with fifteen dollars' worth of wood which
had been cut at Black Mountain. As the women worked, a group of
men gathered by the barn to rest. Wilson watched the fire.

---

[9]Note the differences between these cake preparations and the *'alkaan* recipe given by
Flora Bailey, "Navaho Foods and Cooking Methods," *American Anthropologist*, XLII, No. 2, Part I
(April–June, 1940), p. 281. They may also be compared with the *'alkaan* recipe collected in Crown-
point, given in Appendix E.

Removing the Lumps from the Batter

When the stirring had been completed, the women began to rub the batter between their hands to remove the lumps. After a while Isabelle ceased rubbing and utilized an egg beater.

Wilson cleaned the pit again at 3:00 P.M. While the author was observing this, Augusta Sandoval informed her that only a modified version of this ceremony would be conducted when her daughters had their Kinaaldá. She said that a cake would be made, but it would only be large enough to enable everyone to have a piece. There would be no running.

Preparing the Cornhusks

3:20 P.M. Ruth Yazzie entered the hogan with a kettle of water in which bundles of cornhusks were soaking. She spread a cloth in the north and sat behind it, facing south. Geneva said the husks were from last summer's corn. A board was placed in front of Ruth. She removed a bundle and put a dry one in its place in the bucket. Then, taking individual husks from the rag-tied bundle, she tore the butt end in several places so that the husks would lie flat. Then she straightened them and placed them in a pile, with the tips facing her.

Meanwhile, the author had started to rub the mush. After the women had said that men sometimes assisted, Dr. McAllester joined in. At 4:30 P.M., Marie went to her house to sleep. All the lumps had been removed by 4:45 P.M., and there was a lull while the women cleaned their jewelry with brush straws and washed the pans. The batter was allowed to "ferment."

Ruth continued working the husks. When all had been torn and straightened, she took eight and made two crosses by sewing four husks together with white thread in the manner illustrated below.

Another party of four arrived, bringing food. Howard
Mitchell and Timmy Shirley brought dirt from a hole they had dug
near the cabin and piled it close to the rim on the west side of the
pit. The dirt was used to cover the cake in the pit.

Removing the Fire from the Pit

At 5:10 P.M., Rose knelt beside the fire, moistened the dirt
with water, and mixed it with her hands. Rose and Isabelle removed the burning logs from the pit and extinguished the remaining flames with dirt. The American Indian Films Group removed
the ashes.

Pouring the Batter in the Pit

5:20 P.M. A crowd gathered to watch. Rose and Wilson
spread dirt around the edge and raked the bottom of the pit. Two
large planks were placed east to west on the north and south rims.
Some women brought a blanket and spread it near the south rim,
anchoring it with logs.

5:30 P.M. Two pickup trucks arrived, filled with people.

The procession from the hogan began, with many people
helping to carry the eleven buckets of batter. These were placed
at the north side of the pit. The bottom was lined with newspapers. Then Mary, Rose, Ruth, Isabelle, Louise Begay, and one unidentified woman knelt on the boards. Husks were passed to them.
Marie appeared, took one of the two husk crosses that Ruth had
made, gestured with it in the blessing manner[10] over the pit, and
then placed it in the center. Husks were interwoven with the cross
until the central area was covered.

---

[10]When blessing an object with corn pollen, corn meal, or other material, the Navaho
usually motion to the east and back, the west and back, the north and back, the south and back, and
then around the area in a clockwise circle.

When blessing themselves with corn pollen during Kinaaldá, the Navaho took a bit of the
pollen on their fingertips, touched their tongues and the top of their heads, and then made an upward
motion toward the smoke hole in the roof of the hogan.

All references to object and personal blessings in this publication will be references to
the above procedures, unless otherwise stated.

Fig. 8. Tearing the cornhusks.

Following this, Howard and Wilson stood in the north and poured the batter toward the east into a small pan held by Isabelle over the center of the pit. As the batter overflowed, the women added husks around the edges of the pit, with the tips pointing clockwise. The batter was smoothed and husks were added until the pouring was completed. Everyone then added raisins. Next, Marie took corn meal from the ceremonial basket she was holding in her right hand and, from the south, blessed the batter. A layer of cornhusks was then placed on the batter. Finally Marie placed the remaining cross on the top of this, after repeating the blessing motions with it.

Covering the Cake

The cross was covered with husks, a layer of newspaper, and then fresh, moist earth. The boards were removed. Live coals were raked on top of the dirt, and Rose and Lena added chips of wood, which burst into flame.

Fig. 9. Pouring the batter into the pit.

Fig. 10. Completing the covering of the batter by placing the second cornhusk cross in position.

Race Number Three

As soon as the fire was started, Marie left, from the hogan, for her race. Five minutes later, Frank began discussing the soapweed (yucca) root with Diné łbáhí, Jimmy Begay, Wilson, and an unidentified man. Timmy was sent to get the root after Frank instructed him in the procedures for gathering it. He was to go to the other side of the wash and cut a four-inch piece from the bottom and sides of a yucca root. This piece and some of the rocks lying near the plant were to be brought home. Marie returned at 6:30 P.M., accompanied by fourteen individuals. Timmy returned shortly thereafter.

The Fourth Night

Meal

Supper was served. After the men had eaten, some of them filled the pit with the dirt that remained piled around it. At 9:00 P.M. they started a large fire, which would be kept burning all night.

Preparations in the Hogan

Sometime between 8:00 P.M. and 9:00 P.M., a blanket was hung on the hogan door to signify that a ceremony was in process.

Marie arranged her mattress in her sleeping place in the northwest. A mound of sand was placed in the center under the smoke hole, and a pail of water was brought in. Singers started to arrive. Some lay down to rest while waiting for the strenuous singing to begin.

At 10:00 P.M., Frank entered the hogan and roused the sleeping singers. The American Indian Films Group arrived at 10:20 P.M. Ten minutes later, the men were served a meal of mutton, fry bread, and coffee.

Goods To Be Blessed Are Brought In

Sheepskins, fabrics, deerskins, and a bridle were brought into the hogan. The sheepskins were spread in various places for people to sit on. The fabrics were put to the left of Marie's place, and the bridle and deerskins on the eastern edge of the ceremonial blanket located in the west between Frank and Marie. Two ceremonial baskets were placed in the middle of the blanket. One basket contained a hairbrush and a knotted white rag; the other, a concho belt and pollen pouch.

At 11:00 P.M., Frank entered and sat down in his place. Others came in; the women occupied one side of the hogan and the men the other, as shown in the diagram. Augusta brought most of her children; they were to stay up all night since they had "to be up to go to mass real early in the morning anyway." Frank untied the pollen pouch and replaced it in the basket. Isabelle added another, and Frank untied that. A buckskin was also added; it was placed so that it partially covered the bridle. Lena brought in the stirring sticks, now tied into one bundle, and placed them on the blanket. Isabelle removed two small pouches from a suitcase and untied them. Marie put them in the first basket. Isabelle added another. A suitcase was then placed on the pile of goods to be blessed. Ruth added a buckskin and another pouch to the basket.

Singers Enter

11:10 P.M. Three singers, now wearing headbands, joined Frank in the hogan. These were Diné łbáhí, Jimmy Begay, and John Smiley. Five minutes later, Frank began to instruct the singers and then joke with them.

> After each set of songs, we pass the corn pollen. The reason that we do this is that we want to respect it and keep it holy. ...
> I went over to see a sister-in-law and asked that she help. She said, "No, I heard that that is all being done for white people; when you do anything for white people you always get paid for it." When she said this I thought there was no use urging her to come. Then she said that she had gone to a singing on top of the mesa. I wonder how much she got paid for it. [Laughter] Such words are not good.

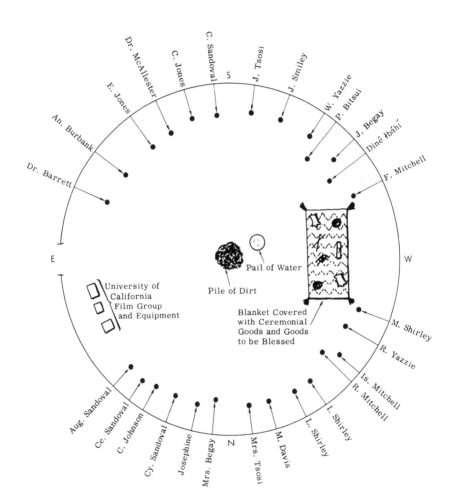

If you talk that way with friends and relatives, it gives them a bad impression. So let us not feel that way toward one another. Let us conduct the ceremony in a friendly manner....

...The first time Marie had a Kinaaldá, we used a set of Home Songs pertaining to the original Hogan Songs. So we will omit those now and use the second set, the Talking God Songs. Now, in the Hogan Songs, there are some Trail Songs. In a certain song in that group, my version differs slightly from yours.

Hogan Blessing

Marie wrapped herself in her blanket. Jimmy Begay took a pollen pouch from Frank and blessed the house, touching the beams in the east, south, west, and north and then scattering pollen around the hogan.[11]

Girl Goes around the Fire

After he sat down, Marie circled the fire clockwise and returned to her place.

People Bless Themselves with Pollen

Frank blessed the goods in front of him with pollen. Marie blessed herself and passed a pollen pouch to the woman on her left. In turn, each woman blessed herself. Then the pouch was returned to Frank. In the meantime, beginning with Frank, on the men's side, a pollen pouch was passed from one man to the next until it reached the man by the door. He blessed himself, and the others did likewise as the pouch was returned to Frank. Both pouches were then placed in one of the ceremonial baskets.

Frank announced that no one might leave the hogan until Marie had departed.

Fixed Singing

Hogan Songs

At 11:20 P.M., the Hogan Songs, *Hooghan bighiin*, began. Nine men sang with Frank. When the sixth song commenced, the

---

[11]The directions occur in a different order in this pollen blessing, since the one doing the blessing of the hogan is walking around the building in a clockwise direction, marking the beams.

tempi and pitches began to vary. By the eleventh song, a real contest was taking place. The young singers were singing the songs faster and at a higher pitch than Frank. After the twelfth song, Frank prayed. Then the following remarks were made:

> **Isabelle:** Do not rush ahead of the leader of the singing. Just follow him.
>
> **Frank:** That makes twelve songs to that point. The belagáanas are white-skinned people. Let these white people talk to us with a corn-pollen voice. We should not say anything that is not friendly. That white man with the white beard [Dr. Barrett, from the University of California] will speak to us with kind words.
>
> From here on, there is another set of twelve songs pertaining to White Shell Woman. Where you mentioned Talking God before, now you say White Shell Woman.
>
> **Isabelle:** Be careful that you just follow the leader in the singing and do not confuse him because all of that is being picked up by the machine, so you have to be careful.

During the last song in this group, Frank turned and passed a pollen pouch to Marie. The women blessed themselves as before, and almost a minute later Frank passed another pouch to the men. This time the people, particularly the women, prayed as they blessed themselves; some had their eyes shut, and most prayed quietly. The two pouches were returned to the basket as before. Then Frank said, *"K'ad ni"* (Now, it is finished), and Marie arose and departed, passing to the left of the fire. Now the people were free to rise and exit.

Free Singing

At 12:50 A.M. Frank Mitchell relinquished his leadership, and others in the group began the "free singing."

> *Group I:* Eight Songs Pertaining to the Pairs, *Bee'itchin da' ya'igíí.* Sung by Wilson, Peter, and Jimmy. 12:50– 1:15 A.M.

During the seventh and eighth songs, the author left the hogan. Many children were playing around the fire; Ivonne and Geneva were not tending it. Clyde Jones came over to tell the author that some people did not welcome her presence.

Fig. 11. The all-night singing.

Before the songs of Group II began, the following conversation took place:

> Frank: There is another set of songs that comes in here, but it
> is up to you. If you are going to sing it, be very careful.
> Peter: Go ahead, sing it for us, then.
> Frank: I am not singing those songs. Someone else is singing
> them. Go ahead and sing a set for us.

Group II: Two Songs of Old Age, *Są́'ą naghei bighiin*. Sung
           by Frank, Diné Łbáhí, Wilson, and Peter. (Isa-
           belle, Mrs. Tsosi, and Mary Davis also sang at
           times.) 1:20 – 1:28 A.M.

After these songs Frank said:

> There's nothing changeable in a song. The words are always
> alike. Now, this set of songs is a sacred set we have to be very
> particular about. That is why most singers skip it, because if they
> did not, they would mess it up. But here, these people have been
> confusing the four mountains. You people, without inquiring more
> thoroughly about it, are just going ahead and singing these songs
> carelessly. You must realize that these non-Navaho are present;
> although they will not use these songs for ceremonial purposes,
> they still would like to preserve them. That is what they are here

for; they are recording it because they want to save it for the future. They have a feeling for the Navaho tribe because they think the *diné*[12] are wonderful people. They say the Navaho have these ceremonies and carry them on for a long time. They are progressive and increasing rapidly. You must realize that other Indians around us, like the Pueblos, are not increasing as we are. These white people here are present to find out what sort of ceremonies, prayers, and songs we have that enable us to increase so rapidly. They also know that our young men went to war for the United States and that their language was used in the far-off countries and was no doubt very useful in most cases. Some of our young people are careless about these ceremonies. They just go wild in these doings; you should not do that.

[Someone interrupts]: Go ahead, my grandfather, keep singing.

Frank: I do not have to do it. I turned it over to you people to carry on from where I stopped.

Group III: Two Songs Pertaining to the Pairs, *Bee'itchin da'ya'igii.* Sung by Jimmy, Wilson, and Peter. 1:31 – 1:35 A.M.

Group IV: Eight Songs for Administering the Pollen.[13] Jimmy, Wilson, Peter, and Clyde sang them. 1:36 – 2:10 A.M.

A break occurred in the middle of this group for a meal.

Group V: One Twelve Word Song, *Naakits'áadah doo'igii.* 2:10 – 2:14 A.M.

Corn pollen was passed. Then Frank said:

That is the reason that these people who are non-Navaho are interested. They are recording to preserve these things. You younger people are not sincere in trying to learn it to carry it on in the future. So it is a good thing white people record it to preserve it for us. You ask why they are here to take pictures, make records, and to preserve the whole ceremony. In the future, someone may be interested in inquiring about it; then he will be able to see it.

Group VI: One Placing of the Earth Song, *Nohodzáán bighiin,* sung by Diné łbáhí and later Jimmy Begay. 2:15 – 2:28 A.M.

---

[12]The Navaho call themselves the *diné,* "the People."

[13]A Navaho name could not be obtained for this group of songs. Chic said that this group belonged to another bigger group, the *Nohodzáán bighiin.*

During this song the dishes were cleared. Marie started to scratch her head, but Frank stopped her. He also made her readjust her blanket, so that it was around her shoulders rather than her waist.

> *Group VII*: Five Songs of the Picking Up of Changing Woman,
> *Asdzą́ą́ nidii yáalgii*.   Sung by Diné łbáhí and
> Frank. 2:30 – 3:05 A.M.

Diné łbáhí's voice was very hoarse by this time. There was much talking and joking and also discussion of myth variation by the two singers.

After the first song of this group, Frank related the story of Coyote finding a baby floating on a lake at the top of Blanca Peak (*supra*, p. 11).

After the second song, Frank repeated the story of the baby on the lake and added:

> Talking God went over there on a sun ray and brought the child out. That is the story that has been passed on from one generation to another. No one is alive now who witnessed that at that time.
>
> We disagree with one another on where Changing Woman was picked up as a baby. This is my father's story that I am telling. My father told me, and that is the reason I mention Blanca Peak first and then Gobernador Knob in the song. Of course, you mention it the other way around; I am not criticizing you; I am just telling you my way.

After Song No. 3, Frank and Diné łbáhí said the following:

> **Diné łbáhí**: They are laughing about us because we are fooling each other here.
>
> **Frank**: Go ahead, brother; you have not gone very far in your songs pertaining to the dressing up of Changing Woman at her ceremony.
>
> **Diné łbáhí**: Well, I was not present when that took place so I do not know about it. I do not know who all contributed their songs to the ceremony. I was not there. I do not have any children I can teach my songs to. I have never taught anybody. Of course, I am sincere when I am singing. I just do not do it for the fun of it.

Corn pollen was passed after the fifth song.

> *Group VIII*: Five Corn Beetle Songs, *'Anłt'ánii bighiin*.
> Sung by John Tsosi. (JT). 3:07 – 3:27 A.M.

After the second song, Frank said, "When Talking God came in when Corn Beetle was decorated, he gazed on it and praised it. Talking God consecrated Corn Beetle Girl in the center of the hogan room."

After the third song, there was a discussion about the time:

Diné łbáhí: Frank is expecting the dawn right now.
Frank: The light is in the east. I wonder if it is dawn now.
Diné łbáhí: Maybe.

After the fifth song, the dawn was again discussed.

Frank: Maybe that is enough now. What does it look like now? We do not want to start in too early, while it is still pitch dark. Let us let it get lighter. How is it? How many more have you got to sing?
John Tsosi: I am finished. I sang all the songs.
Frank: Pass the corn pollen. Go ahead and eat the pollen. Just one more person needs to sing. That will be sufficient.

Group IX: One Horse Song, *Łį́į́ bighiin.* Diné łbáhí and
Frank. 3:30 – 3:34 A.M.

During this song Mrs. Tsosi[14] left her place, went to the basket, and sat down, facing northwest. She then began to pound the soapweed root with two rocks. These were the ones which Timmy had brought from the area where he had cut the yucca.

After the song, everyone decided that dawn had come. (It was now 3:34 A.M.) However, Frank ruled that Marie should wait until there was more light before running her race.

[Someone said]: It is getting too late; it is getting too light.
Frank: Well, go ahead and prepare the soap; who is going to fix the soapsuds? Are you turning the singing back to me now?
[Several answered]: Yes, it is dawn.

Fixed Singing

Hair-Washing

Four Dawn or Washing Songs, *Yołkááł bighiin,* were sung by Frank, 3:35 – 3:53 A.M. During the first song, 3:35 – 3:39 A.M.,

---

[14]Mrs. Tsosi was now attending Marie. May Holtsoh refused to return after the first day because of the cameras.

Marie wrapped herself in her blanket. Ruth passed a pan of water to Mrs. Tsosi, who filled the basket. It began to leak, and they placed more dirt under it. When this did not suffice, the basket was lined with a plastic bag. Mrs. Tsosi rubbed the root between her hands.

Diné łbáhí started the second song at 3:40. During its five-minute duration, Mrs. Tsosi produced a lather and Marie removed her glasses and her blanket. Isabelle told her to remove her jewelry. Mrs. Tsosi continued to work the lather according to Frank's instructions. Marie moved and knelt in front of the basket. Mrs. Tsosi removed Marie's necklaces and her bracelets, first from the right arm and then from the left, starting each time with the bracelets closest to the elbow. She untied the hair string, while Marie unsuccessfully tried to remove her rings. Mrs. Tsosi washed the jewelry. The necklaces were taken from the basket, then replaced and rewashed. These and the bracelets were rinsed with plain water. The concho belt, sash, and hair string were not washed.

More water was added to the basket, and Marie began to wash her own hair, while Mrs. Tsosi straightened the jewelry on the blanket. Mrs. Tsosi and Ruth held the basket.

Between 3:46 and 3:49 A.M., many people helped sing the third song, known as The Song of the Birth of Dawn, *Yikai yischį yisin*. Marie washed her hair and face. Then Mrs. Tsosi rinsed her hair with clear water and squeezed it. After Marie had also wrung it, Frank passed the hair string to Mrs. Tsosi. Marie put on her concho belt. Mrs. Tsosi reached under Marie's right arm, looped the hair string over her concho belt, and tied it in a square knot.

As the fourth song was sung, 3:50 – 3:53 A.M., the jewelry was replaced in the same manner and order as before. Mrs. Tsosi tightened the bracelets and made sure that the necklaces were pinned in place. Marie wrung her hair once more and then shook it. Next, she wrapped herself in her blanket. Then the small children were awakened in order that they would be ready to run.

Final Race

After receiving instructions from Frank, Marie left for the final race of the ceremony. Frank and others sang four Racing Songs, *Jaadesin*, during this time (3:55 – 4:35 A.M.).

During the first song, Mrs. Tsosi took the basket to the west wall and emptied it in a northerly direction. The plastic bag was left next to the wall, but the basket was returned to the blanket. The author and others went outside. It was now 3:55 A. M. Ruth and Augusta had cleaned the fire from the pit so that the cake would begin to cool.

The first song was followed by a conversation:

> Frank: They will go a long way.
>
> John Tsosi: Maybe they will go to Chinle.
>
> Diné łbáhí: They will go to the cottonwood grove.
>
> Frank: Did one of the film men go there?
>
> Chic: No; they are sleeping in the car.
>
> Frank: I thought they were going to set up a camera where she turns around.
>
> Chic: That is what I thought, too, but they did not.
>
> Jimmy Begay: What about raking off the hot ashes and coals from the cake?
>
> Frank: Oh, yes, we had better do that now.
>
> Isabelle: It has already been done.
>
> Frank: Well, then, let us have a jug of wine.
>
> Mary: Leave that [evil] stuff alone.
>
> Frank: Me, maybe.
>
> Diné łbáhí: [Incomprehensible.]
>
> Frank: [turning to a discussion of the songs]: That is the way you should sing these songs. This is not the only time you are going to be singing for Kinaaldá. There are any number of songs that we do for that. Many others are about to come. It will be quite some time before they return because they go quite a distance.
>
> Diné łbáhí: We hear them coming.

The runners, however, were not returning.

Fig. 12. The hair-washing at dawn.

After the second Racing Song (4:07–4:11 A.M.) there was more conversation.

Frank: The next song starts with *násolsį́į́* [the sound is returning]. It will be some time yet before we do that one. We will wait until we hear them coming close. Then the next song will be *natsiltsą́* [it has returned to its starting point]. In this next song your main word is *násolsį́į́*, and you mention returning from the east. In the last song it is *natsíltsá*, and you mention the west. So there are four songs. After we sing *natsíltsá*, that is the end of the set. We are almost finished.

Diné łbáhí: I did not steal any of these songs. I was taught how to sing them. I did not steal them as others do while sitting around at sings.

Frank: That fellow there has been after me to teach him, but he is lying to me; he has never come around to be taught. . . .

That machine is recording; we will ask them to run it back and see what it sounds like. When we listen to it, we will check our-selves and see how many words we missed. I do not think any of us missed any; if there are any missing, it is the machine's fault. Where did Chic drag that man with the beard [Dr. Barrett]?

Diné łbáhí: The old man is over there.

Frank: Oh, is that him over there? Where is Chic?

Dr. McAllester: I wonder if he is running after the girls?

Frank: No, he cannot run. He is liable to stumble and fall. Did you empty the extra water from the basket?

Mrs. Tsosi: Yes.

Frank: Leave those things here for her. Put the *dleesh* in the basket.

The third Racing Song was sung by Jimmy, Diné łbáhí, and Frank between 4:15 and 4:20 A.M. Frank corrected the other singers several times.

Preparation of the White Clay

Mrs. Tsosi took a cylindrical piece of *dleesh* and began shaving pieces from it with a knife into a ceremonial basket. Facing south, she then sprinkled a few drops of water into the basket.

After the third song, Frank said, "Maybe the others do not agree with what we are singing, but that is the way we were taught, and we go according to the way we were taught. We do not add anything."

During the fourth Racing Song (4:30 – 4:35 A.M.) shouts could be heard; Marie and eight runners entered the hogan as Frank completed the song. Chic and Frank requested that all the people come into the hogan. Some explanations followed:

Chic: This will be the last song.

Frank: Now, the only song left is the Twelve Word Song. Here is the way your words in the songs are; you say: [gives text verbally].

Twelve Word Song

As the song was sung, the women were solemn; the white people appeared to have been forgotten. Marie was sitting with her feet straight in front of her, gazing at the smoke hole, still panting from her run. Frank sat facing her, staring at her and occasionally correcting the singers. The song continued from 4:37 to 4:45 A.M. Pollen pouches were passed when the song was completed; all blessed themselves. After the pouches had been returned to Frank, the people went outside and gathered around the cake pit.

Removing and Distributing the Cake

Isabelle swept a portion of the cake with a small brush while Rose sharpened a knife on the mano. When the knife was ready, she began to cut a piece from the eastern edge by moving clockwise. The first piece of cake was about ten inches long and five inches wide. Marie placed it on a newspaper and gave it to Dr. McAllester. It was soft; Rose said that the cake was too hot because the fire had not been removed at the right time. Isabelle continued to precede Rose, sweeping the cake as Rose cut more pieces, first from the east and then from the west. The pieces were put on newspapers and boards, which once again surrounded the pit. Dr. McAllester offered Marie a piece of the cake, but she said she was not allowed to eat it.

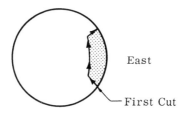

East

First Cut

Meal

After a while, the cutting was terminated, and a meal of fry bread, corn mush, and *'alkaan* was served in the hogan. The author was told to eat in the "cook shack" with the women; this was the first occasion since the beginning of the ceremony that separate eating places for the men and women had been strictly observed.

By 6:10 A.M., all had eaten. John Tsosi and Diné łbáhí departed, after shaking hands.

Combing

At 6:30 A.M. Marie and Mrs. Tsosi returned to the hogan and Marie, who had not eaten, sat in her place, facing east, with her feet extended. The first of two Combing Songs, *Kinaaldá bé'éz-*

hóó ígíí bighiin, was started by Frank. As the song was sung
(6:40 – 6:42 A.M.), Mrs. Tsosi moved behind Marie and began to
brush her hair with the large brush taken from the basket on the
blanket. During the second song, 6:43 – 6:45 A.M., Mrs. Tsosi
continued brushing sections of Marie's hair. Some people left the
hogan to see if the cake had cooled.

Painting

Directed by Frank, Mrs. Tsosi came around the blanket and
faced west. Isabelle handed her some water; she put a few drops
in the basket containing the *dleesh* and stirred it with straws from
the hairbrush. Frank began the White Clay Song, *Dleesh bighiin,*
at 6:47 A.M., and in accordance with the words, Mrs. Tsosi painted
Marie's left and right shoe soles, left and right knees, chest, and
back. Then the left and right shoulders, hands, and cheeks were
painted, the latter being accomplished with an upward motion.
(Marie, of course, remained fully clothed, as she had been for the
entire ceremony.) Finally, *dleesh* was put on the top of her head.
Then Marie rose and pulled her blanket around her shoulders.
Next, she took the basket in her two hands and stood in the middle
of the blanket, facing east. All the people who wanted to be painted
stood up and formed a line. Marie made an upward dab on each
person's right and left cheeks and on his head. Geneva, however,
had her cheeks painted with a downward motion. Frank rubbed his
hands in the *dleesh* basket and then smeared his cheeks and hair.
After this, Marie walked around the hogan and painted all the
people who had not stood in line.

Molding

Everyone went outside for the final molding. Blankets and
other items were spread in front of the door in the following
order: the blanket Marie had been sitting on throughout the ceremony was put down first; then three Pendleton blankets, two jac-
kets, and two deerskins were added. Marie lay down with her
arms spread as before and her head about four feet away from the

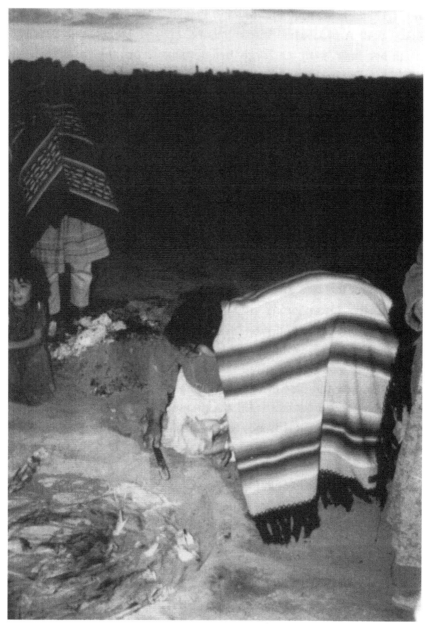

Fig. 13. Removing the *'alkaan*.

door. Mrs. Tsosi molded her, starting with her feet, pressing her legs together, and working up her body, doing first the left shoulder, then the right; the left arm and then the right; the neck; and finally the head. She pulled Marie's hair downward and continued the long, sweeping motion with a wave of the hand over the entire length of Marie's body. When she had finished, Marie rose and returned the blankets and other goods to their owners, who said, "Thank you." Then she went inside the hogan. The public part of the ceremony had been completed.

Subsequent Activities

After the film crew departed, the remainder of the cake was divided, and with much joviality all the women and some of the singers, including Frank, Jimmy, John Smiley, and Wilson, sat by the pit and ate. The author slept for four hours; during this interval the cake was covered with a canvas anchored by tools to protect it from the blowing sand. Only a small portion remained; the people who had helped with the ceremony had either taken their pieces home as they left or come back to get them while the author slept.

The author was absent Sunday afternoon. When she returned, Marie had changed her clothes to dungarees and a yellow blouse. She had argued with Frank again about remaining in Chinle until Thursday, but he insisted that she fulfill the requirement.

Geneva reported that later Sunday afternoon, when the center of the cake was hard enough to be removed, Rose had dug a hole in the center of the pit with her hands. Using a knife, she cut a piece from the center of the cake, which had been removed from the pit and placed in a box. This piece was buried in the hole in the center of the pit. (Rose said later she had removed the piece from the center of the cake with her hands, rather than a knife.)

Fig. 14. The final hair-combing.

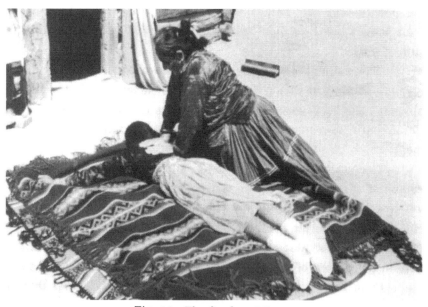

Fig. 15. The final molding.

By Monday afternoon the cooking pit was almost completely filled with dirt. Geneva said, "The wind and weather always do that; the Navaho don't."

Reactions

The author learned that on Sunday afternoon there had been a discussion in the chapter house about the filming of both the Red Ant Way and the Kinaaldá. Many people were disturbed about the white men and the girl who had been "on the scene interfering with the medicine men." Isabelle was at the meeting and spent a long time arguing with the people, explaining that the work being done was for the good of the tribe. Finally, some agreed that these things should be preserved. Geneva said, "That is why there were not more people down here to help with Marie's Kinaaldá. Some of them did not want to be in the 'Hollywood' films, and others did not like the idea of being involved with white people at all."

Augusta later gave additional information in support of Geneva's report. She and Isabelle went to the meeting which had been called to decide who would work on the new ten-mile construction project. However, a discussion of the filming was injected almost immediately. A "Peyote man" from Valley Store, who was a chapter member, began discussing the Red Ant Way. Soon Frank's name was mentioned; the man asked if it were true that he had allowed people to film the Kinaaldá. When this was ascertained, he replied, "Well, what is the matter with him? Doesn't he know he is not supposed to sell out his Navaho religious practices to Hollywood?" Isabelle tried to explain, but many would not listen.

The group said that Frank had forfeited his right to perform ceremonies. When he heard this, he laughed and said, "Watch those people; they will come running when they need one of my sings, but I do not intend to sing any more for the people that talked like that."

Official End of Kinaaldá

Marie's Kinaaldá was officially over at noon on Thursday, June 27, 1963. On Friday she returned to Shiprock, New Mexico.

Comparison between the Ideal and the Actual

Marie's Kinaaldá followed closely the ritual procedures and order of events as described by Frank before the ceremony. There were only five discrepancies. The first of these is of major importance; the ceremony lasted four nights and five days, rather than three nights and four days. The other differences were insignificant: the lifting that occurred on the first day and the cutting of the soapweed root that took place on the afternoon of the fourth day were not mentioned by Frank. Neither were the facts that Marie would return to the hogan to signify the completion of the ceremony on the fifth morning and that the ceremony would not terminate until four days after the cake had been removed from the pit.

The Kinaaldá of Lena Shirley

The Kinaaldá of Lena Shirley, the second one studied, was held in Chinle from July 12 to July 16, 1963. The author was the only non-Navaho present at this ceremony. The Mitchells were more relaxed during Lena's Kinaaldá. Over one hundred people[15] came to help, in contrast to the forty-five or fifty who had attended Marie's ceremony. Joking, gossiping, and a general feeling of friendliness prevailed. In spite of Frank's frequently expressed disapproval of drinking at ceremonials, there was no way of supervising the large crowd and alcohol made its contribution to the good feeling. In general, Lena's puberty ceremony was a happier and livelier one than Marie's.

Lena's Kinaaldá was a *first* one, and, although her parents were not eager to have her puberty celebrated, the girl herself

---

[15]It was impossible to identify all these people.

and other relatives wanted the ceremony performed. Lena started to menstruate on July 8. She informed Geneva and Cecilia as soon as it occurred, but not her mother. Geneva told her mother, Isabelle, on July 9, and she immediately relayed the information to her mother, Rose. Rose said that Lena should start grinding immediately. Lena's mother, Ruth, then said that she did not have the money necessary for the ceremony and that she did not want the Kinaaldá performed. As soon as Frank and the author returned from a Blessing Way ceremony at Black Mountain (the afternoon of July 9), the Kinaaldá was discussed in the hogan by Rose, Frank, Geneva, Frankie Shirley, Lena, several of the smaller children, and the author. Frank and Rose refused to hold the ceremony during the eclipse which would occur during the week-end of July 20−21. Frank suggested July 10 as the starting date, but Rose said they needed time to get the necessary sheep and do the preliminary grinding. It was finally decided that the Kinaaldá would begin on Friday morning, July 12, and the *bijį́* would be on Monday, July 15. Since Lena's first menstrual period lasted for six days, the first two days of her Kinaaldá coincided with actual menstruation.

The author contributed forty-five dollars toward the purchase of the food and wood needed for the ceremony and was given permission to attend, record, and photograph it.

Lena's puberty ceremony was ordered as follows.[16]

First Day: July 12, 1963

> Tie girl's hair. 4:00 P.M. (Mary Davis is attending Lena)
> Dress girl. 4:10 P.M.
> Mold girl.
> Lena and others run. 4:18−4:35 P.M.
> Second run (at sunset). 7:40−7:45 P.M.
> Lena should have ground corn, but did not.
> Lena should have slept in hogan, but did not.

---

[16]Due to spatial restrictions, the detailed account of this Kinaaldá has been omitted.

Second Day: July 13, 1963

> Lena and others run at dawn. 5:00 – 5:10 A.M.
> Grind corn.
> Noon run by Lena and others. 11:30 – 11:45 A.M.
> Grind corn.
> Sunset run by Lena and others. 7:20 – 7:35 P.M.
> Grind corn in hogan. 9:00 – 12:00 P.M.
> Nine sheep and two goats (all newly purchased) arrive 10:30 P.M.
> Lena sleeps in northwest part of hogan after depositing jewelry in scarf.

Third Day: July 14, 1963

> Lena and others run at dawn. 5:15 – 5:20 A.M.
> Grind corn.
> Butcher sheep.
> Noon run. 11:50 A.M. – 12:20 P.M.
> Shop for groceries.
> Lena and others run at sunset. 7:15 – 8:15 P.M.

Fourth Day: July 15, 1963. Bijį́

> Dawn run without yelling. 4:30 – 5:05 A.M.
> Start to dig pit. 5:00 A.M.
> > Pit dug 20 feet west of Marie's; when completed, diameter was 52 inches.
> Start fire. 6:20 A.M.
> Butcher sheep.
> Breakfast.
> Get water.
> Chop firewood.
> Noon run. 12:45 – 1:15 P.M.
> Change clothes.
> Mix mush. 1:30 P.M.
> Fix husks. 4:30 P.M.
> Eat. 6 P.M.
> Put batter in pit. 6:20 – 6:45 P.M.
> Cover batter and bless it.
> Evening run. 6:50 – 7:40 P.M.
> Get soapweed.

Fourth Night

> Eat. 11:20 – 11:35 P.M.
> Clean hogan; hang door blanket and spread one in west.
> Set out corn pollen, *dleesh*, and goods to be blessed.

Bless hogan.
Walk around fire. 12:08 A.M.
Pass corn pollen to all.

Fixed Singing

Fourteen Chief Hogan Songs. 12:10 – 1:15 A.M.
Corn pollen passed during fourteenth song.
Lena goes out and returns.
Frank sings eleven songs related to the fourteen Chief Hogan Songs. 1:18 – 2:08 A.M.
Corn pollen passed; only one pouch used; it is first passed to the women.

Free Singing

Two Women's Songs (*'Asdzáá bighiin*). 2:10 – 2:30 A.M. Sung by Bird Woman.
Eight Songs Pertaining to the Pairs. 2:30 – 3:00 A.M. Sung by Howard, Jimmy, Charlie Watchman, and a friend of Howard's.
(Food break here.)
Two Songs Pertaining to the Pairs. 3:00 – 3:14 A.M. Sung by Jimmy.
Eight Songs for Administering the Pollen. 3:15 – 3:33 A.M. Sung by Howard, Jimmy, and Charlie Watchman.
One Twelve Word Song. 3:35 – 3:50 A.M. (This is a fixed song.)
Corn pollen passed.
Four Unidentified Songs.[17] 4:00 – 4:05 A.M. Sung by Charlie Watchman.
Five Unidentified Songs. 4:10 – 4:14 A.M. Sung by Charlie Watchman.
Corn pollen passed.
Five Unidentified Songs. 4:15 – 4:32 A.M. Sung by Jackie Izzie.
People begin discussing the approaching dawn; washing preparations begun.
Corn pollen passed.

Fifth Day: July 16, 1963

Fixed Singing. Frank takes control again.

Four Washing Songs. 4:35 – 4:50 A.M.
Lena's hair and jewelry are washed during third and fourth song. Water then emptied in rear of hogan.

---

[17]This group of songs and the two following it remain unidentified at present. Charlie Watchman only knew that his songs were Blessing Way Songs. Jackie Izzie refused to work with the author when contacted after the Kinaaldá. Other informants did not know these songs and thus could not help identify them.

Four Racing Songs. 4:51−5:03 A.M.
Lena runs to east for last time.
   Basket reoriented.
Corn pollen passed.
One Twelve Word Song. 5:05−5:15 A.M.
Corn pollen passed.
Cut cake. 5:18 A.M. May Holtsoh cuts first piece; Lena gives it
   to Sam Chee.
Eat mutton, hominy, coffee, store bread, and *'alkaan*.
Cut more cake and distribute it to singers.
Rose makes hole in center of pit and buries four pinches from the
   corners of the cake.
Frank is asleep; people finally leave.
Frank awakens and realizes the ceremony has not been completed.
Frank gives directions for the last steps. Mary returns to the
   Mitchells and Lena is aroused.
Mary prepares *dleesh*; Lena enters. 11 A.M.
Lena's hair is combed while Two Combing Songs are sung. 11:15−
   11:20 A.M.
Lena is painted while one *Dleesh* Song is sung. 11:22−11:25 A.M.
Lena paints others in an upward direction.
Lena is molded outside the hogan.
Lena returns blankets and other goods.
Lena goes inside the hogan; public part of ceremony is complete.
Lena goes home and changes into dungarees.

Official End of the Ceremony

Like Marie, Lena was required to sleep in the hogan, remain quiet, and refrain from her normal activities for four more days. Her ceremony was officially over on Saturday, July 20, 1963. That day she and some other Mitchells went with the author to the Lukachukai rodeo.

Comparison between Lena's and Marie's Kinaaldá

Lena's Kinaaldá, like Marie's, lasted four nights and five days, instead of the shorter three-night, four-day period previously mentioned by Frank. Again, the cutting of the soapweed root, the manner in which the ceremony ended, and the four-day ceremonial period which followed the end of the public part of the ceremony were included, even though not mentioned in the procedures.

Lena's Kinaaldá differed from Marie's in ten respects. The difference in the ceremonial atmosphere has already been mentioned. On the first day, Lena did not lift the children, as Marie had done; she also did not sleep in the hogan nor grind corn that night. The last two omissions were recognized as such and explained to the author as an oversight. The cooking pit was dug further to the west and was smaller than Marie's. The cake batter was not placed in the pit during the midafternoon on the fourth day, but rather near sunset, after supper. One of the races was run without the participants giving the characteristic Kinaaldá yell. In Lena's Kinaaldá the Hogan Songs were different, as Frank had predicted; the Chief Hogan Songs were used, rather than those belonging to Talking God. After these, Frank did not immediately open the singing to the people; instead, he added eleven songs chosen from three sets of songs which, as he had learned, must accompany these fourteen original Hogan Songs.[18]   Finally, Lena was attended by the same "ideal" woman throughout the ceremony.

Acknowledging some omissions in procedure and some minor changes in timing, Lena's Kinaaldá was as it should have been, according to Frank: similar to Marie's except for the Hogan Songs. As such, it differs from its mythological counterpart[19] in the inclusion of the final combing and molding rites. Had Frank not awakened in time to finish the ceremony, the last rites of combing, painting, and molding might very possibly have been omitted, and thus the correspondence would have been closer to Frank's myth and the myths of several other informants.

Comparative Data on Kinaaldá

Source Material

Thirteen published reports of Kinaaldá are available. They range in detail from a brief mention of the ceremonial events to a

---

[18]The composition of the free singing was different from that in Marie's Kinaaldá, but this was expected and is not counted as a difference.

[19]To the author's knowledge, there is no other place in the Kinaaldá literature where the data allow a comparison between one informant's mythological account and actual ceremonial procedures. Many have collected a myth from one singer and then witnessed a ceremony as it was conducted by another, noting the differences between the myth and the procedural account.

complete account of a witnessed puberty ceremony.[20] The sources
include works by Coolidge, Curtis, Driver, the Franciscan Fathers,
Gifford, Hill, Leighton and Kluckhohn, McCombe, Vogt and Kluckhohn, Reichard, Wyman and Bailey, and Young. Two fictional accounts occur: *Dezba* and *Spider Woman*, by Reichard. Besides
these, there is a considerable body of unpublished field data.
From Chinle, Arizona, in addition to the two accounts of the ceremonies witnessed by the author and the data from the author's interviews with Geneva, Marie, Augusta, and Rose, there is an account gathered by McAllester in 1961 from Frank Mitchell. From
Pinedale, New Mexico, reports of nine Kinaaldá are available in
the field notes of Anne Keith. Finally, from Ramah, New Mexico,
fourteen reports of Kinaaldá are available in the Ramah Project
field notes on file at the Laboratory of Anthropology in Santa Fe,
New Mexico.

Comparative Data and Conclusions

As Chart 2 illustrates, an analysis of the accounts indicates
variation in the procedures included in the Navaho puberty ceremony. Nevertheless, there are certain rites that are found in the
majority of the accounts. Ten of the twenty-one possible items
are mentioned in 50 percent or more of the forty-two reports.[21]
These items are:

Item	Percent of Reports Mentioning Item
Fixing the hair	59
Molding	57
Running	91
Corn-grinding	62

---

[20]The only complete account in print is Leland Wyman and Flora Bailey, "Navaho Girl's
Puberty Rite," *New Mexico Anthropologist*, XXV, No. 1 (January–March, 1943), pp. 3–12. Several
sources contain descriptions of the fourth day and night and the fifth (final) morning activities;
among them are the Leightons' Field Notes, July 2–3, 1940; Anne Keith's Field Notes, July 4 and
19, 1963; and Gladys Reichard, *Social Life of the Navajo Indians*, Columbia University Contributions to Anthropology, VII (New York: Columbia University Press, 1928), pp. 137–139.

[21]In analyzing published material, her own notes and those of McAllester, Keith, and the
Ramah Project, the author has included in this case only those accounts which attempt to describe
experienced or witnessed Kinaaldá.

Item	Percent of Reports Mentioning Item
The corncake	83
Baking the cake	74
Biji on the fourth night	57
Singing	90
Washing the hair	59
Taboos connected with puberty ceremony	57

Racing and singing are most often mentioned; the corncake and the activities surrounding it are second in frequency.

Core Progressions

The Kinaaldá accounts also contain information concerning the sequence of order in which rites are performed during the puberty ceremony. Few of the accounts seemed, at first, to follow the same order. However, when the reports were grouped regionally and the order of events ranked, a core sequential progression became evident. Only twenty-nine of the forty-two pertinent reports were treated in this manner because the others lacked information concerning the geographical location from which the data came. Rank orderings were done for three areas: Chinle, Arizona, Pinedale, New Mexico, and Ramah, New Mexico.[22] Since any of these could serve as an illustration, the Pinedale one has been arbitrarily chosen (see Chart 3).

Rank orderings of the available Kinaaldá reports from three regions show that the Pinedale, Chinle, and Ramah areas share a common "most frequent order of events." That common progression follows:

First Day	Second and Third Day	Fourth Day	Fourth Night	Fifth Day
Tie hair	Run	Run	Sing	Wash hair
Dress	Grind	Grind		Race
Run		Bake cake		Cut cake
Grind corn				

---

[22]See Appendix F for a map of these and surrounding regions.

CHART 2

Author / *Event Mentioned*

Author	Fixing the girl's hair	Hair thong: deerskin	mountain lion	unwounded deerskin	sacred	special thong	Jewelry	Molding	Running	Corn-grinding	Corncake	Baking the cake	Biʼį on the fourth day	Blessing the property	Songs	Washing the girl's hair	Painting the girl's face	Lifting the children	Taboos mentioned	Paying the medicine man	Second ceremony
K. Martin	×								×		×	×			×		×				
H. Skeet (1940)	×								×	×	×	×			×	×			×		
B. Thomas	×								×		×	×			×		×				
M. Pino							×	×	×		×	×			×	×	×			×	×	×
B. Lorenzo (1942)											×								×		×
D. Skeet (1941)	×			×					×		×				×				×	×	×
C. Cojo									×		×	×			×					×	
D. Pino										×					×					×	
F. Pino								×							×					×	
J. Henio									×												
D. Skeet (1938)	×			×			×	×	×		×	×	×	×	×	×	×				
J. Pinto															×		×				
M. Bedaga									×		×	×			×		×				
B. Lorenzo (1938)	×	×							×		×	×		×	×	×					
E. Sterns	×						×	×			×	×		×	×	×	×	×	×		
R. Dean	×						×	×	×	×	×	×	×	×	×	×	×		×		
V. Wilson	×						×	×	×	×	×	×	×		×	×	×				
S. Carson	×	×					×	×			×	×			×	×			×		
J. Fernandez	×	×					×	×			×	×		×	×				×		
D. Morton							×	×			×	×	×	×	×	×	×		×		
C. Begay							×	×	×	×	×	×	×	×	×	×	×		×		
J. Marianito	×						×	×	×	×	×	×	×	×		×			×		
R. Mitchell								×	×	×	×	×	×	×	×	×					
A. Sandoval	×						×	×	×	×	×				×	×	×			×	×
G. Kee	×						×	×	×	×	×				×	×	×		×		
M. Shirley	×						×	×	×		×				×	×			×		
Mitchell ceremony, July, 1963	×	×					×	×	×	×	×	×	×	×	×	×	×		×	×	×
Mitchell ceremony, June, 1963	×	×					×	×	×	×	×	×	×	×	×	×	×	×	×	×	×
Mitchell, 1961	×						×	×	×	×	×	×			×	×	×	×			×
Informant																					
Reichard, Spider Woman											×	×	×		×						
Reichard, Dezba	×	×					×	×	×	×	×	×	×	×	×	×		×			
Young							×		×	×	×	×			×						
Wyman-Bailey	×			×			×	×	×	×	×	×	×		×	×	×	×	×		×
Reichard	×	×						×	×	×	×	×	×		×	×	×	×	×		×
McCombe, Vogt, and Kluckhohn									×	×	×	×	×	×							
Leighton-Kluckhohn	×					×			×	×	×	×	×	×	×	×		×			×
Hill		×																			
Gifford							×	×	×	×	×	×	×		×		×		×		
Franciscan Fathers	×								×	×	×		×		×	×	×				
Driver	×								×	×	×		×		×	×	×				
Curtis	×	×							×	×	×	×			×	×		×	×		
Coolidge	×			×					×	×	×	×	×		×	×		×			×

CHART 3 The Sequential Ordering of Kinaaldá Events Pinedale Area Event	*Informant*	Ja. Marianito	C. Begay	D. Morton	J. Fernandez	S. Carson	V. Wilson	R. Dean	E. Sterns
Tie hair		1			1	1	1		
Run		3			3	3		3	3
Run again						4			
Grind		4					3	4	
Dress					4		2	1	2
Run every morning		5						5	
Chew red mixture before run		2							
Grind every day		6	1				4	6	
Put medicine in corn meal		7							
Mix mush		8	2	1	5				6
Sew husks		9							
Put batter in pit		10	3	2			5	7	
Run		11							
Feed people		12							
Bless articles		13	4	3				8	
Sing		14	5	4	6	5	6	9	7
Wash hair		15	6	5	7	6	7	10	4 & 8
Run		16	7	6	8	7	8	11	5 & 9
Run a second time					9	8	9	12	
Run a third time						9			
Cut cake		18		7		10	12	13	10
Dleesh			9	8			10	15	14
Brush hair			8	9				14	1
Mold		17	10	10	2	2	11	2	12
Pass cake		19	11	11	10			16	11
Lift children									13

After the activities associated with the cutting of the cake, no orderly progression is apparent. According to Frank Mitchell, after the cake was served and the people had eaten, the girl was combed, painted with *dleesh*, and molded, and not until the molding was completed would the ceremony be finished. In the two Mitchell ceremonies the author witnessed, this order was followed; but, as previously suggested, in one of these the final rites came close to being omitted. In the four Chinle interviews, the last three rites were not mentioned. Wilson Yazzie, stepfather of both Marie and Lena Shirley, told the author that most people consider the ceremony complete once the cake has been served.

At Pinedale, six of eight informants said that there were activities after the cake-cutting. One said that just molding was needed, one that both *dleesh* and molding were required, and one that *dleesh* and brushing were necessary. The three other informants mentioned three rites: two mentioned brushing, *dleesh*, and molding; and one, molding, lifting the children, and *dleesh*. Since all eight reported a unique order of events, no core progression could be established for the final events in the Pinedale area.

At Ramah, the same diversity was evident. Five of nine informants mentioned *dleesh*; three, the combing; and two, the molding. Again, each reported order of events differed from the rest, and the final Kinaaldá rites could not be sequentially patterned.

In summary, there was a common core progression by which Kinaaldá in three regions—Chinle, Pinedale, and Ramah—were ordered. The core included activities of the first day through the cutting of the cake on the final morning. After the latter rite, only diversity was evident; no sequential pattern could be developed to summarize the remaining rites in any of the three regions.

Regional Differences in Kinaaldá

The author had initially hoped to identify regional complexes for Kinaaldá throughout the reservation.[23] An analysis of the data showed that while major differences do not exist, there are variations in the execution of secondary rites that can be classified regionally.

Pinedale

There are numerous differences between Chinle and Pinedale puberty ceremonials.[24] In the Chinle area, the ceremony may be postponed if the time or conditions are not right for its execution when the girl actually reaches puberty. In the Pinedale area, however, the ceremony must be held at puberty or not at all.[25] At Chinle, the girl's hair is brushed and tied in a pony tail on the first day and then not touched until the final night, when it is washed in yucca-root shampoo. At Pinedale, the hair is brushed and tied every morning before the girl runs. In the Pinedale area, the girls run once a day and do not necessarily increase the length of their subsequent runs. The race is run at dawn toward the east. On the last day, some girls run twice. In the Chinle area, three races are run each day, with the distance supposedly increased each time. The races are held at dawn, noon, and sunset, except on the fourth day, when the second race occurs after the cake is placed in the pit. The direction is eastward, as in Pinedale. On the last day at Chinle, songs are sung during the dawn race. The singing is co-ordinated with the racing; the last song is being

---

[23]On the basis of secondary source material, Harold Driver, in "Girls' Puberty Rites in Western North America," *University of California Anthropological Records*, VI, No. 2, Culture Element Disbributions: XVI (1941), pp. 21–90, attempted to establish differences for eastern and western Navaho Kinaaldá. Edward Gifford, using original material, attempted a similar division in "Apache-Pueblo," *University of California Anthropological Records*, IV, No. 1, Culture Element Distributions: XII (1940), pp. 1–207. Since Driver's and Gifford's results were not categorized as specifically as the author's, they could not be used to support or contrast with her data.

[24]In the field notes of Anne Keith for July 5, 1963, there is some indication that the Pinedale people consider those from Chinle to be more old-fashioned: "The people in Chinle are different. They speak real Navaho there, not slang. I can't even understand them. They do things more in the old way. I can't say that we are better than them but I think they are a little more backward" (Ja.M).

[25]Keith interviewed one girl (RD) who had had her Kinaaldá postponed. Everyone else said that this was never done.

completed as the girl returns. At Pinedale, the last race is also accompanied by singing; here, however, there seems to be no attempt to co-ordinate the two events; if girls return from their races before the singing is complete, they are told either to run again or to wait outside the hogan until the songs have been terminated.

The *'alkaan* is a necessary part of the ceremony at Pinedale, whereas at Chinle, if corn is not available, bread and canned goods are substituted. At Pinedale, the women sew a complete circle of husks to line the pit before the batter is poured.[26] At Chinle, the husks are put in one by one; only the crosses are sewn. The Chinle and Pinedale husk crosses are constructed differently:

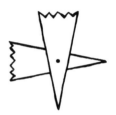

        Chinle   Pinedale

The distribution of the cake also varies; the Pinedale girl serves pieces from a ceremonial basket to the people filing past her as she stands either in or in front of the hogan; the Chinle girl distributes the pieces directly from the pit to some people; others help themselves. The Pinedale girl serves fruit and candy in addition to the *'alkaan*, whereas the Chinle girl only distributes the corncake.

Molding is done once in the Pinedale area; at Chinle, it occurs twice, on the first day and the final morning. At Pinedale, the rite includes hitting the girl on the mouth so she will not talk too much.

Dleesh rather than *chííh* (red ocher) is used for painting in both areas. *Chííh* is, however, related to Kinaaldá in Pinedale: "You take something—it's red and it tastes salty. They say if you

---

[26]A similar husk mat is made in Crownpoint, New Mexico.

do that your menstruation will not smell. It's just red and salty
and you have to eat it. Every time you run, you have to take it.
It is called *chííh dikǫǫzh*. You take it after you run for all eight
days'' (Ja.M).[27]

In the Pinedale area, the girl applies *dleesh* to herself; she
may paint various parts of her body in the ceremonial manner, or
only her cheeks. In the Chinle area, painting is done by the ideal
woman; she must mark the girl's body in the ritually prescribed
manner.

In both areas, the Kinaaldá continues for four days after the
cake is distributed, even though the public ceremony is complete
and the people have gone home. At Chinle, the girl must remain
at home, sleeping in the ceremonial hogan as she did during the
Kinaaldá and refraining from her usual activities. At Pinedale,
these last four days include more than quiet contemplation. The
girl has her hair brushed and tied each morning, runs and eats
chííh dikǫǫzh, and continues to wear her jewelry. However, her
ceremonial dress, like that of the Chinle girl, may be changed.

Few Pinedale girls celebrate their second Kinaaldá. In
contrast to the Chinle ideal, the people at Pinedale feel that while
a second Kinaaldá has desirable effects, one puberty ceremony is
sufficient.

Lukachukai

Limited observations and interviews held in Lukachukai
indicated some differences between Chinle and Lukachukai puberty
ceremonies. The hair-combing is done in Lukachukai so that
swirls are formed around the girl's ears and on her forehead.
Because of these, much of the girl's face is often hidden from
view. The body is ceremonially painted as at Chinle, but at
Lukachukai, evidently both *dleesh* and *chííh* are used. ''They
come up from the bottom with *dleesh*. Then they put a spot of red
on each cheek before putting *dleesh* in upward streaks on her face.

---

[27]Anne Keith, Interview, July 9, 1963.

The Red Ocher Songs, as well as the White Clay ones, accompany the painting'' (MCS).

In contrast to Pinedale, the *'alkaan* is not necessary at Lukachukai. "If the crops are not good or if the people are lazy, they can get canned goods and pass them around instead of cake" (MCS). In contrast to Chinle, where cloth is never distributed, the Lukachukai group may use "calico and other types of material in addition to food" (MCS).

Chinle and Lukachukai puberty ceremonies differ musically. The *Chíih bighiin*, or Red Ocher Songs, have already been mentioned. Another difference is in the combing, ceremonial dressing, and racing on the first day; at Lukachukai, songs accompany these rites, while at Chinle there is no singing until the fourth night. Lukachukai people were amazed and some were upset when they learned that songs were not sung at Chinle. They believe that these songs must accompany the activities of the first day if the Kinaaldá is to be done correctly.

> There should be singing on the first day. They [the Chinle] people definitely should sing on the first day (MCS).

> What's the matter with them? Don't they know that's not right? When Changing Woman had her first Kinaaldá, Hashch'éłti'i came there and did the singing. They dressed her up, molded her, and she ran. He sang all this time (DT).

Ramah

The available reports of Kinaaldá in the Ramah area suggest that puberty ceremonies in this region are similar in many ways to those at Pinedale. The girl runs only at dawn, to the east, and there is some evidence for running twice on the final morning. Molding is done once, on the last day, and the girl is hit on the mouth. Fruit and candy are distributed with the *'alkaan*, which is placed in a ceremonial basket.

Unlike Pinedale, and in accordance with Lukachukai practices, songs are sung in Ramah on the first day. Here, however, the songs do not seem to include racing ones, for only those used for the "fixing up of the girl" are mentioned. As at Chinle and Pinedale, only *dleesh* is used in the painting of the girl. However, at Ramah usually only the cheeks are painted. As at Pinedale, a red mixture made partially from *chííh* is also employed. At Ramah, though, this is not eaten; instead, the girl blows on it after each run.

> *Cih dokoz.* They reached down in the salt lake where they could touch the ground and get something a little like dirt; they called that *tałah adan*. The next thing they got was salt; this is right on top of the water and it looks soft; it is called *aski bizhi* (salt voice). They brought that home. They also went to where antelopes and deer get salt and got a piece of that, too. They added all these things together and ground it with red clay. Any time a girl gets her first menstruation, just as soon as they tie her hair up, they tie a little bundle of that red clay on the girl's right hip. They make the bundle by cutting off a little unshot buckskin and tanning it. The first morning, after the girl races and comes back, she unties that and opens the little bundle; then she blows on it. When the girl does this, a little spit goes in. This is done every morning for four days when she races. When the Kinaaldá is finished, they put that bundle away; that's what is called *cih dokoz* (DS).[28]

Some of the Ramah Navaho believe, as do those in Chinle, that it is necessary to have another Kinaaldá performed at the girl's second menses.

Summary

The regional variations discussed above are summarized in Chart 4. It is obvious that while the Navaho at Chinle, Pinedale, Lukachukai, and Ramah conduct their Kinaaldá according to a core progression of events, there are levels of comparison at which the data support a theory of regional variation in certain Kinaaldá rites.

Reasons for Variation

Although many singers said that Kinaaldá could be performed in only one way (their own), variation in the puberty ceremony has been found to be widespread and obvious. Since there is

---

[28] Clyde Kluckhohn, Field Notes, 1941.

a definite relationship between the myth and the ceremony in all Navaho religious activities, and since discrepancies have already been established in Kinaaldá mythology, the variation found in the execution of the ceremony is not surprising.

Reasons for this variation have already been suggested in the first chapter; they are "the principle of many reasons" and the essence of Navaho formalism per se. Other explanations, however, need to be considered. Willie Marianito (WM), when asked by Keith if it were possible for him to perform Kinaaldá in different ways, replied affirmatively. According to him, the content of the ceremony was adjusted to conform with the financial resources of the family of the girl.[29]

From the published and unpublished Kinaaldá accounts, other factors capable of controlling the content and order of Kinaaldá emerge. The first of these concerns availability of materials needed for the ceremony, such as *dleesh, chííh*, corn, wood, cornhusks, sheep, flour, corn pollen, jewelry, and man power. For example, in Augusta Sandoval's second Kinaaldá, *dleesh* was not available, so Frank used *chííh*. In Rose Mitchell's second Kinaaldá, no corn was available, so food bought at the store was substituted for the *'alkaan*, and cloth was distributed.

Environmental factors also influence Kinaaldá to a certain extent. One ceremony conducted in Chinle during the summer of 1963 was held at a nonrelative's hogan because the sand in the vicinity of the girl's home made running impossible. Frank said that if a girl can run to the east, she should do so; however, if sand, snow, or fences make this impossible, she may run toward the west.

If a relative dies during Kinaaldá, the ceremony is stopped and held at a later time.

> If there is a death of a member of the family or a close relative, the Kinaaldá must be terminated. When it is taken up again, they have to start all over from the beginning of the ceremony (FM).

---

[29]Anne Keith, Field Notes, July 5, 1963.

But they had two sings for Thomas Aunt's daughter. Her name is Bessie Martine, and the sings were for "becoming a woman." The first sing she had was the time when my dear brother, John Leed, died on the twenty-sixth of October. That spoiled her sing. Then it happened again; on the night of the twenty-first of December, Leo Pino's mother died. So they are planning to have another one pretty soon to straighten it out for her (BL).[30]

In Chinle, a relative died two nights before the *biji* of Alice Billie's Kinaaldá. The family did not learn of the death until the fourth night (the *biji*). Everyone wished to cancel the ceremony, but Mrs. Dajool, the owner of the house where the Kinaaldá was being held, insisted that they proceed with the all-night sing. This was done against the wishes of the family. The following morning, Alice ran only a short distance and without giving the characteristic Kinaaldá shouts. The ceremony was finished quickly and quietly, and the family left immediately.

School attendance is another factor influencing Kinaaldá. In the Pinedale region, it often means that the ceremony cannot be performed; in this area, the Kinaaldá must be held at the incidence of puberty or not at all. In Augusta Sandoval's case, at Chinle, school attendance necessitated the reduction of her first Kinaaldá to three days—a week-end event. Others did the work normally assigned to the girl. Augusta came home, had her hair tied, ran, had *biji* the next day, and then returned to school. At present in the Chinle region, Kinaaldá are postponed if puberty occurs during the school term and are held the following summer during vacation.[31]

The wishes of the girl and her family are also responsible for some variation. This is especially true in cases where Kinaaldá are not held. Even if the finances are available, the girl may not desire the ceremony. Some do not like "being stared at"; others dislike the "hot clothes and the heavy jewelries," and still others hate the work involved. Hence, some girls do not tell when

---

[30]Clyde Kluckhohn, letter from Bertha Lorenzo, December, 1942.

[31]In so doing, the Navaho seem to be approaching the Chiricahua Apache situation, where all puberty ceremonies are celebrated in one major public event, the Girls' Dance, held every summer on July 4.

they start to menstruate, or if they do, they may openly refuse to have the ceremony. An example of the latter evidently occurred at the Mitchells after the author left at the end of the summer of 1963; in a letter, she was told: "We are just wondering how we can do all that in the Kinaaldá such as the running and grinding. Ivonne had her first period last week, but she did not want to do it, so it was like that" (GK).

The puberty ceremony varies, therefore, not only for reasons inherent in Navaho culture and philosophy, but also for more immediate, observable reasons--those of available material, economic welfare, personal preference, environmental conditions, death of relatives, school restrictions, and regional customs and beliefs. Therefore, variations occur in performance as well as in myth recitations rationalizing the ceremony.

While diversity exists, though, improvisation is restricted, and an essential core in both myth and ceremony can be established. Although the rites which are mentioned in more than 50 percent of the Kinaaldá accounts are not, in all cases, the same as those appearing with the same frequency in the myth, nevertheless a content core is there. This extends to the ordering of the Kinaaldá rites as well, for a sequential progression that surpasses regional boundaries can be discovered.

The same progression that establishes a reservation-wide unity also reveals, on another level of analysis, contrasting regional orders. The data indicate that smaller patterns—those concerned with the execution of specific rites—are shared only within certain areas; hence Kinaaldá in several regions (those of Chinle, Pinedale, Lukachukai, and Ramah) can at this stage of research, anyway, be distinguished from one another.

Thus, in ceremony, as in myth, Navaho formalism is offset by the persistent occurrence of regional and individual variation.

CHART 4*

Event	Chinle	Pinedale	Lukachukai	Ramah
Ceremony may be postponed	Y	N	Y	0
Songs used on the first day	N	N	Y	Y
Hair brushed and tied daily	N	Y	0	0
Hair brushed and tied only on the first day and the last morning	Y	N	0	0
Hair combed over some of the girl's face	N	Y	Y	0
Run at dawn, noon, and sunset	Y	N	0	N
Run only at dawn	N	Y	0	Y
Each run increased in distance	Y	N	0	0
Run only toward the east	Y	Y	0	Y
Girl eats a red mixture of *chííh* and other materials after running	N	Y	N	N
Girl blows on a red mixture of *chííh* and other materials after running	N	N	N	Y
Dawn run on the last morning may be done twice	N	Y	0	Y
Songs sung during the running on both the first day and the last morning	N	N	Y	N

*Y stands for "Yes" and N for "No." Zero (0) indicates insufficient information. It is obvious that more regional investigations and comparisons need to be made.

Event	Chinle	Pinedale	Lukachukai	Ramah
Songs used only for the final morning run	Y	Y	N	Y
Girl ends her last race by running into the hogan and sitting down while the Racing Songs are being finished	Y	N	0	0
Girl returns from her last race and waits outside the hogan, not entering until the Racing Songs have been completed	N	Y	0	0
Cake pit lined with separate husks	Y	N	Y	0
Cake pit lined with a sewn husk circle	N	Y	N	0
Cross:	N	Y	0	0
Cross:	Y	N	0	0
Cake distributed from a ceremonial basket	N	Y	0	Y
Cake distributed directly from the pit	Y	N	0	N
Other food distributed with the corncake	N	Y	Y	Y
Cake is a necessary part of the ceremony	N	Y	N	0

Chart 4 (continued)

Event	Chinle	Pinedale	Lukachukai	Ramah
Only food can be substituted for the cake	Y	Y	N	0
Cloth as well as food can replace the cake	0[†]	N	Y	0
Molding done twice, on the first day and on the last morning	Y	N	Y	N
Molding done on the last morning only	N	Y	N	Y
Molding includes hitting the girl on the mouth	N	Y	0	Y
Dleesh used for painting	Y	Y	Y	Y
Dleesh and *chííh* may be used at the same time for the painting	N	N	Y	0
Chííh may serve as a substitute for *dleesh* if the latter is unavailable	Y	0	0	0
Ceremonial painting of various parts of the body	Y	Y	Y	N
Only the cheeks are painted	N	N	N	Y
Girl applies paint to herself	N	Y	0	0
Ideal woman paints girl	Y	N	0	0
Songs sung during the painting	Y	Y	Y	0

[†] In Rose Mitchell's second Kinaaldá, which was held in Chinle, where her family lived during the summer, corn was not available; at that time, cloth and food (purchased at the trading post) were distributed. In spite of this, the Mitchells say that cloth can never be substituted for the *'alkaan*.

Chart 4 (continued)

Event	*Chinle*	*Pinedale*	*Lukachukai*	*Ramah*
Ceremony continued for four days after the public part is finished	Y	Y	0	0
Ceremonial clothing may be changed	Y	Y	0	0
Jewelry may be removed	Y	N	0	0
Girl continues to race every day	N	Y	0	0
Girl continues to eat red mixture after running	N	Y	N	N
Girl continues to blow on red mixture after running	N	N	N	0
Girl must remain quiet and refrain from regular tasks	Y	Y	0	0
Girl's hair brushed and tied up every morning	N	Y	0	0
Second Kinaaldá is necessary	Y	N	0	Y

CHAPTER THREE

The Music

General Discussion of Navaho Music

TO those who are unfamiliar with the unique sounds and the subtle intricacies of Navaho music, the songs sung during the puberty ceremony and, indeed, any Navaho songs may seem incomprehensible. The literature, even that by anthropologists, is full of reports of the "weird," "odd," "monotonous singing" to be heard on the reservation. For this reason, before discussing the specifics of Kinaaldá songs, a brief summary of the characteristics of Navaho music seems apropos.

The music of the Navaho is both secular and sacred. It is vocal music, which may or may not be accompanied by drums, rattles, and whistles, according to its context. If a drum is called for, it will be one of two types. The first, a pot drum, is made by covering a small earthen pot with a buckskin. This drum, which contains water, is struck with a looped drumstick. The second kind is a basket drum.[1] This is made by inverting a ceremonial basket and tapping it with a moccasin, straight stick, belt, or the regular drumstick of plaited yucca. The basket drum can be used with a resonator; in the nine-day Red Ant Way Ceremonial, for example, the basket is inverted over a hole scooped out of the hogan floor.

---

[1]See Washington Matthews, "The Night Chant, a Navaho Ceremony," *Memoirs of the American Museum of Natural History*, VI (May, 1902), 59−61, for a discussion of this drum.

Rattles of hide, hoof, or gourd are used in many chants. The hide, which may be buffalo, badger, or rawhide, is

> shaped and sewed when moist and the handle is platted [plaited] of the same material as the rattle. Small pebbles of white shell, turquoise, abalone, cannelcoal and red-white stone are inserted to produce a rattling sound. The gourd rattle is made of a hollow gourd with a stick attached for a handle. It is decorated with figures of the sun, moon, or some constellation.[2]

Flutes are presently nonexistent, although formerly corn was supposedly ground at the war dance in time to "a flute made of the stalk of the sun flower and provided with four keys."[3] According to the Franciscan Fathers, whistles are used in both the Bead Chant and *Hóchǫ́ǫ́ji*, or Evil Way.

> The one used in the Bead Chant is made of the leg bone of a jack rabbit killed by an eagle. This is spliced [sic], and removing the marrow, a piece of the inner ear of the jack rabbit is laid between the two pieces of bone and wound with sinew.[4]

Whistles are also used in Peyote ritual, the Shooting Way, Red Ant Way, and other ceremonies.

The music of the Blessing Way Ceremony, and hence that of the Kinaaldá, is unaccompanied. The songs are sung in a style characterized by nasality, vibrato, a tense, rigorous manner, medium to high pitch level which rises steadily during the night, occasional indefiniteness of certain note pitches, a few ornaments, sharp emphases, and much individual variation. The element of falsetto which characterizes *Yeibichai* songs and some Squaw Dance Songs is rarely in evidence in the songs of the puberty ceremony.

While women may and often do sing, ceremonial practitioners are almost invariably men.[5] Wearing ceremonial headbands (in the case of the leaders), they typically sing in a seated

---

[2]Franciscan Fathers, *An Ethnologic Dictionary of the Navaho Language* (St. Michaels, Ariz.: St. Michaels Press, 1910), p. 402.

[3]*Ibid.*, p. 511.

[4]*Ibid.*

[5]The reader is referred to Clyde Kluckhohn, "Navaho Women's Knowledge of Their Song Ceremonials," in Richard Kluckhohn (ed.), *Culture and Behavior. The Collected Essays of Clyde Kluckhohn* (New York: The Free Press of Glencoe, 1962), pp. 92-96.

position, with eyes closed and fists clenched. Frank Mitchell said the eyes are shut so the songs can be remembered more accurately. Singing is usually a group activity; it contrasts with the unified singing of the neighboring Pueblos in its "wild freedom."[6] As McAllester says:

> [The Navaho] perform a song with a kind of extempore group artistry. Not all the singers seem to know the song equally well nor do they all seem to be singing exactly the same version of the song. The strongest voices determine the song to be sung next and the version to be used, but there is always a trailing edge of "error" (perhaps "variation" is a better word since nobody seems to be distressed by this). The impression is of a group of individualists who tune their differences to each other at the moment of singing in a dynamically creative way which is very hard to describe.[7]

In this individualism and variation, Navaho medicine men exemplify the oral tradition, which, as Albert Lord points out,[8] is characterized by these qualities.

> We cannot correctly speak of a variant since there is no "original" to be varied .... Our greatest error is to attempt to make "scientifically" rigid a phenomenon that is fluid.[9]

To Lord, a "singer of tales" is one who is a singer, performer, composer, and poet all at once.[10]

> All singers [of tales] use traditional material in a traditional way, but no two singers use exactly the same material in exactly the same manner. The tradition is not all of one mold.[11]
>
> ... The singer of tales is at once the tradition and an individual creator.[12]

The Navaho medicine man qualifies as "a singer of tales."

Variation in singing is recognized and openly discussed among the Navaho. However, while variation is sometimes perfectly acceptable, in other instances it is not permissible. In contrast to the Yugoslavian Epic singers discussed by Lord, Navaho

---

[6] David McAllester, "Enemy Way Music," *Papers of the Peabody Museum of American Archaeology and Ethnology, Harvard University*, Vol. XLI, No. 3 (1954), p. 74.

[7] *Ibid.*

[8] Albert Lord, *The Singer of Tales*, Harvard Studies in Comparative Literature, No. 24, (Cambridge, Mass.: Harvard University Press, 1960).

[9] *Ibid.*, p. 101.

[10] *Ibid.*, p. 13.

[11] *Ibid.*, p. 63.

[12] *Ibid.*, p. 4.

medicine men sing within a framework of ceremonial formalism. Songs can be lengthened or shortened, and verses within them ordered differently or even omitted, as in the epics. But the details of ceremonial songs per se may not be changed. Characters must retain their original names, costumes, and habitats; they must pursue their established journeys and perform determined acts. Perhaps the difference in the amount of variation that is allowed stems from a basic difference between the transmission of sacred and secular songs in the oral tradition. In any case, while the Navaho "singer of tales" is a "creative artist as well as a preserver of tradition,"[13] the stronger emphasis is usually on the tradition.

The melodies of Navaho songs are generally restricted in range and built on rather limited tonal systems which emphasize the major triad. The melodic lines of religious music do not tend to start high and move down, as do those of the secular music. Instead, they follow a variety of contours. Movement is both by steps and skips. The latter may be large or small, but those using intervals of thirds, fourths, and fifths occur most often. The phrases are short and often repetitive. The melodic material is highly integrated. Ornamentation is occasional; it consists of grace notes, slides, and/or vocal pulsations.

Tempi in Navaho music vary with the singer and the type of song being performed. However, with the exception of Peyote Songs, most Navaho music is sung quite rapidly. The Kinaaldá singing ranges from M.M.[14] ♪ = 138 to ♪ = 184.

The rapidity of the singing is enhanced by the frequent use of eighth notes. In Navaho music, note types are limited to quarters and eighths, with occasional sixteenth or ♪. ♪ figures being interjected. Navaho rhythms are highly fluid. The basic unit often appears to be a duple one, but many times it is interrupted by a

---

[13]Paraphrase of a statement in *ibid.*, p. 29.

[14]M.M. refers to "Maelzel's Metronome." See *Grove's Dictionary of Music and Musicians*, H. C. Colles, ed. Third Edition (New York: Macmillan, 1927), III, 447–449.

subtle shift to a triple grouping. Phrases vary in their total number of beats. Singers take breaths and end phrases in such a way that the steady, metronomic pulsation is constantly interrupted.

Some of the Kinaaldá songs have a structure not unlike that found in other Navaho ceremonial music. McAllester has described this structure as follows:

> After a brief introduction of vocables (words without meaning such as 'e ne yanga) sung on the tonic or base note of the scale, the most common form of Navaho sacred chant begins with a phrase repeated a number of times in what might be called a chorus. The main body of the song follows; it is usually made up of two parts separated by another rendition of the chorus. The chorus is sung once more to end the song. There may be from five to as many as thirteen or fourteen lines in each of the two parts in the body of the song and each of these lines ends with a burden-like repetition of certain musical and textual material, usually the last two bars of the chorus. The whole picture then, is:
> Introduction; Chorus (burden)
> 1st part: line 1 . . . . (burden)
>   line 2 . . . . (burden)
>   line 3 . . . . (burden)
>   etc. . . . .
> Chorus (burden)
> 2nd part: line 1 . . . . (burden)
>   line 2 . . . . (burden)
>   line 3 . . . . (burden)
>   etc. . . . .
> Chorus (burden)
> In nearly all cases the repetitions of the Chorus are identical musically. Parts one and two of the body of the song are likewise nearly identical; in each line the burden is the same and the musical material which precedes it contains only a slight amount of melodic and rhythmic variation to accommodate differences in text.[15]

The Navaho are, however, too subtle to use any one plan consistently; thus, it is no surprise to find other Kinaaldá songs organized as follows:

---

[15]David McAllester, "The Form of Navajo Ceremonial Music," in Mary Wheelwright, *Texts of the Navajo Creation Chants* (Cambridge, Mass.: Peabody Museum of Harvard University, n.d.), p. 36.

Introduction		Introduction
Chorus	or	Chorus
Verses		Verses (with last verse
Closing Chorus		slightly extended)

In these structures, the verses are not arranged so the male elements in the text are given first and then balanced by their female counterparts after an intervening chorus. Rather, the sexes alternate with every verse change. Even here, variations derived from pairings, reversal of symbolic order, and the like are frequent.

Few Navaho ceremonial songs exist as separate entities. Instead, they are grouped in sets which usually must follow each other in an established order. Musically, the songs exist as cycles bound together by unifying elements, such as the pitch curve which continues to rise during the night. Textually, the songs are bound by the myths each set relates. According to Matthews, the myths help the medicine man remember the song sequence; in other words, they are his mnemonic key.[16]

The songs are sung in ceremonial Navaho, which differs in some respects from spoken Navaho. The texts are composed of words and vocables which are generally considered to be meaningless syllables. A feeling of motion and action characterizes most of them. Through constant repetition, images are accumulated and ideally perfect harmony and complete identification with specific deities is attained.

Kinaaldá Music

The primary function of song is to preserve order, to coordinate the ceremonial symbols; a secondary purpose must be

---

[16]Washington Matthews, "Songs of Sequence of the Navajos," *Journal of American Folklore*, VII, No. 26 (July—September, 1894), p. 186. Gladys Reichard cited an instance where the reverse was true.

"Although the story has several functions, it is not an indispensable part of the chanter's lore. Many chanters today sing before learning the myth, but if they wish to 'be sure' of their technique and want a secondary guide to the song series to fix the items and events quite thoroughly in mind, they learn the tale and are able to tell it in minute detail.

. . . .

"... tł'á·h depended on his songs to recall parts of the Hail Chant myth; he remembered the song though he forgot the plot. Moreover if a chanter learns the songs though not the myth, he may perform the ceremony; if he knows the myth but not the songs, he is considered incapable of carrying out the chant—he is simply in possession of miscellaneous information."—*Navaho Religion* Bollingen Series XVIII (New York: Pantheon Books, 1950), I, 276, 283.

enjoyment, if we may judge by the effort exerted by the lay Navaho to attend and participate in the ceremony, for it is unlikely that he knows the deepest significance of the songs.[17]

To the Navaho, song is a necessity; it is an inspiration, a hope, a protection and comfort, a guide, to one in want of a procedure, a means of transforming frustration into power.[18]

In Kinaaldá, music is used during the activities of the first day in some regions and during the final night in all reported areas. The songs sung for the ceremony are numerous and varied; some are short, others are long; some accompany specific rites, others do not. The songs comprise many different categories; a few of these include Hogan Songs, Corn Beetle Songs, Songs for the Placing of the Earth, Twelve Word Songs, and Songs for Administering the Pollen.

In spite of the differences, however, the songs are similar in two ways. Since the Kinaaldá is a subceremony in the Blessing Way Ceremonial Complex, all the puberty songs are Blessing Way Songs.[19] As such, they are sung without drum or rattle accompaniment. Then, too, all belong to one of two categories: either "fixed" or "free" songs. There are certain songs which must be sung at fixed points in the ceremony and by a specific singer. These fixed songs may or may not accompany rites. The other songs, the free ones, are those sung by the singers who are present after the main singer has temporarily relinquished his control. These are sung until dawn begins to appear, and then the singing is "turned back to the main singer" and the songs become fixed once again. The free songs never accompany rites.

Approximately seventy-five songs are sung for Kinaaldá. In the two ceremonies fully recorded by the author, seventy-two

[17]*Ibid.*, p. 288.

[18]*Ibid.*, p. 291.

[19]Some of these songs are used in Kinaaldá only; these include the Racing and Painting Songs, among others. While all the songs relate portions of the Blessing Way myth, the ones specific to Kinaaldá concentrate on the events of the original puberty ceremony, the Kinaaldá of Changing Woman. Both a general and a specific myth are delineated by the song texts.

The subjects of the Navaho Kinaaldá songs contrast with those used in Apache puberty ceremonies. The Chiricahua Apache songs portray the girl's passage through the four stages of her life: girlhood, young womanhood, middle age, and old age. See Morris Opler, *An Apache Life Way* (Chicago, Ill.: University of Chicago Press, 1941), p. 117, and Harold Driver, "Girls' Puberty Rites in Western North America," *University of California Anthropological Records*, VI, No. 2, Culture Element Distributions: XVI (1941), p. 34.

and seventy-three songs were used. These were from a region where singing was not used on the first day. Anne Keith recorded sixty-five songs in her partial taping of the final night of Carla Begay's Kinaaldá in Pinedale. Investigation in Lukachukai suggests that when songs are used on the first day, from two to five are sung.

Singing is continuous throughout the final night. The first songs are started around 11:00 P.M., and from then until about 3:30 A.M. only short breaks occur, for joking, passing the corn pollen, and perhaps for a single meal. After 3:30 A.M., the singing is interrupted more often; from there on, most of it is done in connection with rites and is timed according to their execution. A break of several hours usually occurs before the final three songs, in order that the *'alkaan* can be distributed and a meal eaten.

Kinaaldá songs were recorded by Mary Wheelwright, and the Navaho texts and English translations of these are available; the music, however, is not.[20] Dr. George Herzog transcribed at least one of these songs from the original cylinders, and the author was able to copy the transcription, which is on file at the Museum of Navajo Ceremonial Art in Santa Fe, New Mexico. The majority of the songs discussed in this chapter were recorded by the author in the field in 1963 and 1964 in ceremonial and/or solo performances. Her tapes have been supplemented by those of Anne Keith and Dr. David McAllester. A complete list of the Kinaalda music[21] available to the author for study follows:

Johnson: *Ceremonial Recordings*

1. Kinaaldá of Marie Shirley. *Singer*: Frank Mitchell, 72 songs.

---

[20]A search for the recorded cylinders which are at the Peabody Museum, Harvard University, Cambridge, Massachusetts, is presently under way. Wesleyan University's collection of some of the recordings from Wheelwright's *Creation Chants* does not include Kinaaldá songs. An outline of the Kinaaldá part of the collection, as derived from the Wheelwright texts, is in Appendix G.

[21]The Kinaaldá songs are not the only Navaho songs which deal with menstruation. There are "Songs of the Menstruants" in the Flint Way. See Father Berard Haile, "Origin Legend of the Navaho Flintway," *University of Chicago Publications in Anthropology*, Linguistic Series. (Chicago: University of Chicago Press, 1943), pp. 268–270, and additional notes on pp. 36, 39, and 317–318.

2. Kinaaldá of Lena Shirley. *Singer*: Frank Mitchell, 73 songs.

Solo Recordings

1. Chief Hogan Songs. *Singer*: Frank Mitchell, 14 songs.
2. Three sets which follow the Chief Hogan Songs. *Singer*: Frank Mitchell, 21 songs.
3. Songs of the first day and selected songs from the final night. *Singer*: Blue Mule, 19 songs.
4. Selected songs from the first day and final night. *Singer*: Totsoni Mark, 17 songs.

Keith: *Ceremonial Recording*

1. Partial tapes of the final night of Carla Begay's Kinaaldá. *Singer*: Willie Marianito, 65 songs.

McAllester: *Ceremonial Recording*

1. Tapes of a 1957 Blessing Way. *Singers*: Frank Mitchell and Gray Eyes, 25 Talking God Hogan Songs.

Solo Recording

1. Corn-grinding and Racing Songs. *Singer*: Baánzizba; 1957, 10 songs.

Herzog: *Transcription*

1. Racing Song from Wheelwright cylinders. 1 song.

Wheelwright: *Texts of Kinaaldá Songs*

1. Wheelwright's *Creation Chants* as done in solo recordings by Tł'aáh[22] (Left-Handed One) (T), 1929; specifically, the Kinaaldá Song texts, 39 songs.

Goddard: *Texts of Kinaaldá Songs*

1. One text each of a Hogan Song, Dressing Song, and Dawn Song in "Navajo Texts," *Anthropological Papers of the American Museum of Natural History*, XXXIV, Part I (New York: American Museum of Natural History, 1933).

---

[22]Mary Wheelwright refers to this informant as Hasteen Klah (Mr. Left-Handed) in *Navaho Creation Myth*, Navajo Religion Series, Vol. 1 (Santa Fe, N. Mex.: Museum of Navajo Ceremonial Art, 1942), p. 9. Reichard (*Navaho Religion*, I, 283) calles him *tłá·h* (Left-Handed One). The Franciscan Fathers (p. 122) give *tł'a* as the name for "the left-handed one." In conjunction with Reichard and the government system of transcription, this informant's name will appear here as Tł'aáh (Left-Handed One).

Haile: *Texts of Kinaaldá Songs*

1. 14 Chief Hogan Song texts, 6 Talking God Hogan Song texts, Songs of First Day. 2 Dressing and 4 Racing Song texts from "Blessingway," Version I, 1932 (Informant: SC).

Spatial restrictions at this time permit only a discussion of the fixed songs: those that must be sung by the main singer at specific times during the ceremony. These songs include those used on the first day, the Hogan and Twelve Word Songs used during the fourth night, and the Dawn, Racing, Combing, and Painting Songs sung on the final morning.

Songs of the First Day

Songs are known to accompany the first day's activities of Kinaaldá in Lukachukai and Ramah. The two recordings available are from the first region made respectively in July, 1963, and August, 1964, in solo performances by Dzaa nééz dootł'izhi, Blue Mule (BM), and Totsoni Mark (TM). Seven other Blessing Way singers and the families of four more were contacted in this region, but all who were available refused to record Kinaaldá songs. Examples of some of their reasons follow:

> My granduncle, who was my teacher, never did such things as record, so I don't either (JB).

> If I do that, people will start bad rumors that I am selling my ceremonies (AB).

> If I give my songs to you and that machine, you'll take them far away and then they won't be my songs any more (DT).

The number of songs that these singers use for the first day evidently varies. Archie Begay said he had either two or four songs that he used when "fixing the girl up" on the first day. Diné Tsósí (Slim Man) said he used five. Blue Mule recorded nineteen. Of these, five were specified as songs used during the first day, four for dressing up the girl, and one for racing. However, only two or three of these are actually used.

We never sing all four of them in one singing. We may use two
out of a set of four this time and then on the last morning we'll use
the ones we didn't use before. That's the way we work it. It de-
pends on how fast they're fixing up the girl. That's the main thing.
You just watch them working on the girl; if you think you have
enough time to sing one song, well, you sing that; if you have more
time, then you do another song. You use one or two songs, but
never all four of them. Of course, they're in sets of fours (BM).

Totsoni Mark, in contrast with Blue Mule, used different sets of
Combing and Racing Songs for the first and final mornings. He
mentioned a set of ten songs that were used for the combing on the
first day and a set of six for the first race.

When singing accompanies the rites of the first day, it is
timed accordingly. From one to ten songs are sung as the girl's
hair is combed and she is dressed in her ceremonial sash, belts,
and jewelry; then between one and six songs may be given as she
runs. "After the girl has been prepared and gone off on her run,
that completes the first day. From this time until the final night,
there is no singing" (BM).

The songs for the first day fit into two categories: Combing
Songs and Racing Songs. Since there are other songs in both of
these categories which are sung during the last morning, discussion of these first-day songs will be postponed until later in the
chapter, when they can be treated comparatively.

The Hogan Songs

Ceremonial Usage

On the final night of the Kinaaldá, the people gather in the
ceremonial hogan. The dwelling is blessed with corn pollen, and
then buckskin pouches containing pollen are passed to all those
present so they may bless themselves. After the pouches are returned to the ceremonial basket in the west, the singing begins
with the main singer leading the Hogan Songs, or *Hooghan bighiin*.
There is confusion as to whether these songs refer to the "home"
or the "structure." At one time Frank said the "structure" was

meant; but later he said, "When we say Hogan Songs we mean home or Hogan Songs. Hogan means habitation, a place where people are living, such as a tent, open shack, or under a tree—any place that is somebody's home. Hogan also means structure. I don't know which they mean in the songs, home or structure."

According to Father Berard Haile, Hogan Songs occur only in the Blessing Way Ceremony.[23] Research at Wesleyan, however, has shown that Hogan Songs may also be found in the Enemy Blessing Way, the Night Chant, and the Shooting Way Chant. Many of these songs vary with individual singers, but there are similarities from one ceremonial to another in melodies and texts.

Function

The function of these songs, like all *Hózhǫ́ǫ́jí* songs, is prophylactic rather than curative. They are sung "to make conditions in general safe and pleasant, or even to prevent unpleasant developments in the future."[24] The texts of the Hogan Songs are concerned with either the building of the original conical-shaped hogan or the sanctification of the ceremonial hogan and the gradual identification of it with the home of a particular deity. As they relate either story, the songs bring blessing on the hogan and the people and property gathered inside.

Kluckhohn and Wyman, in "An Introduction to Navaho Chant Practice" (1940), designate a House Blessing Ceremony as one of three subceremonies within the Blessing Way Complex. While Hogan Songs may have once been used to consecrate a new hogan, Frank Mitchell and Chic Sandoval deny the existence of any such House Blessing Ceremony as well as this use of the Hogan Songs.[25]

---

[23]Father Berard Haile, *A Stem Vocabulary of the Navaho Language* (St. Michaels, Ariz.: St. Michaels Press, 1951), II, 154.

[24]*Ibid.*

[25]However, when Frank participated in the dedication ceremonies for new school buildings in Chinle, Arizona, in 1961 and 1964, he sang Hogan Songs. James Smith, of Ganado, Arizona, sang Hogan Songs during the dedication of the stadium of the Inter-tribal Ceremonial at Gallup, New Mexico, in 1940.

The Hogan Songs as Special Songs

The Hogan Songs are regarded as special songs by the Navaho themselves. In many instances in the literature, the main singer in the Kinaaldá is designated as "the one that did the singing of those Hogan Songs" (VW)[26] or as "the one who sang those beginning special songs" (ES).[27] Frank Mitchell does not allow the singing of the Hogan Songs to be interrupted by people leaving the hogan. Once these songs start, although entering is permissible, no one can leave until they have been completed, when the girl is told to go out by the main singer and then return. "The girl opens the door for the people by doing this. Now they can come in and go out all night long as they wish regardless of the singing" (FM). The only reason that could be ascertained for this restriction was that it was a "custom." Perhaps Frank and other singers believe that while entering can only increase the number receiving the blessing, leaving before the sanctification of the hogan and its occupants is completed will detract from the total desired effect and make it impossible to establish fully an effective blessing.

The songs are regarded as special in at least two other ways. Willie Marianito requested to hear only the Hogan Songs that Anne Keith had taped during the Kinaaldá he had sung for Carla Begay. As he explained through his daughter Jannette, "These first songs are the important ones. Those are the ones that *have* to be done right."[28] Both John Bull and Diné Tsósí refused to record Hogan Songs. In explaining their refusals, each said that while it would perhaps be permissible to record the "Kinaaldá Songs" (such as the Racing and Combing Songs), songs that were part of the regular Blessing Way Ceremony, such as the Hogan Songs, could not be sung for a recording machine; they were "too special."

---

[26]Anne Keith, Field Notes, June 26, 1963.

[27]*Ibid*, July 19, 1963.

[28]*Ibid*, July 4, 1963.

Origin and Number

Most informants agreed that the Hogan Songs originated during the first Kinaaldá (that of Changing Woman), and some implied that they were the first Blessing Way songs ever sung. There was less agreement, however, about the number originally sung. The various myths mention twelve, fourteen, twenty-four, and twenty-five Hogan Songs. Present-day practices vary as well. Ceremonies using fourteen and twenty-five were witnessed in 1963. When informants gave a number to the Hogan Songs, however, most of them reported that twelve were used.

Classification

According to Frank Mitchell and other informants, there are three kinds of Hogan Songs: the Chief Hogan Songs, the Hogan Songs of Talking God, and those pertaining to White Shell Woman's home in the west. In discussing them, however, the songs of Talking God and White Shell Woman are usually grouped into one set, the Talking God Hogan Songs. The two kinds, Chief and Talking God Hogan Songs, are discussed on the following pages.

The Chief Hogan Songs

I am planning for it, I am planning for it.

Under the east, I place my first main beam in position,
Under the west, I place my second main beam in position,
Under the south, I place my third main beam in position,
Under the north, I place my main beam firmly in the earth in position.

I am planning for it,
It is being placed in position according to my command.[29]

(From Song No. 4, FRANK MITCHELL, Lena Shirley's Kinaaldá, 1963)

---

[29]The song text given at the beginning of the discussion of each song group is representative of the group, but is a reduced version of a particular song within the set.

Origin and Number

The *Naat'á hooghan bighiin*, or the Chief Hogan Songs, are the original Hogan Songs. They were created before the first hogan was built and were first used to bless it and the newly created chiefs within it. "At the time of the first Kinaaldá, the Hogan Songs of Talking God had not yet originated, therefore they sang the chief Hogan songs."[30] The Chief Hogan Songs are sung at present when a girl celebrates her first Kinaaldá, when medicine bundles are blessed, or when a Blessing Ceremony is held for paraphernalia from another ceremony. They may be used as optional alternants for the Talking God Hogan Songs in other Blessing Way ceremonies, except those for pregnancy, which require the use of the latter type (FM).

There are fourteen Chief Hogan Songs, according to Frank Mitchell, Chic Sandoval, and Willie Marianito. In contrast to those of Talking God, the Chief Hogan Songs are not owned by any particular deity.

> The first Kinaaldá took place at the rim of the Emergence Place in the First Woman's home. All kinds of Holy People were there. The original Hogan Songs are not known to have one person owning them. We can't really say whose songs they were. The second set does, however, really belong to Talking God. The first set is like the early settlers of America who came over the ocean and set up the government together without anyone owning it (FM).

The Subject of the Song Cycle

The fourteen Chief Hogan Songs are concerned with the building of the original conical-shaped hogan. For two songs, the construction is thought about and discussed. In the third and fourth, the beams are put in position. Instructing is done as the construction goes on "below and above the first layer" in Song No. 5 and then "by the fire" in Song No. 6. The furniture is

---

[30] Father Berard Haile, "Origin Legend of the Navaho Enemy Way," *Yale University Publications in Anthropology*, XVII (1938), p. 87.

brought in and the people settle down in Songs Nos. 7–9. Hashch'-
éłti'í (Talking God), who knows nothing about the house, arrives in
Song No. 10 and, looking around the hogan, says, "I have come to
a holy house." In Song No. 11, the god says he will occasionally
return to this holy house. Songs Nos. 12–14 are his decree that
conditions are always to remain the same in the house; no trash
is to accumulate; it is to be brushed out whenever necessary.

The Three Related Sets

Frank learned[31] that three other sets of songs must accompany the fourteen *Naat'á hooghan bighiin*:

> It is compulsory for me to add three sets on top of these four-
> teen songs. Others do not learn these, so they only sing these
> first fourteen.
> These three sets of songs pertain to the original inhabitants of
> the earth, what they should do and acquire as they go along, such
> as selecting a chief for the people, choosing the garments to be
> worn for instructing the people, and things to be put in their mouth
> so wisdom will be evident when they speak (FM).

The first set concerns the appointing of the chiefs in the
home of First Man and First Woman.

> At the rim of the Emergence Place ... the people were foolish;
> they had no sense; they did not plan ahead. They got together and
> began to discuss how they should have leaders to guide them. Now
> these songs pertain to the selection of leaders as guides for the
> people (FM).

The second set discusses the garments the chief wears to
instruct the people. The discussions take place in the home of the
Sun and White Shell Woman. After the chief is dressed, all the
people sit down together and smoke and laugh. The third set
concerns what is produced there (at the home mentioned above)
and the Sun and Moon instructing the two Monster Slayer Boys.

---

[31]Frank learned the Blessing Way from two teachers: his own father, Hastiin Tábahá, from
Chinle, Arizona, and his wife's father, Hastiin Delaghooshi, from Saline Springs Mesa (possibly
Balukai Mesa, Arizona). Totsoni Mark learned from his teacher, Adiłdiłii, that a set of songs
known as *Adiłdiłii bighiin* is compulsory after the Talking God Hogan Songs. Totsoni could not give
the number of songs in this set.

"Monster Slayer is mentioned in these songs, even though these things happened before his time" (FM).

Frank described the organization of the original Hogan Songs as follows:

Fourteen original Chief Hogan Songs

plus

Set One: Eight songs
Set Two: Eight songs
Set Three: Five songs

The three sets were not identified as any particular song type; instead, Frank referred to them as numbered sets concerned with the content given above. He said it was compulsory for him to sing these twenty-one songs after the fourteen *Naat'á hooghan bighiin*, and when he recorded the original Hogan Songs in solo performance, he did just that. However, during Lena Shirley's Kinaaldá (a first Kinaaldá), he picked and chose from the three sets, following the Chief Hogan Songs at this time with eleven of the twenty-one "compulsory songs." The selection was not surprising, however, since Frank had mentioned it before the ceremony: "You can omit some of the others ⌊of the twenty-one⌋, especially the longer ones in a ceremony. During Lena's, I'll sing some of the shorter ones from these three sets because of the time." The selection was thus premeditated and purposeful.

Available Recordings

Frank Mitchell's Chief Hogan Songs were recorded in two versions, solo and ceremonial. As mentioned before, thirty-five songs were recorded the first time and twenty-five the second; the variation was located in the three compulsory additional sets, rather than in the number of Chief Hogan Songs performed. Anne Keith's tapes include Willie Marianito's ceremonial version of the fourteen Chief Hogan Songs. In addition to these recordings made during the study of Kinaaldá, texts for fourteen are available in Father Berard Haile's "Blessingway." Then, too, twenty-one Chief Hogan Songs can be found in the "Creation Chant" singing of Tł'aáh. Finally, there are thirty-two of these songs in Blessing

Way collections; sixteen are sung by Tł'aáh and sixteen by Naat'-áanii. Rather than attempt to treat all the available versions comparatively, only representative samples from those Chief Hogan Songs used in Kinaaldá[32] will be discussed.[33]

Chart 5

Chief Hogan Songs Used in Kinaaldá

Mitchell: solo		Mitchell: ceremonial		Marianito: ceremonial	
	14		14		14
Three	8		4 (Nos. 1, 2, 5, 6)		
additional	8		4 (Nos. 1, 4, 5, 8)		
sets	5		3 (Nos. 1, 3, 5)		
	35		25		14

Groupings

Frank Mitchell's fourteen Chief Hogan Songs can be musically grouped as follows: Nos. 1–2, 3, 4, 5, 6 (the Fire Song), 7, 8–9, 10–11, 12–13, and 14. Song No. 1 is given here, and four others (Nos. 4, 8, 12, and 14) are on pp. 132–139.

Chief Hogan Song No. 1
FRANK MITCHELL
Solo Recording; 1963

heye nene yaŋa bana tsedze keene tsene

bana tsedze keeya tse   bana tsedze keene tse

---

[32]A comprehensive study of Hogan Songs is being made in the Laboratory for Ethnomusicology at Wesleyan University, Middletown, Connecticut.

[33]Discussions of these songs and all other categories in the present book are based on full transcription, charting, and analysis of all available Kinaaldá examples. Copies of all the tapes and transcriptions are on file at the Laboratory for Ethnomusicology, Wesleyan University. Appendix H contains a key for the symbols used in the transcriptions.

The next three verses use different openings and then proceed as verse 1, with the changes noted below.

3.

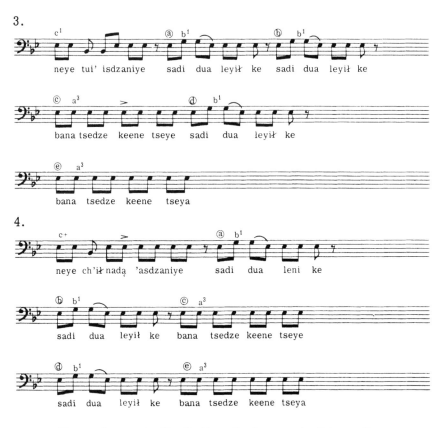

Verse 4 runs to the *; then it changes to this ending:

Formulas and Structure

There are characteristic musical elements in these songs. All are built around certain formulas. The introductions are flat in contour, three beats long (♩♩ ♩♩ ♩♩), and use the Navaho vocables *heye nene yaŋa*. The structure for most of them is as follows: introduction; opening chorus, ending with the vocable *holaghei* (71 percent); four verses with a partial chorus at the end of each; and a closing chorus which ends with the "vocable"[34] *golaghanane* (71 percent) and a musical idea that retards and slides downward.

Ending of Song No. 1[35]

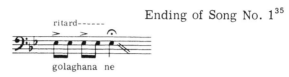

golaghana ne

Ranges

The songs have a range of an octave or more; six use an octave; one, a ninth; six, a twelfth; and one, a thirteenth. Introductions are sung on one note, and the verses are usually within an octave range. It is in the choruses that the widest ranges are most often displayed.

Tonal Systems, Note Types, and Ornamentation

The tonal systems vary, but in all, the emphasized intervals are those of the third, fourth, fifth, and sometimes the sixth, and eighth.

Tonal System-Song No. 1   Tonal System-Song No. 11

The note types are restricted to quarters, eighths, and sixteenths, with only one song including a few grace notes and another two or three, dotted eighths. Ornamentation is conspicuously absent in these songs. Pulsations are rare, and the downward slides heard so often in Navaho music occur in 85 percent of the songs, but only at the end of the final choruses.

---

[34]*Golaghanane* has long been viewed as a vocable formula; the author obtained a meaning for it, however, as will be discussed shortly (see p. 118).

[35]It should be understood that almost every note sung by Frank Mitchell is slightly tremoloed. Due to this consistency, only the slower, more emphasized tremolos are indicated by the sign, ⁓.

Contours

The contours of the introductions, opening choruses, and final choruses reveal the flat *heye nene yaŋa* and *holaghei* and the sliding terminal formula already mentioned. While they are too varied to suggest one or more patterns of design for whole chorus and verse sections, they do illustrate the fact that in these songs the melodic movement is wider in the chorus and more apt to be above the tonic than below it, as in the verses. A few examples of the numerous chorus and verse patterns follow.

Opening Choruses

Song No. 1    ← (tonic level)

Song No. 9

First Verses

Song No. 8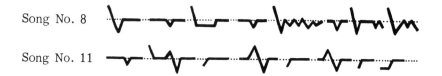

Song No. 11

Internal Structure

The internal structure of these songs is interesting, for while each verse is made up of many small musical phrases, a number of these phrases are related. Hence, while built on many musical ideas, each song is a unified entity. The internal structure of Song No. 1 as diagramed below can serve as an illustration:

Introduction	x
Opening Chorus	a b a^1 a^2
Verse 1	c a/1 b^1 a^3
	c^1 b^1 a^3
	c^2 c^2 + b^1 a^3
	(Middle Chorus a^1 b^2 a^1 a^2)

Verse 2 $c\ a/1\ b^1\ a^3$
                           $c^1\ b^1\ a^3$
                           $c^2\ c^2 + b^1\ a^4$
                           (Middle Chorus $a^1\ b^2\ a^1\ a^2$)

Verse 3   See verse 1

Verse 4 $c\ a/1\ b^1\ a^3$
                           $c^1\ b^1\ a^3$
                           $c^2\ c^2 + b^1\ a^3$

Final chorus $a^1\ b^2\ a^1$

Concluding Formulas $x^1\ x^1$

Texts

As mentioned before, the Chief Hogan Songs relate how the construction of the first Navaho hogan was planned and accomplished. The songs are grouped textually as follows.

Nos. 1−2. Thinking about and planning the construction.
Nos. 3−6. Placing the beams in position.
No. 7. Bringing in the furniture.
Nos. 8−9. The moving in and settling down of the people.
Nos. 10−11. The arrival of Talking God and his admiration.
Nos. 12−14. Talking God's command to keep the place clean.

Unlike the texts of the Talking God Hogan Songs, those of the Chief Hogan Songs are not structured so they present a set of male words and then a comparable set of female ones. Instead, the majority of them are concerned with four ideas, either those of the four directions—east, west, south, and north—or four female deities—Wood Woman, Mountain Woman, Water Woman, and Corn Plant Woman. Father Berard Haile commented on the importance of the latter group by pointing out that "without the mountain woman the Navaho hogan would be impossible; timber woman furnishes the main and minor poles of the hogan; water woman keeps the water supply flowing for the home and also the fields where corn woman reigns."[36]

Of the Chief Hogan Songs, three have more than four verses; two of these, Nos. 5 and 14, extend these four ideas: Song No. 5

---

[36]Haile, *A Stem Vocabulary*, Vol. II, paraphrase of the material on p. 294.

with two more directions, "below" and "above," and Song No. 14 with two more deities, Corn Pollen Boy and Corn Beetle Girl. Song No. 7 is special in its listing, in nine verses, of the furnishings of the hogan.

As in other Navaho songs, the texts are composed of meaningless syllables, or vocables, as well as words. The verbs show a change from the indefinite third person to a definite first person. The singer becomes one with the deity who sang these songs at the first Kinaaldá. In these songs, however, there is a return to the indefinite verb form when, in Songs Nos. 8 and 9, the people move in. Then Talking God arrives, and the singer becomes one with him.

The text of Song No. 1 is given below; it is designed to furnish the Navaho as sung, the spoken form of the same material, and a literal English translation, as well as a possible free translation. Free translations of the texts of Songs Nos. 4, 7, 10, and 14 can be found on pp. 128–132.

Chief Hogan Song No. 1
FRANK MITCHELL
Solo Recording, 1963

	heye nene yaŋa
(Sung Navaho)	bana tsedze keene tsene
(Spoken Navaho)	baa ntsékees
(Literal English)	about it one is thinking[37]

bana tseze keene tse	bana tsedze keene tse
baa ntsékees	baa ntsékees
about it one is thinking	about it one is thinking

bana tsedze keene holaghei
baa ntsékees
about it one is thinking

1. neye nehotsaniye	biza deya	sadi	dua leya ke
nohosdzáán	bizaadi	sadii	doleeł
Earth	its main beam	made the main beam	to be

---

[37]Unless otherwise specified, all texts given in three lines herein will follow this format— line 1 being the Navaho as it is sung, line 2, the Navaho as it is spoken, and line 3, the literal English. All song texts given at the conclusion of discussions of specific song groups will appear only as free translations.

                          bana tsedze keene tsene
                          baa ntsékees
                          about it one is thinking

tse'esdzaniye   sadi   dua leya ke
tsį''esdzą́ą́   sadii   doleeł
Wood Woman   made the   to be
                          main beam

                          bana tsedze keene tsene
                          baa ntsékees
                          about it one is thinking

ka   sa'a naghei   ka   bik'e hozhoniye   sadi   dua lenił ke
k'ad są́'ą naghei   k'ad bik'e hózhǫ́ǫ́ [38] sadii   doleeł
now   long life   now everlasting   made the   to be
                          beauty   main beam

                          bana tsedze keene tsene
                          baa ntsékees
                          about it one is thinking

bana tsedze keene tse   bana tsedze keeya tseya
baa ntsékees   baa ntsékees
about it one is thinking   about it one is thinking

                          bana tsedze keene tse
                          baa ntsékees
                          about it one is thinking

                          bana tsedze keene holaghei
                          baa ntsékees
                          about it one is thinking   *holaghei*

---

[38] The Navaho *k'ad są́'ą naghei, k'ad bik'e hózhǫ́ǫ́* is very difficult to translate. Every author decides more or less on his own translation of these terms, which are known as the "sacred words" to some writers. John Ladd's *The Structure of a Moral Code* (Cambridge, Mass.: Harvard University Press, 1957), contains some pertinent information about these words on p. 394:

"[I asked whether word for living a long time was *saą naghai*. They said it was related.]

"*Saą naghai*—that's the word that every song that ends with it. But that's something like one of the Holy People have a word. That's a name. But all the Singers they's kind of afraid to talk about Blessing Way song. They kind of feel bad about it if they talk about. They won't talk about it for nothing. Only time they can talk about it is when Singer is talking song to young man—then he can tell that story there.

"*bikeh hozhon*—goes with that. They hang together. Only the singer who sings Blessing Way and the other Singers—all different way they're singing. They only know this word. But they don't tell it out to the people what it is. They are afraid to talk about those two words. Only time when Singer is learning the Song to another man. When a man is through learning then that comes in behind all these song. Then this man will ask that he wants to learn what's meaning by that two word. Then Singer he has a right to tell that little story to man who learned the Song. He didn't have to tell about it if the man learned just a little bit of the Song. That's only time when man sing the whole Blessing Way. They can talk about good living and living a long life anytime."

Reichard also discusses these words (*Navaho Religion*, I, 45–48). In the present book the author is translating the terms as "long life" and "everlasting beauty."

2. neye dził esdzaniye   biza deya   sadi   dua leyił ke
   dzil esdzą́ą́   bizaadi   sadii   doleeł
   Mountain Woman   its main   made the   to be
                          beam   main beam

                         bana tsedze keene tsene
                         baa ntsékees
                         about it one is thinking

tse'esdzaniye   sadi   dua leyił ke
tsį''esdzą́ą́   sadii   doleeł
Wood Woman   made the   to be
                                     main beam

                         bana tsedze keeye tseye
                         baa ntsékees
                         about it one is thinking

ka   sa'a naghei   ka   bik'e hozhoniye   sadi   dua lenił ke
k'ad   są́'ą naghei   k'ad bik'e hózhǫ́ǫ́   sadii   doleeł
now   long life   now everlasting   made the   to be
                           beauty   main beam

                         bana tsedze kee tseye
                         baa ntsékees
                         about it one is thinking

bana tsedze keene tse   bana tsedze keeya tseya
baa ntsékees   baa ntsékees
about it one is thinking   about it one is thinking

                         bana tsedze keene tse
                         baa ntsékees
                         about it one is thinking

                         bana tsedze keene holaghei
                         baa ntsékees
                         about it one is thinking   *holaghei*

3. neye tui'isdzaniye   biza deya   sadi   dua leyił ke
   tó 'isdzą́ą́   bizaadi   sadii   doleeł
   Water Woman   its main   made the   to be
                          beam   main beam

                         bana tsedze keene tsene
                         baa ntsékees
                         about it one is thinking

tse'esdzaniye   sadi   dua leyił ke
tsį''esdzą́ą́   sadii   doleeł
Wood Woman   made the   to be
                                     main beam

bana tsedze keene tseye
baa ntsékees
about it one is thinking

ka	sa'a naghei	ka	bik'e hozhoniye	sadi	dua leyił ke
k'ad	są'ą naghei	k'ad	bik'e hózhǫ́ǫ́	sadii	doleeł
now	long life	now	everlasting beauty	made the main beam	to be

bana tsedze keene tseya
baa ntsékees
about it one is thinking

bana tsedze keene tse   bana tsedze keeya tseya
baa ntsékees   baa ntsékees
about it one is thinking   about it one is thinking

bana tsedze keene tse
baa ntsékees
about it one is thinking

bana tsedze keene holaghei
baa ntsékees
about it one is thinking   *holaghei*

4. neye ch'ił nadą	'asdzaniye	biza deya	sadi	dua leni ke
ch'ił naadą́ą́'	'asdzą́ą́	bizaadi	sadii	doleeł
Plant Corn	Woman	its main beam	made the main beam	to be

bana tsedze keene tsene
baa ntsékees
about it one is thinking

tse'esdzaniye	sadi	dua leyił ke
tsį''esdzą́ą́	sadii	doleeł
Wood Woman	made the main beam	to be

bana tsedze keene tseye
baa ntsékees
about it one is thinking

ka	sa'a naghei ka	bik'e hozhoniye	sadi	dua leyil ke
k'ad	są'ą naghei k'ad	bik'e hózhǫ́ǫ́	sadii	doleeł
now	long life now	everlasting beauty	made the main beam	to be

bana tsedze keene tseya
baa ntsékees
about it one is thinking

bana tsedze keene tse   bana tsedze keeya tseya
baa ntsékees   baa ntsékees
about it one is thinking   about it one is thinking

bana tsedze keene tse   bana tsedze kees   golaghana ne
baa ntsékees   baa ntsékees   ní
about it one is thinking about it one is thinking   it is
                                                             said

Chief Hogan Song No. 1
Free Translation

heye nene yaŋa
One is thinking about it, one is thinking about it,
One is thinking about it, one is thinking about it,
   holaghei.

Its main beam, Earth is to be made the main beam,
            one is thinking about it,
Its main beam, Wood Woman is to be made the main beam,
            one is thinking about it,
Now long life,   now everlasting beauty are to be made the main
            beam,
            one is thinking about it.

   One is thinking about it, one is thinking about it,
   One is thinking about it, one is thinking about it.

Its main beam, Mountain Woman is to be made the main beam,
            one is thinking about it,
Its main beam, Wood Woman is to be made the main beam,
            one is thinking about it,
Now long life,   now everlasting beauty are to be made the main
            beam,
            one is thinking about it.

   One is thinking about it, one is thinking about it,
   One is thinking about it, one is thinking about it.

Its main beam, Water Woman is to be made the main beam,
            one is thinking about it,
Its main beam, Wood Woman is to be made the main beam,
            one is thinking about it,
Now long life,   now everlasting beauty are to be made the main
            beam,
            one is thinking about it.

   One is thinking about it, one is thinking about it,
   One is thinking about it, one is thinking about it.

Its main beam, Corn Plant Woman is to be made the main beam,
   one is thinking about it,
Its main beam, Wood Woman is to be made the main beam,
   one is thinking about it,
Now long life, now everlasting beauty are to be made the main
     beam,
   one is thinking about it.

  One is thinking about it, one is thinking about it,
  One is thinking about it, one is thinking about it,
   it is said.

Vocables

A study of these texts is a research topic in itself and one
that can only be handled in depth after extensive linguistic training. Thus, only certain facts are mentioned for each set of texts
discussed in this book. In the Chief Hogan Songs, the vocables
were of particular interest to the author. For a long time, many
whole as well as partial texts of American Indian songs have been
dismissed as being meaningless. However, in working with Frank,
the author learned that phrases and words viewed as "meaningless" by some informants might have meanings ascribed to them
by others.[39]

Frank Mitchell recognized that some syllables in the songs
are meaningless, to be sure. These he calls "tones" or "links,"
for "they get you to the next word." At times he also called them
"stretchers": "These stretch out the words and make them last
longer." An example of a "link" or "tone" would be the *aiye* and
eiye in the third verse of Song No. 7.

shi ko aiye	shi ch'iiya eiye
shi kǫ'	shi ch'iyạ'
my fire	my food

A "stretcher" is seen in comparing the opening choruses of Songs
Nos. 8 and 9:

niji nịnowo		niji nịnowowowowa
nijinịnā	*vs.*	nijinịnā
one has settled in		one has settled in

---

[39] These discoveries apply to non-Kinaaldá songs as well. See Charlotte Johnson, "Navaho
Corn Grinding Songs," *Journal of the Society for Ethnomusicology*, VIII, No. 2 (May, 1964), pp.
101–120.

But Frank also viewed other supposedly "meaningless" syllables as having a literary value. The final *golaghanane* found in so many Blessing Way songs is really *ní* (it is said).[40] Other syllables are actually archaic Navaho words with very definite meanings. Examples of these come in later songs. Finally, Frank told of syllables which, while not actual words, have a meaning, since they are the identifiable calls belonging to specific deities. Two examples of these are found in the Chief Hogan Songs: the *howowo* in Song No. 10 is a form of *ho-o*, one of Talking God's calls; the *yaiye aiye* in Song No. 11 is another such call; the *dei a wai* in Song No. 14 means "sweep up right here" in Talking God's language, according to Frank. Thus, the gods have a special speech in addition to their calls.

The Three Sets of Additional Songs

The three sets of songs which Frank is obliged to sing after the Chief Hogan Songs total twenty-one songs. An analysis of them shows, however, that the first eight are essentially one song with minor changes, the second eight, the same, and the last five, three different songs. There are five songs from these twenty-one on pp. 140−168: No. 1, Set I; No. 1, Set II; and Nos. 1, 3, and 5 of Set III.

Length

The songs in the sets vary in length. The first eight songs are short, four having five verses and four having six verses each. In Set II, the length increases almost without a break; the first two have thirteen verses, the third has twenty-five, and the fourth, twenty-six. Songs Nos. 5 and 6 have forty-eight verses, Song No. 7, forty-seven, and Song No. 8, fifty. Frank said the third set had the longest songs, but this was not the case. The verse totals in Songs Nos. 1−5 in Set III are forty-five, forty-

---

[40]Haile also gives a meaning for *golaghanane*: "so it is." See "Origin Legend of the Navaho Enemy Way," pp. 262−263, 319, n. 76.

seven, thirty-three, thirty-three, and ten. In any case, Frank was aware of the lengthening, explaining that the songs were getting longer as he was recording them: "Now these songs are longer. But they're somewhere in the back of my head." Great length evidently makes a song formidable to the lay Navaho, for Frank added, "The people do not care to sing the long ones. They're so long, they keep forgetting them."

Set I

Ranges, Formulas, Note Types, and Skips

The first eight songs are uncomplicated. All share a total range of an eleventh with choruses and verses being sung within the boundaries of an octave. The introductory

is found in all but one, which, for reasons not ascertained, has no introduction. The *holaghei* link found in the Chief Hogan Songs between the opening chorus and verses is not present, nor is the final *golaghanane*. The retarding, downward sliding final is, however. Note types are restricted to quarters, eighths, and grace notes; skips, to intervals of a third, fourth, fifth, sixth, and octave.

Internal Structure

The songs follow an integrated structure:

Introduction	x
Opening Chorus	a b a^1 b^1 a^1 b^1
Verse 1	c d (a^1 b^1)
Verse 2	c d^1 d^2 (a^1 b^1) (Song No. 1)
Verse 3	c d^3 (a^1 b^1)
Verse 4	c^1 d^4 (a^1 b^1)
Verse 5	c^1 d^5 (a^1 b^1)
Final Chorus	a b a^1 b^1

A pattern can be readily observed in even the minor changes which occur each time. Many of the textual and musical changes alternate in such a way that all the odd-numbered and all the even-numbered songs are interrelated. For example, the music and words of the second verse of Song No. 1 are used in the second verses of Songs Nos. 3, 5, and 7, whereas Songs Nos. 2, 4, 6, and 8 use the slightly different form presented in the second verse of Song No. 2.

The Second Verse of Odd-Numbered Songs

ka'atse hastiye bihooghan ya'ałnish dola

The Second Verse of Even-Numbered Songs

ka'atse asdzana bihooghani ya'ałnish dola

Texts

The first set of songs tells the story of the choosing of the four original chiefs for the Navaho people. Here is the text of the first song.

> *heye nene yaŋa*
> Chiefs shall be created it is said,
> Chiefs shall be created it is said,
> Chiefs shall be created it is said.

Now at the rim of the Emergence Place,
       chiefs will truly be created it is said,
Now at the center of the room in the house of First Man,
       chiefs will truly be created it is said,
At the center soft fabrics will be spread,
       chiefs will truly be created it is said,
Now with Monster Slayer, the chief-planner-to-be,
       chiefs will truly be created it is said,
Now long life, now everlasting beauty,
       chiefs will truly be created it is said.

> Chiefs shall be created it is said,
> Chiefs shall be created it is said,
> Chiefs shall be created it is said.

Songs Nos. 2, 3, and 4, respectively, see "Born for Water" named the second chief in the house of First Woman where jewels are spread; "He Who Changes into All Things" named third chief and "Yellow Man," in First Man's house surrounded by soft fabrics; and "One Reared in the Ground" becomes a chief in the earth at the house of First Woman where jewels are spread. Songs Nos. 5 − 8 name the chiefs again, give their numerical rank, and describe their dress.

Set II

Ranges, Tonal Systems, Formulas, Note Types and Structures

The songs in Set II are longer. The total range contracts, though, to an octave which is covered in the choruses. The verses are generally sung within a range of a sixth. The tonal system is reduced still further, and all these eight songs are built on only four tones: I, III, V, and its octave:

The same intervals are emphasized in skips, and in general the same formulas are present. However, now the *holaghei* and *golaghanane* formulas return, with the latter often being given in the rhythmic form characteristic of Frank Mitchell's Talking God Hogan Songs:

Note types expand to include sixteenths and dotted eighths as well as the quarters and eighths used in Set I. The internal structure is integrated in much the same way. This time, though, the set is interrelated from song to song, rather than in an odd-even number pattern. There are many changes in the total verse numbers, but few other variations occur; when they do, they are ones of slight range extensions in the verses, removal of dotted figures, and minor tonal changes.

Texts

The first four songs of Set II tell of the dressing up of the chief in the house of White Shell Woman. Textual alternations occur in color as well as in the type of articles put on the chief. By the end of the fourth song, he has been completely dressed. Then he begins to relax; a smoke is prepared for the chief, who sits right down and starts smoking, finally laughing and becoming happy.

Set III

Ranges and Tonal Systems

The second set leads directly into the third, for when the chief is through smoking, he gets up and begins talking to the people, instructing them. The five songs in this set are, perhaps, the most musically interesting of all twenty-one. In Song No. 1, the range is almost incredible; it covers a seventeenth! In the opening chorus, it is almost as if the singer is searching for a tonic:

heye nene yaŋa towa nana to wo wowi yeye towi nane taŋa

aŋa yeye towi nana tana-- aŋa yeye towi nani tạ 'aŋaye

towi naŋa haŋa holaghei

The verses have ranges anywhere from a sixth to a thirteenth in this song, while the choruses range from an octave to an eleventh.

The tonal system includes twelve pitches:

Finally, in the various segments of Song No. 1, there is much more variation than has been previously observed.

Songs Nos. 2 − 5

Song No. 1 is not the only source of musical surprises. In Songs Nos. 3 and 4, the introductions rise rather than remaining flat in contour:

heye   neye   yaiye

The elaborateness of Song No. 1 does not characterize the entire set; changes in form, tonal system, and range make Songs Nos. 3[41] and 4 simpler and clearer, as does another change in form in the fifth and final song. Throughout all the songs, a subtle balance is achieved between elaboration and simplicity through variation in the amount of ornamentation and melodic movement, the kinds of note types, the shapes of contours, and the definition of the musical and textual formulas per se.

Texts

The third set consists of four long songs and one short one. Of the long ones, two are Planning Songs; two others describe how the chief has become the child of White Shell Woman, the son of the Sun; the child of Changing Woman, and the son of the Moon. The one short song tells of blessing the earth, so the hogan will be a permanent entity.

---

[41]Frank Mitchell sang this song (No. 3 of Set III) at the 1961 school dedication (*supra*, p. 151, n. 25).

Vocables

In the work on these texts with Frank, two more indications of meanings and forces attached to supposed "vocables" were discovered. In Song No. 3, the opening chorus is:

yaghee hai ya'ei
naghei
that thing

Frank said *hai ya'ei* were "just tones, but they give the idea of 'in order to make it holy.'" In the same song, the first verse reads, in part:

yołgai isdzaŋa	aŋa neya	biyaazhji	shinishlį yelagowo
yołgai 'esdzą́ą́		biyáázhi	shi nishlį́
White Shell Woman		her little one	I, I am

Yelagowo would not be used in speaking, according to Frank, but it makes *shi nishlį́* more emphatic in the song.[42]

A free translation of the final song in Set III follows.

> *heye neye yaŋa*
> The earth's surface, the earth's surface,
> The earth's surface, the earth's surface.

Now with the dawn, I have become a young man,
  he who lies within the interior of the dawn,
    Talking God, he has put rock crystal, exactly beautiful,
      he has put the pollen of dawn with the pollen
        of the soft fabrics into my mouth.
    By means of it you talk, by means of it you plan.
    The elder listens to it; he pays attention to it.
Now long life and everlasting beauty,
  he who lies within the interior of the dawn.

Now with the sun coming up, I have become a young man,
  he who lies within the interior of the dawn,
    Hogan God,[43] he has put turquoise, exactly beautiful,
      he has put the pollen of the sun with the pollen
        of jewels into my mouth.

---

[42]Note the correspondence of this material with Reichard's and Haile's.

"Furthermore, AB [Adolph Bitanny] insists that there are no 'nonsense' syllables, that all have meaning. Possibly the syllables constitute another kind of symbolism which a full analysis of the songs may prove to exist. Perhaps Father Berard's informant agreed with AB when he said, 'The words have no meaning, but the song means, "Take it, I give it to you."'" Reichard, *Navaho Religion*, I, 281, quoting from Haile, "Origin Legend of the Navaho Flintway," p. 293, 69n. excerpt.

[43]Reichard and Goddard feel that Haashch'éhoognan (Hogan God) is an untranslatable name. See Reichard, *Navaho Religion*, II, pp. 502–504, and Goddard, "Navaho Texts," pp. 149, 151

By means of it you talk, by means of it you plan.
The old woman listens to it; she pays attention to it.
Now long life and everlasting beauty,
    he who lives within the interior of the dawn.

3. The same as verse 1, but use "young man" instead of the "elder."
4. The same as verse 2, but use "woman" instead of the "old woman."
5. The same as verse 1, but use "the children" instead of the "elder."
6. The same as verse 2, but use "the chief" instead of the "old woman."

Before me it is blessed, behind me it is blessed
    it listens, it pays attention,
Below me it is blessed, above me it is blessed,
    it listens, it pays attention,
All around me it is blessed, my speech is blessed,
    it listens, it pays attention,
Now long life, now everlasting beauty, I am a young man,
    it listens, it pays attention.

The earth's surface, the earth's surface,
The earth's surface, the earth's surface,
The earth's surface.

A Comparison of the Chief Hogan Songs as Sung by Frank Mitchell

Given the Navaho characteristic of much variation and the fact that nine singers in addition to Frank were present, it is not surprising that none of the fourteen songs was sung for Lena's Kinaaldá exactly as it had been previously sung for the solo recording session. The pitch curve, which had actually dropped in the latter singing, rose in true Navaho style in the ceremonial performance of the song sequence. The first few songs were pitched a minor third higher than before.

The opening choruses were the scene of most of the musical changes. Here, phrases were altered, skips were expanded, and repeats of the whole section were added or subtracted. As the tonic rose, the opening choruses were changed so that their previous ranges were restricted. Intervals were contracted and lines flattened in many instances. In studying the changes, there seemed to be a level beyond which upward skips of any kind were to be avoided and stepwise progressions used consistently. The pivotal point in these songs was around d'[44]; while this was not the upper limit of Frank's range, it was, at least on that night, the point beyond which he was not particularly comfortable.

Other changes occurred; several of the songs added closing choruses where they had not had them before. Within the verses, melodic lines were also occasionally altered. In general, the changes were musical rather than textual; in only a few cases were individual words altered in their textual position or vocable composition.

A Comparison of the Three Additional Sets

In singing the three subsequent sets, Frank, as mentioned earlier, used eleven of the twenty-one possible songs. During the ceremonial performance of Songs Nos. 1, 2, 5, and 6 from Set I, few changes occurred other than minor tone alterations. This was true for the first two songs, Nos. 1 and 4, Set II. Then, however, verses began to be changed and even omitted. After singing songs Nos. 5 and 8, Set III was begun. In Song No. 1, the search for a tonic mentioned above was evident, but the resolution was smoother. Verses were consistently run together with additional vocables, and some of the original text was omitted. The second song which was sung started as if it were Song No. 4, but after the second verse it became Song No. 3. Rose Mitchell was singing these songs with Frank, and during this one she was singing at a *minor ninth* above him! Whenever he made a mistake, she stopped singing, not starting again until he had corrected it and re-established the continuity. In Song No. 5 from Set III, the choruses as well as many details in each verse were changed.

In the ceremonial performance of these sets, the changes again occurred more often in the music than in the texts. In contrast to the differences found between the solo and ceremonial versions of the Chief Hogan Songs, those in the three additional

---

[44]The Tablature system being used throughout this book is the one generally used by musicians. It is given on pp. 143–144 of Louis Elson, *Elson's Pocket Music Dictionary* (Philadelphia, Penna.: Oliver Ditson, 1909).

sets were not localized in one section, and they became more frequent in the latter songs.

Comparison of Willie Marianito's and Frank Mitchell's Chief Hogan Songs

The Willie Marianito Chief Hogan Songs sung for Carla Begay's Kinaaldá are very similar to those of Frank Mitchell. The first six songs are especially close to the solo versions Frank recorded. The only variations are Willie's tendencies to repeat the opening chorus, to use *dạ'asdzaniye* (Corn Woman) in the fourth verse instead of Frank's *ch'ił nadą̄'asdzaniye* (Corn Plant Woman), and to alter one or two notes. Willie explains the first song as "This is the beginning of the building of the hogan" and the sixth as "This is where they build a fire."

There are more changes in Songs Nos. 7–14. The opening choruses vary, and most of them emphasize the minor triad. Final choruses are left out of songs that use them in Frank's versions. Song No. 14 appears to be a dissection of Frank Mitchell's song. The opening chorus is changed musically, and all of the choruses are lengthened. In contrast to the Mitchell version, found on pp. 137–139, the verses in Willie Marianito's fourteenth song follow this form:

yeye bihoghaniye ntsis kł'ah doiye weiye (etc.)
neye shihoghaniye ya'ałniyish doiye weiye
neye shihoghaniye honeshlaŋash doiye weiye
neye shihoghaniye bahaskł'ash doiye weiye
neye shihoghaniye che'etinish doiye weiye
neye shihoghaniye binadeeyish doiye weiye
yelaŋa heye aŋ ne hodizho golaghanane

In spite of these differences, the Marianito and Mitchell Chief Hogan songs resemble each other quite closely. That this should be true is surprising when the singers' histories are considered. While they have heard of each other, they are from different sections of the reservation. They learned from different teachers who were unrelated and who were also from different parts of the reservation.

A possible explanation of the similarity is that the Blessing Way Chief Hogan Songs may exist in essentially one version. Research on the general topic of Hogan Songs at Wesleyan University is revealing similarities among Mitchell, Marianito, and other Blessing Way singers such as Naat'áanii and Tł'aáh.

Chief Hogan Song No. 4

FRANK MITCHELL

Solo Recording, 1963

heye nene ya'a
I am planning for it, I am planning for it,
I am planning for it, I am planning for it,
I am planning for it,
It is being placed in position according to
        my command.

Under the east, I place my first main beam in position,
Long life, everlasting beauty, I am planning for it,
It is being placed in position according to my command.

Under the west, I place my second main beam in position,
Long life, everlasting beauty, I am planning for it,
It is being placed in position according to my command.

Under the south, I place my third main beam in position,
Long life, everlasting beauty, I am planning for it,
It is being placed in position according to my command.

Under the north, I place my main beam firmly in the earth
        in position,
Long life, everlasting beauty, I am planning for it,
It is being placed in position according to my command.

I am planning for it, I am planning for it,
I am planning for it, I am planning for it,
I am planning for it,
It is being placed in position according to
        my command.

Chief Hogan Song No. 7

FRANK MITCHELL

Solo Recording, 1963

heye nene yaŋa
I fully understand it, I fully understand it,
I fully understand it, I fully understand it.

Now with my doorway, now with my door curtain,
    the house has come into being it is said.
        I fully understand it, I fully understand it,
        I fully understand it, I fully understand it.

With the door frame, now with the cross beam,
    the house has come into being it is said.
        I fully understand it, I fully understand it,
        I fully understand it, I fully understand it.

With my fire, with my food,
    the house has come into being it is said.
        I fully understand it, I fully understand it,
        I fully understand it, I fully understand it.

With my pot, with the stirring sticks,
    the house has come into being it is said.
        I fully understand it, I fully understand it,
        I fully understand it, I fully understand it.

With my dish, with my gourd ladle,
    the house has come into being it is said.
        I fully understand it, I fully understand it,
        I fully understand it, I fully understand it.

With the quern, with the broom,
    the house has come into being it is said.
        I fully understand it, I fully understand it.
        I fully understand it, I fully understand it.

With my woven mat, with my bedding,
    the house has come into being it is said.
        I fully understand it, I fully understand it,
        I fully understand it, I fully understand it.

All kinds of soft fabrics, all kinds of jewels
    were brought into the interior, it is said.
        I fully understand it, I fully understand it,
        I fully understand it, I fully understand it.

Now long life, now everlasting beauty,
    were brought into the interior, it is said.
        I fully understand it, I fully understand it,
        I fully understand it.

        I fully understand it, I fully understand it,
        I fully understand it, I fully understand it,
                it is said.

Chief Hogan Song No. 10
FRANK MITCHELL
Solo Recording, 1963

heye nene yaŋa
howowo aiye ye (Call of Talking God and vocables),
It is a holy house that I have come to,
   it is a holy house that I have come to,
howowo ai yeye aiye,
It is a holy house that I have come to,
howowa ai ne,
It is a holy house that I have come to, *holaghei.*

Now I have come to the home of the Earth,
Now I have come to a house built with wood,
Now I have come to a house built with all kinds of soft fabrics,
I have come to a holy house, the holy house of long life,
   now of everlasting beauty.

 (Call of Talking God and vocables),
 I have come to a holy house,
 I have come to a holy house,
 I have come to a holy house.

Now I have come to the home of Mountain Woman,
Now I have come to a house built with wood,
Now I have come to a house built with all kinds of jewels,
I have come to a holy house, the holy house of long life,
   now of everlasting beauty.

 (Call of Talking God and vocables),
 I have come to a holy house,
 I have come to a holy house,
 I have come to a holy house.

Now I have come to the home of Water Woman,
Now I have come to a house built with wood,
Now I have come to a house built with all kinds of gathered
   rain waters,
I have come to a holy house, the holy house of long life,
   now of everlasting beauty.

 (Call of Talking God and vocables),
 I have come to a holy house,
 I have come to a holy house,
 I have come to a holy house.

Now I have come to the home of Corn Plant Woman,
Now I have come to a house built with wood,

Now I have come to a house built with corn pollen,
I have come to a holy house, the holy house of long life,
            now of everlasting beauty.

    (Call of Talking God and vocables),
    I have come to a holy house,
    I have come to a holy house,
    I have come to a holy house, it is said.

Chief Hogan Song No. 14
FRANK MITCHELL
Solo Recording, 1963

heye nene yaŋa
    From now on, keep it swept clean; beauty extends out,
    From now on, keep it swept clean; beauty extends out,
    From now on, keep it swept clean; beauty extends out,
                        holaghei.

In the rear of the home of the Earth,
        keep it swept clean; beauty extends out,
Now in the house of long life, now of everlasting beauty,
        keep it swept clean; beauty extends out.

        From now on, keep it swept clean; beauty extends out,
        From now on, keep it swept clean; beauty extends out,
                        holaghei.

In the center of the home of Mountain Woman,
        keep it swept clean; beauty extends out,
Now in the house of long life, now of everlasting beauty,
        keep it swept clean; beauty extends out.

        From now on, keep it swept clean; beauty extends out,
        From now on, keep it swept clean; beauty extends out,
                        holaghei.

By the fire in the home of Water Woman,
        keep it swept clean; beauty extends out,
Now in the house of long life, now of everlasting beauty,
        keep it swept clean; beauty extends out.

        From now on, keep it swept clean; beauty extends out,
        From now on, keep it swept clean; beauty extends out,
                        holaghei.

In the east corner of the room in the home of Corn Plant Woman,
        keep it swept clean; beauty extends out,

Now in the house of long life, now of everlasting beauty,
  keep it swept clean; beauty extends out.

  From now on, keep it swept clean; beauty extends out,
  From now on, keep it swept clean; beauty extends out,
            holaghei.

By the doorway of the home of Pollen Boy,
  keep it swept clean; beauty extends out,
Now in the house of long life, now of everlasting beauty,
  keep it swept clean; beauty extends out.

  From now on, keep it swept clean; beauty extends out,
  From now on, keep it swept clean; beauty extends out,
            holaghei.

All around the home of Corn Beetle Girl,
  keep it swept clean; beauty extends out,
Now in the house of long life, now of everlasting beauty,
  keep it swept clean; beauty extends out.

  From now on, keep it swept clean; beauty extends out,
  From now on, keep it swept clean;
  Beauty is all over the horizon surrounding the house,
            it is said.

Chief Hogan Song No. 4
FRANK MITCHELL
Solo Recording, 1963

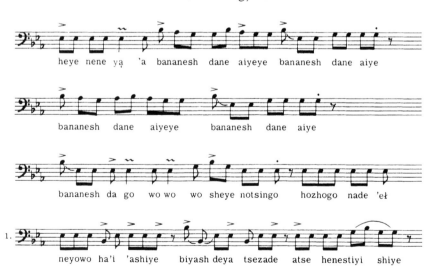

heye nene yą 'a bananesh dane aiyeye bananesh dane aiye

bananesh dane aiyeye bananesh dane aiye

bananesh da go wo wo wo sheye notsingo hozhogo nade 'eł

neyowo ha'i 'ashiye biyash deya tsezade atse henestiyi shiye

sa'a nagha-'a yeye bik'e hozhowo neya

bananesh da go wo wo wa sheye notsingo hozhogo nade - 'eł

neyowo bananesh dane aiyeye bana dane aiye

bananesh dane aiye yeye bananesh dane aiye

bananesh da go wo wo wo sheye notsingo

hozhogo nade - 'eł neyowo

Chief Hogan Song No. 8
FRANK MITCHELL
Solo Recording, 1963

heye nene yaŋa ni-ji-ni nowo niji-ni nowo ni-ji-ni na -'aŋa

ani - ji - ni ŋa - 'ana - 'a ne-yo-wo

k'ad no-ho-tsani beye ne-ji-ni na -'aŋa - 'a neyowo

The song continues with three more verses. The music remains the same; the text changes in the opening portion of lines 1 and 3 of each verse.

2. k'ad dził 'isdzani beye
ntł'iz iłtas eiye beye

3. k'ad tui'isdzani beye
to'o lanashchini beye

4. ch'ił nadą'asdzani beye
(add one more eighth note on *d*)
k'ad tadidini beye
(remove last group of sixteenths)

On the final *neyowo* of verse 4, there is a ritardando.

Chief Hogan Song. No. 12
FRANK MITCHELL
Solo Recording, 1963

t - 'aŋa   hoteeli   neye   t - 'aŋa   hoteeli   ne

t - 'aŋa   hoteeya   t - 'aŋa   hoteeli   holaghei

neye   nehot-sa-ni-ye   bihooghana   de - hoteela   neya

tsi - 'isdza -niye   yebaghan   lade   hoteela   neya

yodi   iłtas   ei   ye   yebaghan   lade   hoteela   neya

k'a sa-'a   naghei   k'a bik'e   hozho - niye

bihooghan   lade   hoteela   ne   t - 'aŋa   hoteeli   ne

t - 'aŋa   hoteeli   neye   t - 'aŋa   hoteeli   ne

t - 'aŋa   hoteeli   holaghei

The song has three more verses. The openings of lines 1 and 3 of each verse change, almost exactly as they did in Song No. 8.

2. neye dził 'isdzani beye   3. neye tui'isdzaniye
   ntł'iz iłtas ei ye   to'o lanashchiniye

4. neye ch'ił nadą'asdzaniye
   tadidiniye

After the fourth verse, the opening chorus is sung once again, beginning after the introduction and using a new ending which is shown below along with the other musical changes that occur throughout the song.

Chief Hogan Song No. 14
FRANK MITCHELL
Solo Recording, 1963

esdzą doiye wei ye yela ŋaha howozhowo deya

esdzą doiye wei ye yela ŋaha howozhowo holaghei

ⓐ
1. yeye nihotsa - ni- ye biho - gha - ni - ye

ⓑ ⓒ
nitsis tł ash doiye wei ye yela ŋaha howozhowo de

k'a sa'a naghei yi-ye k 'a bik'e hozho - ni - ye biho - gha-ni - ye

ⓑ
nitsis tł'ash doiye wei ye yela ŋaha howozhowo de

ⓓ ⓔ
esdzą doiye wei ye yela ŋaha howozhowo de

ⓕ
esdzą doiye wei ye yela ŋaha howozhowo holaghei

Five other verses follow the one above, using these textual and musical changes:

ⓐ ⓑ
2. neye dził 'isdza - ni - ye ya' ałniyish doiye wei ye

esdzą doiye wei ye   yela ŋaha... yela ŋaha...

3.   neye tui-'isdzą - ni - ye   honesh lanash...

4.   yeye ch'ił nadą - 'asdza - ni - ye   bahastł -'anash...

esdzą doiye wei ye

5.   yeye tadi - dini esh-kiye   ch'e' etinish...   esdzą doiye wei ye

6.   yeye enił - tani et - 'e - de   binadeeyish...

yela ŋaha howozhowo deya esdzą doiye wei ye

yela ŋaha howo - zhowo deya

yelaŋa keyi aŋa na hodizho golaghana ne

Songs Which Must Follow the Chief Hogan Songs
Set I, No. 1
FRANK MITCHELL
Solo Recording, 1963

heye nene yaŋa nana da doleel jini daŋa ai - ye

nana da doleel jini daŋa ai yeye nana da doleel

jini daŋa ai yeye

1. k'a hajai-yi-nai-ye tsibi da dola nana da doleel

jini daŋa ai yeye

2. k'a atse hastinye bihooghan ya'aɬnish dola nana da doleeɬ

jini daŋa ai yeye

3. yodi beho - steli tsibaka dola nana da do-leeɬ

jini daŋa ai yeye

4. neiye nei-yi-gha-ni-la ni-la-jai-yi nana da do-leel

jini daŋa ai yeye

5. nana k'a sa'a naghei nana k'a bik'e hozhogola

nana da do-leel jini daŋa ai ye

nana da do-leel jini daŋa ai ye

nana da do-leel jini dạ-a ai ye

Songs Which Must Follow the Chief Hogan Songs

Set II, No. 1

FRANK MITCHELL

Solo Recording, 1963

heye neye yaŋa k'a bina-nata eyi-lowo k'aŋa ni-ji-ni-la

yeye k'a bina-nata e-yi-la ka'a ne-ji-ni laŋa

Songs Which Must Follow the Chief Hogan Songs
Set III, No. 1
FRANK MITCHELL
Solo Recording, 1963

heye nene yaŋa towa nana to wo wowi yeye towi nane ta - ŋa

aŋa yeye towi nana ta - ŋa aŋa ye-ye towi nani tạ 'anaye

towi naŋa haŋa holaghei

1. neye k'a esda hai yołgai yisdzana bihoo-ghani- ya'ałnish

nani ta - ŋa

2. aŋa yeye yołgai yeye bihooghani ya'ałnish nani ta - ŋa

3. aŋa yeye yołgai ye beho - ste-li tsiba - kado nani ta - ŋa

4. aŋa yeye yo-di beho - ste-li tsiba - kado lani ta - ŋa

5. aŋa yeye naiyai yołgaiye beye e - ke - ke hoshchini tsiba - kado

nani ta - ŋa

aŋa yeye towa ŋaŋa to wo wowe yeye towe nane ta - ŋa aŋa yeye

towi naŋa ta - ŋa aŋa yeyi towi nani ta̧ - ' aŋa-ye

ritard.

towi nani ta gola - ghana ne

Songs Which Must Follow the Chief Hogan Songs

Set III, No. 3

FRANK MITCHELL

Solo Recording, 1963

heye nene ye'o hiiya hiiye aiye hai - ye

yaghei yana aiye haiye ai - ye   yaghei yena ai ye haiye aŋa haiye

ya̧' iiye haiye haiye hai - ye   yaŋa yena aiye haiye ai ye

yaŋa yaŋa ai-ye haiye aŋa haiye

yena gowa k'a yikai et'ee - ya   yena gowa shila-bani ya - ŋa

26. aŋa aiye aigi beye nitł'iz iltas a - ŋa   aŋa aiye aigibe

bitsi howo-sti - ye   yena gowa k'a la yiye tsa - ŋa

yena gowa k'a yikai et'ee - ya   yena gowa shi-labani ya - ŋa

27. aŋa aiye aigi beye łį'iltaŋas a - ŋa   aŋa aiye ai-gibe

bitsi howo-sti - ye   yene gowa k'a la yiye tsa - ŋa

yena gowa k'a yikai et'ee - ya   yena gowa shi-labani ya - ŋa

28. aŋa aiye aigi beye dibe iltas a - ŋa   aŋa aiye ai - gibe

bitsi howo - sti - ye   yene gowa k'a la yiye tsa - ŋa

yena gowa k'a yikai et 'ee - ya   yena gowa shi - labani ya - ŋa

29. aŋa aiye aigi beye di-ni-jį iltaŋas a - ŋa   aŋa aiye ai - gibe

bit-si howo - sti - ye   yene gowa k'a la yiye tsa - ŋa

yena gowa k'a yikai et'ee-ya   yena gowa shilaba-ni ya-ŋa

30. aŋa aiye aigi beye yisna iltas a - ŋa   aŋa aiye ai-gibe

bitsi howosti - ye   yena gowa k'a la yiye tsa - ŋa

yena gowa k'a yikai et'ee-ya   yena gowa shilabani ya-ŋa

31. aŋa aiye aigi beye beye yaŋa tsitsiji hozho-wo

yaŋa gowa shi-laba-ni ya - ŋa

32. aŋa aiye aigi be shikeshdę hozhowo   yaŋa gowa shila-bani ya-ŋa

33. aŋa aiye aigi beye nana ka sa'a nagha-ŋa

aŋa yeye nandah bik'e hozhowo   owa neya ka lashinishliya

heye   ya-'aiye haiye haiye hai-ye

yaŋa yena aiye haiye ai - ye

yena yaŋa aiye haiye aiye haiye

Songs Which Must Follow the Chief Hogan Songs
Set III, No. 5
FRANK MITCHELL
Solo Recording, 1963

heye nene yaŋa neye ai aiyi yeye neye ai ya - ni ya - na eh

neye eiyi yaŋayei neye'eh niya aghai yiye heye

1. eyi - laŋa ka bił hai-yolkaŋałe tsełke haŋa natsisliyigo

hai - yolkałiye biyi giyi - stiniye ka hascheyalti'i'eh

tsegha dini - diniiye tsegha dinizhowone iye yayai ya'a

haiyol - kałiye bahadi - diiyi-ne yodi iltas ei ye

beye   yanilti   lakah   beye   nantah   lakah

hahaznaiyone   asdzaŋane   yiyiltsą   hahaznaiyone tsełke   niyo

yiyiltsą   yiyiltsą   ai   yeye   heye   eiye   nana   ka   sa'a   naghei'i'ye

ka bik'e   hozhoniye   hadzo'ałal   haiyołkałiye   biyigi   yistiniye

ka   hashcheyaltiyi'e   tsegha   dini - diniiye   tsegha   dini - zhowone

haiyolkal   baha-didiyi - le   yodi   iltas   ei   ye   ka   baha-didi-yi -łe

yiiyis zaiyis   ala - ne   yiiyiz   tsesai   yaiye   ana - go

beye   yanilti   lakah   beye   nantah   lakah

hahasnayone   tsełke   niyo   yiyiltsą   yiyiltsą   ei   yeye   heye

eiyi   naŋa   ka   binaŋa   ka bił   hadzo' ałiye   tsełke   hai   natsisljyi - go

eigi beye shikigi hozhowogo yiyiltsą yiyiltsą ei yeye heye

9. eiye naŋa eigi beye shinade ta'aɬtso hozhowogo eigi beye

tsizadę hozhowogo yiyiltsą yiyiltsą ei yeye heye

10. eigi beye ka sa'a naghei ka bik'e hozhoni tseɬke hai

shinishįl-yi - go yiyiltsą yiyiltsą ei yeye heye

neye ei -- ye yiye neye ai ya-ni ya-ŋa ei

neye ei -- ye yiye neye'eh neye eiyi yaŋa heya

Talking God Hogan Songs

With these she moved, with these she moved.

Now from the Emergence Place, with these she moved,
Now with white corn, with this she moved,
Now with many kinds of blue small birds, with these she moved.

With these she moved, with these she moved.

Now from the Emergence Place, with these she moved,
Now with yellow corn, with this she moved,
Now with Corn Beetle, with him she moved.

With these she moved, with these she moved, it is said.

(From Song No. 13, FRANK MITCHELL, Blessing Way, 1957)

Different Hogan Songs are sung when the second menses are celebrated, and according to Frank it is these songs themselves that distinguish the first Kinaaldá from the second. The second kind of Hogan Songs belong to Talking God, one of the major deities in Navaho religion.

Origin

The myths, when they include references to the first use of the Talking God Hogan Songs, *Hashch'éłti'i Hooghan bighiin*, agree that the songs were given at the second rather than the first puberty ceremony. However, once again there is no consistency in the number of songs reported for this set.[45]

> On the appointed day all assembled. The first matter to decide was the number of songs to be sung. Some wished fourteen, others thought twelve would be sufficient. Haschelti, Talking God, sang the songs and chose to sing fourteen.[46]

> It was then [after arriving at the second Kinaaldá] that Talking God remarked; "My mouth is not used to it, my grandchildren, so I shall make just four Hogan songs of it!"
> They had just agreed to this, when they discovered, that First Scolder was among them. "What does this mean, just four Hogan Songs?" he asked. "Don't be talking!" he replied. "I'll just say one more word. Why not make just four of your tail feathers? Instead, your tail feathers number twelve! Don't you give that a thought? Really their number ought to govern the number of these songs!" he said. "Be it so, then" Talking God immediately agreed.[47]

According to Frank, Talking God came to the second Kinaaldá in order to sing his Hogan Songs. After he had done so, he "turned the singing over to the rest of the people."

Frank said that there are twenty-five Talking God Hogan Songs and that they consist of two sets: "Twelve songs of Talking God, twelve songs pertaining to White Shell Woman's home in the west, and then one long song."

---

[45]The field accounts of the number of Talking God Hogan Songs sung are no more consistent than they were for the Chief Hogan Songs.

[46]Edward Curtis, *The North American Indian*, Vol. 1, *Apache, Jicarillas, Navaho* (Cambridge, Mass.: The University Press, 1907). p. 94.

[47]Haile, "Origin Legend of the Navaho Enemy Way," p. 89.

You have these two sets, then another that has to go with it. This song has five words [verses] about the insides of the hogan; then it tells about the outside. There are about sixteen words [verses] in that song. They vary too; they're not all alike. Dif-, ferent singers have different numbers. Mine is a sixteen word [verse] song.[48]

Talking God's Hogan Songs were created at Ch'óol'í'í, the home of Changing Woman in the west. When Frank was asked about the twelve songs pertaining to White Shell Woman's home and whether these were sung when Talking God finished her home, he replied:

There is no real story about that. I just know that the home was built for the use of Changing Woman at Gobernador Knob where First Man and First Woman were living. The baby was brought there to them to be raised. I don't really know how they got the idea.

There is no detailed story about the house. We only know it was there. When people migrated to the present earth from the bottom world, they brought mountain earth up from there and set up mountains, the place known as Gobernador Knob being called "the heart of the earth," and the Huerfano Buttes being called "the lungs of the earth." The story only says that there was a home there and that Changing Woman was brought to First Man and First Woman. I only know a bit about the people coming up from below. I only know that they inhabited a single, two, three, four mountains for their home.

Talking God sang at the Kinaaldá. I only know that the directions in the hogan are east, which is dawn, south, which is blue sky, west, the twilight, and north, darkness. The beams are marked with an upward motion. I do not know about any singing when the house was built. The people of the present world are the ones who originated the marking of the hogan.

Ceremonial Usage

According to informants, the Talking God Hogan Songs must be used for Hózhǫ́ǫ́ji done for pregnancy as well as for the second puberty ceremony. In other instances they may be interchanged with the Chief Hogan Songs, according to the singer's preference and the kind of Blessing Way being conducted.

---

[48]McAllester, Field Notes, July 19−20, 1961, pp. 8a and 8b. Neither Frank Mitchell nor Chic Sandoval made distinctions between the words, lines, and verses of a song. This is understandable since in many songs the verses differ from one another only by one word.

Subject of Song Cycle

Father Berard Haile said that Talking God Hogan Songs are
the better known of the two kinds.[49]

> This set [Talking God's] consists of twelve songs which ask
> mountain woman for permission to trim the main poles for a cone
> shaped hogan, mention the main parts of the interior, the fireplace,
> cooking utensils, even the old stirring sticks, metates, shelves,
> and nooks between the poles and roof cribbing where small articles
> may be stored away temporarily.[50]

According to Frank and Chic, what Haile has described as
the subjects of Talking God Hogan Songs are actually those of the
Chief Hogan Songs. The Talking God Songs progress as follows:
the house where the Blessing Way Ceremony is taking place first
becomes a ceremonial hogan, a sacred place. This house is next
identified with that of a particular deity; whether the identification
is meant to imply that the house is the actual home of the given
deity or whether it is the house that Talking God built for Changing Woman in the west is, as yet, unclear. In any case, by Song
No. 13, the house has become that of Changing Woman (and White
Shell Woman), and this deity is moving toward it. In Song No. 25
she reaches the house, which is now thoroughly beautified and
sanctified through decorations, various kinds of prayer offerings,
and the presence of many deities. At this point, the person referred to in the song text is no longer "she"; instead, it is "I"—
an "I" which is now completely identified with the chief Kinaaldá
deity. Thus, the song cycle progresses through various stages to
a culmination of glorification and complete identification.

Frank summarized his Talking God Hogan Songs as follows:

Twelve Talking God Songs.
    Three mention the hogan.
    Three mention the trail.
    Three mention moving along the trail.
    Three mention the trail.
Interlude of passing the corn pollen and praying.

---

[49]Haile, *A Stem Vocabulary*, II, 154.
[50]*Ibid.*, p. 294.

Twelve Songs of White Shell Woman: "Where you previously mentioned Talking God, you now say White Shell Woman."
One long song mentioning the interior and the exterior surroundings of the beautiful house.

Source Material

Four versions of these Talking God Hogan Songs are available; one from the 1957 Blessing Way recorded by McAllester,
one from Marie Shirley's Kinaaldá, another from Carla Begay's
Kinaaldá, and the last from Totsoni Mark.[51] The discussion here
is based on a detailed analysis of the 1957 recordings,[52] with
comparisons from the other versions. The texts that are available for Talking God Hogan Songs include those mentioned above,
one from Goddard's "Navajo Texts," and six from Haile's
"Blessingway," Version I.

Similarities Between the Talking God and Chief Hogan Songs

The Talking God Hogan Songs can be grouped both musically
and textually as follows: Nos. 1–6, 7–9, 10–12, 13, 18, 19–24,
and 25. The music of Songs Nos. 1, 7, 10, 13, 19, and 25 are given
on pp. 189–209. In many respects, these songs are stylistically
similar to the Chief Hogan Songs which have already been discussed. To mention only a few details, the same musical formulas are generally used at the same places, the note types, skips, and
tonal systems are similar in their restrictions and emphases,
verses show the same internal structure,[53] and the songs stand as
a musical set or cycle, unified by shared meters, note values,
textures, timbres, registers, and formulas.

---

[51]There are a few fragments of sets of Talking God Hogan Songs in existence. At Wesleyan
University, on discs made by Gladys Reichard, there are four Talking God Hogan Songs by the
singer James Smith, from Ganado, Arizona. In Natalie Curtis, *The Indians' Book* (New York:
Harper, 1907), pp. 356–358 and 382–388, there is one Talking God Hogan Song. The ones Reichard
collected from James Smith, however, do not correspond with any of the above.

[52]Johnson, "Talking God's Hogan Songs" (MS), 1963.

[53]As mentioned, *ibid.*, pp. 11–19, the verses consist of three segments both textually and
musically. The author is calling the short phrase which occurs as the final segment in each verse
"the burden." The burden recurs in each verse without much change, if any. It is by comparing
the burdens of consecutive songs that the verbal tense and aspective changes readily become
obvious.

Differences between the Two Kinds of Hogan Songs

In the Talking God Hogan Songs, the singing style is more ornamented. Pulsations occur in 60 per cent of them, grace notes in 35 per cent, and downward slides in 95 per cent. The slides are not restricted to a position of finality in these songs; they occur at the end of many verses, often seeming correlated with nasalizations in the texts. Then, too, they occur in the middle of verses, especially whenever an octave skip is to be found in the melodic line.

Formulas

While 92 per cent of the introductory formulas are flat in contour and use the three-beat duration found in Chief Hogan Song introductions, they do not use just one textual formula. The *heye nene yaŋa* of the Chief Hogan Songs is not to be found in the list of textual introductions used in the Talking God Songs.

1. he neye haŋa	6 songs
2. haiye naiye yaŋa	5 songs
heye neye yaŋa	6 songs
naiye naiya yanai	1 song
3. ai yai ya naŋa	2 songs
4. he ne yaŋa	3 songs
hai nai yaŋa	2 songs

The closing formula in these songs is the same retarding slide figure found in the Chief Hogan Songs. Here, though, the figure is rhythmically defined as

76 per cent of the time, in contrast to the 7 per cent usage of this pattern in the Chief Hogan Songs.

Structure

In structure, the Talking God Hogan Songs also contrast with the Chief ones; the balanced plan described by McAllester (an introduction, opening chorus, male set of verses, short intervening

chorus, female set of verses, longer closing chorus, and conclusion) is quite common. Each of the first six songs has a total of
sixteen verses, the first eight being male, and the second eight
their female counterparts. Songs Nos. 7—9 have eighteen verses
and Nos. 10—12, sixteen. Songs Nos. 13—24 contain eighteen verses
each, divided nine and nine. The last song is the exception to the
plan described above. It has twenty-two verses (in contrast to the
sixteen Frank said it had). The first six concern the house, the
next eleven focus on the gods and the natural surroundings outside the hogan, and the last six are a group concerned with directions. In this song, the male-female alternation principle occurs
in immediate groups of twos, when it is evident. For example,
the verse concerning White Corn Boy is balanced by the next
verse, which mentions Yellow Corn Girl.

Performance

Finally, the singing of these songs is always interrupted
after Song No. 12 for a corn-pollen blessing. After the singer and
others have prayed in their own words, asking Talking God to
guide them, the singing continues.

Three Focal Points

When studying these Talking God Hogan Songs in 1962—1963,
the author became interested in three ideas, among others: the
ways in which the texts of these songs exemplified the Navaho concept of motion, the difference between sung and spoken Navaho, and
the twenty-five songs as a musical cycle. The results of studying
these three topics are summarized below.

The texts of the songs can be grouped as follows:

Nos. 1—6.   The idea of things being "sacred places" or "blessed
            paths."
Nos. 7—9.   "Setting forth on the road."
Nos. 10—12. Emphasis on "the road" by itself.
Nos. 13—18. Movement, or movement "with these things."
Nos. 19—24. "She moved," "with it she is all moved," "the
            woman moved." (Nos. 23—24) "in beauty she
            moved," "in beauty with these things she moved."

No. 25 Descriptions of the inside and outside of the hogan surroundings; traveling with sacred power and beauty in
all directions is now done by "I."

Examples of seven of these texts, those of Songs Nos. 1, 7,
10, 13, 15, 19, and 25, are included in pp. 183-189. These songs
have already been shown to portray the Navaho religious idea of
complete identification with a deity. They also illustrate the concept of motion described by Margot Astrov.[54]

Navaho Concept of Motion

As mentioned in "Talking God's Hogan Songs":

In the first song, the house becomes a ceremonial hogan, or a
sacred place. The second song is more active textually, for now
"blessing is being sought." The sacredness becomes a topic of
discussion in the third song where the activity shifts to the actual
speech of unidentified people; "it is sacred, they say." Motion is
carried further in the next song by substituting "door path" for
"road" and by the introduction of the idea of "leading out." In
song #5, the action is forward-looking, for the burden emphasizes
the future; "it will be a blessed path." A return to the present
tense and use of actual speakers once again in the sixth song provides motion; "it is blessed they say."
...In song #12, which follows the prayer, the emphasis is
openly on movement; the actual word "moved" is mentioned for
the first time....Motion is further defined and made more complete in song #14 "she has moved." Song #15 adds direction to the
motion; "over there she moved." ...Song #23 gives the old motion a new focus. "She" is again used instead of woman, but now
the way in which she moves is qualified: "in beauty, she moved,
she moved." In a way, "she" is a fitting change since it complements the abstract state of being, "in beauty."
...Although a change is suggested, the extent of the one occurring in song #25 is hardly anticipated in #24. For the first time
since song #8, the action becomes progressive: "with my sacred
power, I am traveling." The word "traveling" implies more extensive movement over a longer space of time, than does the word
"move." The inner verse content is also completely revised; no
longer are there sixteen or eighteen verses. First, the hogan is
shown in its complete glorification. A description of the beauties
of its surroundings follows as well as the mention of both familiar

---

[54]Margot Astrov, "The Concept of Motion as the Psychological Leitmotif of Navaho Life
and Literature," *Journal of American Folklore*, LXIII, No. 247 (January-March, 1950), pp. 45-56.

and new deities. In reality, this concluding song seems to contain a maximum amount of textual movement.[55]

Textual motion in these twenty-five Talking God Hogan Songs seems to bring about either complementary musical motion or a contrasting reduction of motion which in itself enhances *hózhǫ́ǫ́* (inherent balance). While the author realizes that it is almost impossible to investigate and demonstrate this phenomenon fully enough to regard it as a regular principle of Navaho ceremonial music, one of her earlier ideas still seems to have enough value to warrant inclusion.

In song #7, the increase in action seen in "I set forth on the road" is reflected in a rise in the pitch curve, an increase in possible variation in the first segment (of the verse) and a general increase in action in the second segment. In song #9, where blessedness and peace define the tone, minute analysis shows that the music is again complementary. Small fragments from first segments used in earlier songs reappear, bringing harmony and unity with them.

The music of song #11 complements the text in some ways. The absence of the third segment reflects the textual sparseness. However, the music also balances this reduction of movement by increasing the number of inner segment changes and variations found in the repeat. The principle of *hózhǫ́ǫ́* is again reflected in the music of song #20. The text is tightening up, and in opposition, the music expands. The pitch level changes, the first segment increases in length, more skips are used, and vocables are more frequent. Interestingly enough, though, while doing this, the music is also tightening in the number of ideas used, the interrelatedness shown among the verses within the song, and the amount of motion in the burden.

In song #23, there is only a slight reflection of the long-awaited textual change. There is a small increase in the smoothness and fluidity of the contours of the second and third segments. This increase makes me wonder if there is a correlation between fluidity and beauty in Navaho aesthetics. Song #23 is also interesting when one notices that both it and #24, in extending the use of the burden, suggest a closing which is not implied in the text.

The final song, #25, is another in which the musical material complements and contrasts with the text. One musical reflection of the great textual change is the extension of phrases; a contrast

[55]Johnson, "Talking God's Hogan Songs," pp. 29-32.

to this change can be found in the increased amount of formality, achieved through an extensive use of burden-like segments.[56]

Sung and Spoken Navaho

In studying the texts of these songs, one of the first things that became obvious was the difference between the sung and spoken Navaho forms of specific words. A total of eighty-seven words are used in these twenty-five songs, and over half of them differ from the spoken form when sung. The treatment of *'atiin*, the word for "road," is a representative example.

Navaho—Sung Form	Navaho—Spoken Form	English—Meaning
etai	'atiin	road
etaiya		
etaiye		
etaiyi		
eti		
etinainai		
etiye		
etiyine		
etiyineye		
etiyiyeye		
tineye		
wotai		
yaiyina		
yaiyinana		

A study of the eighty-seven words in their two forms suggests that certain "rules" govern the changes that are made when singing in Navaho. These rules can be tentatively defined as follows:

1. A vocable of one syllable is often placed between two similar vowels (a long vowel).

2. Vocables added to the ends of words are usually of one or two syllables. If the word ends in a consonant, then the vocable is constructed with a vowel, consonant, vowel; if the reverse is true, the vocable will read consonant, vowel, consonant, vowel, and so on.

3. Terminal *d* is usually omitted entirely in sung Navaho or replaced by *ya*.

---

[56]*Ibid.*, pp. 32−33.

4. If the spoken word contains a glottal stop, it will be removed, closed by a vowel-consonant combination, or left after a consonant is added, before the first vowel. Example: *bik'eh* becomes *bike*.

    a. If there are two glottal stops in one word, the first one will be omitted in singing. Example: *ch'é'étiin* becomes *che'etiin*.

5. One-syllable words often become two-syllable words when sung. Example: *bee* becomes *beye* or *beni*.

6. Vowels will be changed in sung possessive adjectives. Example: *shi* becomes *she*.

7. Anything that ends in *gai* in its spoken form will become *gaiye*, or *gan*.

8. Spoken *káál* endings become *ka, kan, kaliye,* or *kanale*.

9. A word cannot end in the spoken form of *ei, oi,* or *ai*. These will be changed by adding *ye* or *ya* to the word.

10. Spoken ending *iin* becomes *niye* in sung version. Example: *schiin* becomes *shiniye*.

11. The directions of east and west will change their vowels and lengthen their spoken forms through the addition of *ash*. Example: *ha'a'aah* becomes *ha'i'ashiye*.

12. "Corn" will always appear as "corn plus *at* plus color." Example: *naadaa'algai*.

13. The sung version of "road" will usually start with *'e* and contain three or four syllables of vocables. Example: *'etiyine*.

14. The burden will usually appear in its correct spoken form in the phrase directly preceding the concluding vocable.

15. Speech tones are disregarded in sung Navaho. Occasionally when the vowels should be long ones, length is acquired by adding vocables.

16. Possessive adjectives are not elided in sung Navaho. Example: Spoken *shaghan* becomes *shi hoghan* when sung.

17. Sung Navaho shows a preference for the vowel *e* above that of *a* for beginning words. Example: *'antt'ánii* becomes *'enittani* when sung.

18. Spoken words ending in *he* end in *she* or remove the whole *he* in the sung version.

19. Verbs that are of two syllables (low, high) when spoken are either sung the way they are or with the addition of two or three vocables on the end.

    a. Two-syllable verbs which are high, high, are sung with an addition of two vocables on the end.

20. Two similar vowels are always broken up when sung. Example: *hadaa* becomes *hadana*.

21. Specific verbs:

    ninná: The syllabic *ń* is always spelled out in sung form. The middle *n* usually becomes *l*. Example: *nilina*. The word can be preceded by one vocable, and one vocable can be interjected between the second and third syllables.

nashá: The word will be imbedded in vocables. Example: *lanashanaye*.

nijinna: Syllabic *n̈* is spelled out. Vocables can be attached before the final syllable or after the word has appeared.

22. Nasalizations are avoided in sung Navaho. Example: *zlį* becomes *zlini*, *dáá déé* becomes *dana ge*, *'isdzą́ą́-nanai*, *'asdzą́ą́* becomes *'asdzo*.

23. Long *i* word endings are not allowed in sung Navaho, and even short *i* endings are avoided. Example: *'ashkii* becomes *'eshkiya*, *shiyaagi* becomes *shiyage*, *nizhóni* becomes *nizhogo* or *nijowo*.[57]

Other differences between spoken and sung Navaho are also suggested by these songs. As mentioned above, speech tones seem to be absent in sung versions, and musical lines do not reflect any recognition of their original existence. The very use of vocables is, of course, another difference. Then, too, in sung Navaho there seems to be little of the syntactical reference found so frequently in spoken Navaho in the word *jini* (it is said).

The Songs as a Musical Cycle

That these Talking God Hogan Songs are a cycle, or a unit in which one segment logically leads to the next and in which many elements are interrelated through various unifying devices, is obvious. The songs are unified by several means, the first of which is the text.

The songs share a common textual emphasis, with separate songs actually being only slightly different in content. The songs are further unified by definite textual groupings existing within the main plan. As pointed out earlier ... these serve to divide the texts into smaller groupings: Nos. 1−6, 7−9, 10−12, 13−18, 19−24, and 25. These smaller divisions serve as key structural points and control musical development quite thoroughly ....

There are many ways in which the song cycle is musically unified. Shared meters, note values, textures, timbres, registers, interval emphases, and singing styles all help provide unification. The carry-over of specific musical formulas between songs adds

---

[57]From *ibid.*, pp. 38−39.

much integration; so does the tonality, which follows a slowly ris-
ing curve, tying together not only all the songs at any given tonal
level but, in actuality, all the twenty-five songs.

Interestingly enough, while hearing the whole cycle at one time
suggests the presence of much unity, it also implies the opposite,
namely, the presence of many elements providing variety . . . .

Variety is, of course, a feature of each song individually as well
as of groups of songs. No two songs are exactly the same; there
are always slight variations in the amount of ornamentation, number of slides, types of skips, vocables, and so on. Furthermore,
no song which can be transcribed by designating the female verses
as a repeat of the male verses contains an exact repeat; minute
parts of the verses will always be changed. Hence, while unity is
provided in the individual songs by an over-all A B A' B' A''
scheme, through formulas for separate parts of the song, definite
key structural points, and a strophic setup, a large amount of variety is also subtly achieved.

. . . .

. . . Just as Classicists, Romanticists, and other musical styl-
ists had definite ideas, formulas, and techniques through which
they achieved a sense of development in their works, so do the
Navaho, whether or not it is conscious. These twenty-five Hogan
Songs suggest that Navaho musical development is achieved
mainly through alternation of ideas and contrasts between simplicity and complexity. This development principle can be sum-
med up in the Navaho concept of *hózhóó*, inherent balance.[58]

A Comparison of 1957 and 1963 Mitchell Versions of the Talking
God Hogan Songs

The two versions are highly similar. This is amazing in a
sense, since Frank in 1963 was accompanied by nine other singers
who, much of the time, were singing their own variations on these
songs. In the 1963 performance, a singing competition developed
in which the younger singers kept pushing Frank's tempo faster
and his tonic level higher. In some cases, due to this pressure,
Frank was forced to contract certain skips that would have necessitated falsetto singing; at such times, melodic alterations did, of
course, occur. More often, however, he firmly maintained his
own version; the result was polytonal singing, a rarity in Navaho
music. Sometimes this lasted throughout a whole song; at other
times, the younger singers yielded to the main singer.

---

[58] From *ibid.*, pp. 45 – 47.

On listening to the musical conflict, there seem to be as many versions as there are participating singers. In some instances, the numbers are equivalent. See, for example, the following transcription of the *nitłiz iłtas an* section in the fifth, female verse of Song No. 24, as sung during Marie's Kinaaldá.

FRANK MITCHELL, 1957

neyowo nitliz iłtas a   na ŋa   naŋa yei

FRANK MITCHELL, 1963

neyowo nitliz iłtas aŋ   a ŋa   naŋa yei

W. YAZZIE, 1963

neyowo nitliz iltas aŋ   a ŋa   naŋa yei

C. JONES, 1963

neyowo nitłiz iłtas aŋ   a ŋa   naŋa yei

J. SMILEY, 1963

neyowo nitliz iłtas aŋ .a ŋa   naŋa yei

P. BITSUI, 1963

neyowo nitliz iłtas aŋ   a ŋa   naŋa yei

J. BEGAY, 1963

neyowo nitliz iłtas aŋ   a ŋa   naŋa yei

J. TSOSI, 1963

neyowo heye neye ya ŋa ŋa   naŋa na

DINÉ ŁBÁHÍ, 1963

[He had lost his voice by this point.]

In spite of this example of variety and the many more like it, an interesting phenomenon was observable. In the songs where Frank either dropped out or did not sing at all, the remaining singers achieved a sound which, while not a complete unison, was quite near one. And, while continuing to sing faster and at a higher tonic than Frank's, they did manage to sing the songs in a way almost identical to his 1957 recording. It was as if they knew Frank's version, and once the occasion for contest over the tonic and tempo was removed by his not singing, they were willing to unite and sing in the manner of the main singer.

Thus, aside from instances where slight changes became necessary because of the group situation, the 1963 rendition of the Talking God Hogan Songs is almost identical with the 1957 one.

A Comparison of the Marianito and Mitchell Talking God Hogan Songs

In a few instances, Willie sang the songs so the ranges of an opening or a final chorus were extended, skips were diminished, and melodic contours were drawn more squarely. In one instance, the Marianito version contains an extra verse. But all these differences are minor ones; essentially, the Marianito and Mitchell Talking God Hogan Songs are musically the same.

Functionally, however, the songs are different. Willie used these Hogan Songs in a *first* Kinaaldá. He began the night with the Chief Hogan Songs and followed these fourteen with one Twelve Word Song (the next song type to be discussed). Then, however, he sang eleven Talking God Hogan Songs which correspond to Nos. 15–25 of Frank's series. Following these, the singing was "turned over to the people."

Information is insufficient in this case to establish the reason why this was done. Perhaps Willie always sings the Hogan Songs in this manner. Perhaps it is one of the ways in which he adjusts his Kinaaldá singing to correlate with variables such as fees received. Or perhaps Pinedale singers always include both sets of Hogan Songs, since many people in the region feel that only one Kinaaldá is necessary.

At present, it is not known whether Willie Marianito was shortcutting or whether the Talking God Hogan Songs to him mean eleven songs which, in fact, are comparable to Frank's Nos. 15–25. There is also no way of knowing, at present, how he might sing the Hogan Songs for a second puberty ceremony.

Talking God Hogan Song No. 1
FRANK MITCHELL
Blessing Way, 1957

he neye naŋa
Here at this house, it is a sacred place,
Here at this house, it is a sacred place,
Here at this house, it is a sacred place,
Here at this house, it is a sacred place,
holaghei.

The house under the east is a sacred place,
Now the home of Talking God is a sacred place,
The house made of dawn is a sacred place,
The house made of white corn is a sacred place,
The house made of all kinds of soft fabrics is a sacred place,
The house made of gathered rain waters is a sacred place,
The house made of corn pollen is a sacred place,
Now it is the house of long life and everlasting beauty;
it is a sacred place.

Here at this house, it is a sacred place,
Here at this thouse, it is a sacred place,
holaghei.

The house under the west is a sacred place,
Now the home of Hogan God is a sacred place,
The house made of afterglow is a sacred place,
The house made of yellow corn is a sacred place,
The house made of all kinds of jewels is a sacred place,
The house made of gathered spring waters is a sacred place,
The house made of corn pollen is a sacred place,
Now it is the house of long life and everlasting beauty;
it is a sacred place.

Here at this house, it is a sacred place,
Here at this house, it is a sacred place,
it is said.

Talking God Hogan Song No. 7
FRANK MITCHELL
Blessing Way, 1957

heye neye yaŋa
I set forth on the road, I set forth on the road,
I set forth on the road, I set forth on the road,
I set forth on the road, *holaghei*.

The door path under the east, on it I set forth,
Now the door path of Talking God, on it I set forth,
The door path made of dawn, on it I set forth,
The door path made of white corn, on it I set forth.
The door path made of all kinds of soft fabrics, on it I set forth.
The door path made of gathered rain waters, on it I set forth.
The door path made of corn pollen, on it I set forth,
Now it is a door path of long life and everlasting beauty;
                              on it I set forth,
Before me it is blessed; behind me it is blessed.

        I set forth on the road, I set forth on the road,
        I set forth on the road, *holaghei*.

The door path under the west, on it I set forth,
Now the door path of Hogan God, on it I set forth,
The door path made of afterglow, on it I set forth,
The door path made of yellow corn, on it I set forth.
The door path made of all kinds of jewels, on it I set forth.
The door path made of gathered spring waters, on it I set forth,
The door path made of corn pollen, on it I set forth,
Now it is a door path of long life and everlasting beauty;
                              on it I set forth,
Behind me it is blessed, before me it is blessed.

        I set forth on the road, I set forth on the road,
        I set forth on the road, it is said.

Talking God Hogan Song No. 10
FRANK MITCHELL
Blessing Way, 1957

heye nene yaŋa
This is the road, this is the road, the road,
This is the road,
The road which is blessed, the road which is blessed.

The door path under the east,
Now the door path of Talking God,
The door path made of dawn,
The door path made of white corn,
The door path made of all kinds of soft fabrics,
The door path made of gathered rain waters,
The door path made of corn pollen,
Now it is a door path of long life and everlasting beauty.

> This is the road, the road,
> This is the road which is blessed,
> The road which is blessed.

The door path under the west,
Now the door path of Hogan God,
The door path made of afterglow,
The door path made of yellow corn,
The door path made of all kinds of jewels,
The door path made of gathered spring waters,
The door path made of corn pollen,
Now it is a door path of long life and everlasting beauty.

> This is the road, the road,
> This is the road,
> The road which is blessed, the road which is blessed.

Talking God Hogan Song No. 13
FRANK MITCHELL
Blessing Way, 1957

ai yai ya naŋa
With these she moved, with these she moved,
With these she moved, with these she moved,
With these she moved, with these she moved,
With these she moved, with these she moved,
> *holaghei.*

Now from the very edge of the Emergence Place, with these she
    moved,
Now White Shell Woman,[59] with these she moved,
Truly with the dawn, with this she moved,
Now with white corn, with this she moved,
All kinds of soft fabrics, with these she moved,
Truly with gathered rain waters, with these she moved,

---

[59]According to Frank Mitchell, White Shell Woman is always mentioned before Changing
Woman in Blessing Way Songs. See McAllester, Field Notes, July 19−20, 1961, p. 8a.

Truly with corn pollen, with this she moved,
Now with many kinds of blue small birds, with these she moved,
Now long life and everlasting beauty, with these she moved.

With these she moved, with these she moved,
With these she moved, with these she moved,
holaghei.

Now from the very edge of the Emergence Place, with these she moved,
Now Changing Woman, with these she moved,
Truly with the afterglow, with this she moved,
Now with yellow corn, with this she moved,
All kinds of jewels, with these she moved,
Truly with gathered spring waters, with these she moved,
Truly with corn pollen, with this she moved,
Truly with Corn Beetle, with Her she moved,
Now long life and everlasting beauty, with these she moved.

With these she moved, with these she moved,
With these she moved, with these she moved, it is said.

Talking God Hogan Song No. 15

FRANK MITCHELL
Blessing Way, 1957

heye neye yaŋa
Over here, she moved; over here, she moved,
Over here, she moved; over here, she moved, *holaghei.*

Now from the very edge of the Emergence Place, she moved,
Now White Shell Woman, she moved,
Truly with the dawn, she moved,
Now with white corn she moved,
With all kinds of soft fabrics she moved,
Truly with gathered rain waters she moved,
Truly with corn pollen she moved,
(Now long life)[60] now with many kinds of blue small birds she moved,
Now with long life, now with everlasting beauty, she moved.

---

[60]All the songs in the present book are given as they were at the time specified in the title. Parentheses are used to enclose words and phrases which were designated as "mistakes" by the singer when he listened to the tapes of his performance. Brackets enclose material that was omitted in the original performance, but added by the singer during the tape playback. In the process of working out the texts, the author collected several different opinions as to the order of words and other possible changes in these songs, especially in those of Blue Mule. These opinions have not been included, since a discussion of the canons of Navaho ceremonial chant must wait for another time.

Over here, she moved, *holaghei.*

Now from the very edge of the Emergence Place, she moved,
Now Changing Woman, she moved,
Truly with the afterglow she moved,
Now with yellow corn she moved,
With all kinds of jewels she moved,
Truly with gathered spring waters she moved,
Truly with corn pollen she moved,
Truly with Corn Beetle she moved,
Now with long life, now with everlasting beauty, she moved.

> Over here, she moved; over here, she moved,
> Over here, she moved; over here, she moved,
> Over here, she moved, it is said.

Talking God Hogan Song No. 19
FRANK MITCHELL
Blessing Way, 1957

haiye naiŋe yaŋai
She moved, she moved,
She moved, she moved,
She moved, she moved.

From the Emergence Place, she moved, she moved,
White Shell Woman, she moved, she moved,
Now with the dawn she moved, she moved,
With white corn she moved, she moved,
With all kinds of soft fabrics she moved, she moved,
With gathered rain waters she moved, she moved,
Now with corn pollen she moved, she moved,
With many kinds of blue small birds she moved, she moved,
Now with long life, now with everlasting beauty, she moved, she
    moved.

From the Emergence Place, she moved, she moved,
Changing Woman, she moved, she moved,
Now with the afterglow she moved, she moved,
With yellow corn she moved, she moved,
With all kinds of jewels she moved, she moved,
Now with gathered spring waters she moved, she moved,
Now with corn pollen she moved, she moved,
Now with Corn Beetle she moved, she moved,
Now with long life, now with everlasting beauty, she moved, she
    moved.

She moved, she moved,
She moved, *e yo wo.*

Talking God Hogan Song No. 25
FRANK MITCHELL
Blessing Way, 1957

haiye naiye yaŋa
With my sacred power, I am traveling,
With my sacred power, I am traveling,
With my sacred power, I am traveling.

At the back of my house, white shell prayer offerings are placed;
          they are beautifully decorated;
With my sacred power, I am traveling,
At the center of my house, turquoise prayer offerings are placed;
          they are beautifully decorated;
With my sacred power, I am traveling,
In my house by the fireside, abalone prayer offerings are placed;
          they are beautifully decorated;
With my sacred power, I am traveling,
In my house, in the corners by the door,
          black jewel prayer offerings are placed;
With my sacred power, I am traveling,
In the doorway of my house, rock crystal prayer offerings are
    placed;
          they are beautifully decorated;
With my sacred power, I am traveling.

All about my house is Talking God; He is beautifully clad;
With my sacred power, I am traveling.
All about my house is Hogan God; She is beautifully clad;
With my sacred power, I am traveling.
All about my house, bushes are growing;
          they are beautifully leafed out;
With my sacred power, I am traveling.
All about my house, trees are growing;
          they are beautifully leafed out;
With my sacred power, I am traveling.
All about my house, rocks are standing;
          their surfaces are beautiful;
With my sacred power, I am traveling.
All about my house, mountains are standing;
          their sides are beautiful;
With my sacred power, I am traveling.

All about my house, springs are flowing; they are beautiful;
    With my sacred power, I am traveling.
All about my house is White Corn Boy; He is beautifully clad;
    With my sacred power, I am traveling.
All about my house is Yellow Corn Girl; She is beautifully clad;
    With my sacred power, I am traveling.
All about my house is Corn Pollen Boy; He is beautifully clad;
    With my sacred power, I am traveling.
All about my house is Corn Beetle Girl; She is beautifully clad;
    With my sacred power, I am traveling.
With beauty before me, I am traveling,
    With my sacred power, I am traveling,
With beauty behind me, I am traveling,
    With my sacred power, I am traveling,
With beauty below me, I am traveling,
    With my sacred power, I am traveling,
With beauty above me, I am traveling,
    With my sacred power, I am traveling,
Now with long life, now with everlasting beauty, I live.
    I am traveling,
    With my sacred power, I am traveling.

    With my sacred power, I am traveling,
    With my sacred power, I am traveling,
    With my sacred power, I am traveling, it is said.

Talking God Hogan Song No. 1
FRANK MITCHELL
Ceremonial Recording, 1957

he heye naŋa dzaŋade hoghaneyi laŋa hozho hoghaŋaŋe

dzaŋa - de hogha - ne - yi - lạ hozho hoghaŋa neye

dzaŋa - de hogha - ne - yi - lạ hozho hoghaŋa neye

dzaŋa - de hoghan ne - yi - la - ŋa hozho hoghaŋa holaghei

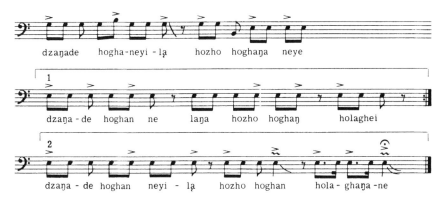

Two musical changes occur in the sixth verse during the repeat:

There is one musical change each in the seventh and eighth verses during the repeat:

Talking God Hogan Song No. 7

FRANK MITCHELL

Ceremonial Recording, 1957

1.

neye ha'i - 'ashi - ye   biyashjiyi che'e-ti - ne   kiye de yaŋa ye
i'i - 'ashi - ye

2.

ka hashcheyałti che'eti - ne - kiye de yaŋa ye
hasche'oghan [1]

3.

hayoł - ka-łi - ye   bik'e che-'eti - ne - kiye de yaŋa ye
hoho - tsoi - ye

4.

dạ' ałgai ye [2] bik'e che-'eti - ne - kiye de yaŋa ye
dạ' ałsoi ye

5.

yodi iłtas ei   ye [3] bik'e che-'eti - ne - kiye de yaŋa ye
nitliz iłtas ei ye

6.

to'o łanaschini - ye   bik'e che - 'eti - ne - kiye de yaŋa ye
to biyashiye [4]

7.

tadi - dini - ye   bik'e che-'eti - ne - kiye de yaŋa ye

8.

k'a sa'a naghei   k'a bik'e hozhon - e

che - 'eti - ne   kiye de yaŋa ye

shi-tsiye jiye hozhǫwone   shikeyesh deya hozhǫwone
shikeyesh deya hozhǫwone   shitsiye deya hozhǫwone

ti-ne— kiye de yą ye 5
yaŋa ye

ti-ne-ye ki de yaŋa yeye tine kiye de yaŋa holaghei

tine - ye ki de yaŋa yeye tine kiye de yą holaghalaŋa

Certain musical changes occur in the opening phrase of the second, fourth, fifth, and sixth verses during the repeat:

ka hashche'oghan dą - ał - soi ye

nitliz iłtas ei ye to biya - shiye

During the repeat, the burden of verse 5 changes to:

ti-ne - kiye de yaŋa ye

Talking God Hogan Song No. 10
FRANK MITCHELL
Ceremonial Recording, 1957

heye nane yaŋa esdi diye etai-ya esdi diya etaiye etaiya

esta diya etai   hozhǫgo wotai   hozhǫgo   e-ti-yi-ye-ye

1. neyowa   ha'i - 'ashi-ye   biyash-jiyi   che'e - tine
           i'i - 'ashi-ye

2. ka hashcheyałti   che'e - tine
    hashche'oghan[1]

3. hayoł - kałi - ye   bik'e   che'e - tine
   noho - tsoi - ye

4. dą'ałgai   ye [3]   bik'e   che'e - tine
   dą'ałsoi   ye

5. yodi iłtas ei   ye   bik'e   che'e - tine
   nitliz iłtas ei   ye

6. to'o   łanashchini - ye [4]   bik'e   che'e - tine
   to   biya - shi - ye

7. tadi - di-ni-ye   bik'e   che'e - tine

8. k'a sa'a naghei k'a bik'e hozhǫne   che'e - tine

esdi diye e-ti-ye e-ti-ye esdi diye e-ti-ye
esdi diye etai[5]

hozhǫgo wotai hozhǫ gowo giye yaya

hozhǫgo wotai hozhǫ gowo ti ye ya yǫ e yogho

Certain musical changes occur in the opening phrase of the second, third, fourth, and sixth verses during the repeat:

ka hashche'oghan noho - tsoi - ye

dǫ-'ał - soi ye to biya - shiye

There is a musical change in the final chorus during the repeat:

esdi diye etai

Talking God Hogan Song No. 13
FRANK MITCHELL
Ceremonial Recording, 1957

ai yai ya naŋa yala ne na yeye yala ne nina

8. yaye k'a ayash dootliyi - ji   yala neni na

9. yaye k'a sa'a naghei   k'a bik'e hozhowogo   yala neni na

yeye yala neni naŋa ya   yala neli - la   yela neni naŋa ya

yala   ni-ni laŋa   holaghei

1. neya k'a haji - yinai - ye ts'idi daŋa - ge   yala neni na

2. yaye k'a isdza - nadlee - she   yala neni na

3. yaye ts'ida nao - soi - ye   yala neni na

4. yaye k'ana daŋa soi - ye   yala neni na

5. yaye nitliz iłas aŋa yai   yala neni na

6. yaye ts'ida to biya - nazhe   yala neni na

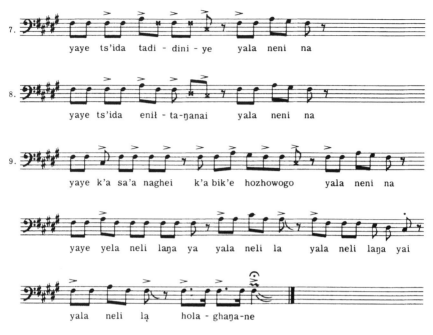

7. yaye ts'ida tadi - dini - ye   yala neni na

8. yaye ts'ida enił - ta-ŋanai   yala neni na

9. yaye k'a sa'a naghei   k'a bik'e hozhowogo   yala neni na

yaye yela neli laŋa ya   yala neli la   yala neli laŋa yai

yala   neli   lą   hola - ghaŋa-ne

Talking God Hogan Song No. 19

FRANK MITCHELL

Ceremonial Recording, 1957

haiye naiŋa yaŋai yene ni no -- wo wo   wowo   woye

yaŋai   ni no-- wowo woye   yaŋai ni no -- ŋaŋaŋa neyowo

yeni   ni no -- wo wo   wowo woye yeni ni no -- wowo woye

yaŋai   ni no -- ŋaŋa - ŋa

2. neyowo   isdzana - dlee   yeye   ye yeye   she

yeni   ni   no   wowo   woye   yanai   ni   ŋa   ŋaŋaŋa

3. neyowo   k'ana   no   so - o   wo   wowo   woye

yeni   ni   no   wowo   woye   yanai   ni   ŋa   ŋaŋaŋa

4. neyowo   nada   na   so - o   wo   wowo   woye

yeni   ni   no   wowo   woye   yanai   ni   ŋa   ŋaŋaŋa

5. neyowo   nitliz   iłtas   'ą   'a   ya   ŋa   a   ŋane

yeni   ni   no   wowo   woye   yanai   ni   ŋa   ŋaŋaŋa

6. neyowo   k'a   to   bi - yash   ei   ye   yeye   yene

yeni   ni   no   wowo   woye   yanai   ni   ŋa   ŋaŋaŋa

7.

neyowo   k'a tadi - de - e ye   yeye   yene

yeni   ni no   wowo woye   yanai ni ŋa   ŋaŋaŋa

8.

neyowo   k'a enił - ta-na   ŋa   ŋa ŋaŋane

yeni   ni no   wowo woye   yanai ni ŋa   ŋaŋaŋa

9.

neyowo k'a sa'a naghei k'a bik'e hozho - ho wo   wowo   wone

yeni   ni no   wowo woye   yanai ni ŋa   ŋaŋaŋa   neyowo

yeni   ni no -- wo wo   wowo woye   yeni ni no - wowo woye

ritard.

yeni   ni ŋa   ŋaŋaŋa   eyo wo

Talking God Hogan Song No. 25
FRANK MITCHELL
Ceremonial Recording, 1957

haiye naiye yaŋa she' he   ye yeye   ala   leli   laŋa shaŋa ye

bine 'enizho-go she' he yeye a-la leli ŋaŋa shaŋe yeyi

4. naŋa she hoghan niya baha-stla kina-aŋa

bashjinei k'et a-niye shini ye eya ai-i-ye

bine 'enizho-go she'he yeye a-la leli ŋaŋa shaŋe ye-yi

5. naŋa she hoghan niya che'e-tigi laŋa

tsagha dena deni ye k'et 'aniye shini ye eya ai-i-ye

bine 'enizho-go she'he yeye a-la leli ŋaŋa shaŋe ye-yi

6. naŋa she hoghan niya bina de-ya ka hashcheyałti'i ye

eshi nana ze-ni ye bine 'enizho-go she' he yeye

a-la leli ŋaŋa shaŋe ye-yi

7. naŋa she hoghan niya bina de-ya ka hashch'ogha —— niye

eshi nana ze-ni ye bine 'enizho-go she' he yeye

a-la leli ŋaŋa shaŋe ye-yi

8. naŋa she hoghan niya bina de-ya chi'il

eshi nani ch'o ziye bine 'enizho-go she' he yaiye

a-la leli ŋaŋa shaŋe yeyi

9. naŋa she hoghan niya bina de-ya t'sin

eshi nana 'ai -- ye bine 'enizho-go she' he yaiye

a-la leli ŋaŋa shaŋe ye-yi

10. naŋa she hoghan niya bina de-ya tseye

Actions Correlated with the Completion of the Hogan Songs

As the relevant Hogan Song set comes to a close, corn pollen is passed around the hogan. Everyone present prays in his own words or the words of the songs for whatever end he chooses. When the corn-pollen pouches have been returned to the main singer and placed in the ceremonial basket, the girl is instructed to rise and go out of the hogan, passing the fire on the north side. She then returns, coming around the fire's south side, and resumes her ceremonial position. As mentioned before, the girl does this to "open the door" for the people. Once this has happened, they are free to enter and leave the hogan all night long, regardless of the singing.

Free Singing

While the Hogan Songs do not accompany any of the major Kinaaldá rites, the prescribed actions of pollen-blessing and "opening the door" closely follow their termination. Once these are completed, the ceremonial practitioner is free to turn the singing over to the people. If he has more songs he himself wants

to contribute, he may do so; if not, the other singers start giving
their songs. According to Frank, either these singers can be designated by the main singer or anyone that knows the songs can
start in.

> There are two ways of doing the last night of the singing. Who-
> ever is in charge looks around and sizes up the people, seeing who
> can sing. If you know somebody who knows the Hózhǫ́ǫ́ji pretty
> well and knows the songs as well as the main singer, you point him
> out and tell him to do the singing.... Now, we don't do this very
> often any more. Now everyone who has a song to sing sings out
> until the dawn.

There is much mention of the free singing in the literature,
including mythological references to the free singing which was a
part of the first Kinaaldá. As the reader will recall, Frank spoke
of it in his Kinaaldá myth (*supra*, pp. 11–15). In 1961, he told
McAllester:

> Anyone is permitted to sing as many as he cares to during this
> time; four, six, or maybe a whole set of twelve songs. Of course,
> the beginning of the Kinaaldá was with Changing Woman when she
> had her first menstruation. At that time, there were no humans
> on the earth; it was just the supernatural people who congregated
> there for that occasion. It was decided to do that from then on, in
> order to revive the holiness of that time. Nowadays, some people
> come to Kinaaldá just to grab some of that cake; some just put on
> a show. Others come sincerely to revive the holiness of the songs.
> At the first Kinaaldá, they sang, of course, all night until around
> daybreak. Then the singing was terminated, and the whole thing
> was turned back to the leader.[61]

Other myths also mention the free singing.

> When Talking God finished, each of the Holy People sang six
> songs making in all two hundred eighty-two. An entire night was
> thus consumed.[62]

> Following these songs, all persons attending this ceremony
> contributed sets of songs which purposed to again bring man into
> being and to enable him to give birth to his kind.[63]

Informants also frequently mentioned the free singing when
talking about the Kinaaldá.

---

[61]McAllester, Field Notes, July 19–20, 1961, p. 5b.
[62]Edward Curtis, I, 94.
[63]Haile, "Origin Legend of the Navaho Enemy Way," p. 91.

After that he just turns it over to the people and all the people just sing their own songs (TS).[64]

Of course at this Kinaaldá my father was the main leader in the singing that night; he was the leading man at that particular time. After he had sung the Songs of the Hogan, just anyone could sing what songs he wanted to sing or songs that he knew .... Of course on an occasion like this, all are welcome. Anyone wishing to sing at a Kinaaldá is welcome. When they do come and contribute their songs to Kinaaldá, then, of course, they receive a piece of cake. That I remember (RM).

When he finished those twelve songs (Hogan Songs) he told the people he was leaving the singing with them. Anybody who has a song and who is willing to sing for the people is the next one to sing (N).[65]

The main singer keeps urging those present to give their songs until it is dawn. It is worth while reviewing some of the comments from Marie's and Lena's Kinaaldá to show how this is done.

Kinaaldá of Marie Shirley

(Before Group III of the Free Singing)

[Somebody breaks in]: Go ahead, my grandfather, keep singing.
FRANK: I do not have to do it. I turned it over to you people to carry on from where I stopped.

(Before Group IX of the Same)

FRANK: Maybe that is enough now .... What does it look like now? We do not want to start in too early while it is still pitch dark. Let us let it get lighter .... How many more have you got to sing?
JOHN TSOSI: I am finished; I sang all the songs.
FRANK: Pass the corn pollen ....Just one more person needs to sing. That will be sufficient.

Kinaaldá of Lena Shirley

(Before Group VI of the Free Singing)

CHARLIE WATCHMAN: Are you through singing your songs?
FRANK: Sure, my in-law. I have some more songs, but you go

---

[64]Dorothea Leighton, Field Notes, March 4, 1940.
[65]Alexander and Dorothea Leighton, Field Notes, February 2-3, 1940.

ahead....Who-all has sung so far? Jimmy, did you sing? Is it almost dawn?

(Before Group VIII of the Same)

FRANK: It's a long time before dawn; go ahead and continue the songs. Is somebody else waiting to sing? Go ahead and sing. ...If someone else wants to donate a song, he should go ahead. If not, continue yours. It's getting daylight. I'll help you. Well, you can follow me.

According to Frank and other informants, the songs used can be any of the many that are connected with the Blessing Way Ceremony. Among the kinds mentioned specifically are Mountain, Horse, Bead, Sheep, Soft Fabrics, Jewels, Journey, Earth, and Corn Songs, Songs Pertaining to Bad Dreams, and the Songs of the Grasshopper, Women, Talking God, Hogan God, and the Water Men. "The songs may even concern gambling. If a woman wants to sing, she can sing the Bouncing Stick Game Song. Yes, this is really true" (FM).

Examples of the content of free-singing sections in Kinaaldá are available for the ceremonies of Marie and Lena Shirley and Carla Begay. During Marie's, the free singing included:

8 Songs Pertaining to the Pairs
2 Songs of Old Age
2 Songs Pertaining to the Pairs
8 Songs for Administering the Pollen
(1 Twelve Word Song [Fixed])
1 Placing of the Earth Song
5 Songs of the Picking Up of Changing Woman
5 Corn Beetle Songs
1 Horse Song

In Lena's ceremony, the free songs were:

2 Women's Songs
8 Songs Pertaining to the Pairs
2 Songs Pertaining to the Pairs
8 Songs for Administering the Pollen
(1 Twelve Word Song [Fixed])
4 Unidentified Songs
5 Unidentified Songs
5 Unidentified Songs

Once again, due to a lack of help from Kinaaldá singers when contacted after the ceremony, only some of the songs on the partial tape of the free singing in Carla Begay's Kinaaldá could be identified.

6 Songs Pertaining to the Pairs
2 Songs Pertaining to the Pairs
1 Song for Administering the Pollen
4 Unidentified Songs
3 Unidentified Songs
6 Unidentified Songs
2 Unidentified Songs
3 Unidentified Songs
6 Unidentified Songs
3 Songs Pertaining to the Pairs
3 Unidentified Songs

While informants reported that songs could be given in any order during the free singing, investigation has shown that in the case of Frank Mitchell the first Twelve Word Song always occurs after four sets of songs in the free singing and that the two sets that precede it are, respectively, Songs Pertaining to the Pairs and Songs for Administering the Pollen.

Women can sing during the night, just as the men can, and, in addition to the Bouncing Stick Game Song, informants mentioned Sheep, Mountain, Water Men, and Women's Songs as being performed by female singers. One informant, Rosalyn Dean, recalled Kinaaldá singing done by nine men and five women. "The ladies sang and then the men. So it went back and forth like two choruses."[66]

The singers sing as many songs as they wish. Certain rules, however, seem to govern the performances. The singers are expected to sing only their own songs, to know them well, and to be in a condition to sing them correctly. "Don't add what doesn't belong to you. That would bring hardship and misfortune....Don't let them sing the song. If any of you are not feeling too well, don't

---

[66]Anne Keith, Field Notes July 23, 1963.

sing'' (FM on LS's Kinaaldá). Singers should determine the number of songs they contribute by the number of available singers present at the ceremony. "Someone, the parents or anyone, is supposed to keep track of the singing'' (JF).[67] Songs should not be repeated; however, in the free singing in Carla Begay's Kinaaldá, at least three songs were sung twice.

At intervals during the night, the corn-pollen pouches are passed. Janice Fernandez said this happened every hour.[68] Frank Mitchell said this was done after the end of each set of songs in order to "respect the singing and keep it holy.'' Observations suggest, however, that at least in the Mitchell Kinaaldá the timing of the corn-pollen rites is freely defined. As a group of songs is terminated, the singer who is momentarily in charge calls for the pollen if he or she so desires; if not, another set begins without it.

In addition to the singing, such activities as story-telling, the recounting of myths, discussions of differences in ceremonial performances among singers, joking, and eating occupy the night. Individuals smoke cigarettes whenever they wish and occasionally leave in order to drink as well as to attend to other biological functions.

The Twelve Word Songs

He came upon it, He came upon it.

Now he has come upon the Earth,
Now he has come upon Sky Darkness,
Now he has come upon Mountain Woman,
Now he has come upon Water Woman,
Now he has come upon Darkness,
Now he has come upon Dawn,
Now he has come upon Talking God,
Now he has come upon Hogan God,
Now he has come upon White Corn,
Now he has come upon Yellow Corn,
Now he has come upon Corn Pollen Boy,
Now he has come upon Corn Beetle Girl.

---

[67] *Ibid.*, June 22, 1963.
[68] *Ibid.*

Blessedness is behind, blessedness is before,
Blessedness is below, blessedness is above,
Blessedness is extended all around,
    as far as the horizons, it is said.

(From Song No. 1, FRANK MITCHELL, Marie Shirley's
Kinaaldá, 1963)

In the course of the night, the free singing[69] is interrupted by the insertion of a fixed song—one that is led by the main singer, and this time one that is definitely correlated with a specific rite. This song is known as the Twelve Word Song, *Naakits'áadah doo-'ígíí*. It is one of two such songs used in Kinaaldá. The second Twelve Word Song is sung early on the final morning after dawn has begun to appear and the race and the accompanying Racing Songs have been completed. Since the first Twelve Word Song is the only fixed song sung in several hours of all-night singing, both it and its dawn counterpart will now be discussed.

As mentioned above, in the Kinaaldá of both Marie and Lena Shirley, the first Twelve Word Song was sung after four groups of "free songs" had been performed, and each time the two groups which directly preceded it were Songs Pertaining to the Pairs and Songs for Administering the Pollen. The tapes from Carla Begay's Kinaaldá suggest that the first Twelve Word Song may be placed differently by different singers. Willie Marianito sang the first Twelve Word Song early in the evening between the two sets of Hogan Songs and before the free singing began. The tape supply had been exhausted before the second Twelve Word Song was sung.

Blue Mule included both Twelve Word Songs in his solo Kinaaldá recording. The song that is similar to the first Twelve Word Song of both Marie's and Lena's Kinaaldá was sung as the last song in a group of nineteen. The other Twelve Word Song was included earlier, as No. 9, after four songs from the first day and four Racing Songs had been performed. Thus it would seem that Blue Mule might use both songs during the all-night singing, but at

---

[69]Due to spatial restrictions, the textual and musical particulars of the free singing cannot be discussed here.

different times and in an order that is the reverse of Frank's. Whether this procedure, which was demonstrated in solo recording, would be followed in ceremonial situations was not ascertained.

Unlike data for the Hogan Songs, the only reference to the origin of the Twelve Word Songs is contained in Frank's myth (*supra*, pp.11–15), where the songs are said to have originated at the second Kinaaldá.

Twelve Word Songs can be found in many Navaho ceremonials. Those from the Blessing Way, especially the Twelve Word Song from the end of a *Hózhǫ́ǫ́jí*, have special powers.

> This song is called a Twelve Word Song. The Blessing Way has any number of Twelve Word Songs in the ceremony. There are many groups, each with its own Twelve Word Song. They have prayers which have the same words in them as the songs. If you make a mistake, you say the prayer afterward. If you do not miss anything, you do not need any prayers.
>
> The Twelve Word Song from the final part of the Blessing Way is used to conclude all other ceremonials. However, each ceremonial has separate sets of Twelve Word Songs which are used during the duration of the chants. Other ceremonies have their own songs; these are probably misused during the singing. In order to make the ceremony good, they conclude with the Twelve Word Song from the end of the Blessing Way. This way their mistakes are corrected. This song, the Twelve Word Song from the end of the Blessing Way, concludes other ceremonies, and when it is used, it benefits whatever has been used during the ceremony and also benefits those participating in the ceremony (FM).

Twelve Word Songs, especially the one used at the end of a Blessing Way (Twelve Word Song No. 2 in Kinaaldá), are functional. They bring special blessing on the ceremony in process and cancel the effects of previous mistakes. They are also considered to be songs which complete a block of singing.

> The song concluding the Hogan Songs comes at this point. This song [Twelve Word Song No. 1 of Marie's Kinaaldá] concludes all the singing that has been done from the Hogan Songs to this point. It is called a Twelve Word Song. Other songs that are used for Kinaaldá also have a Twelve Word Song which may be used during a *Hózhǫ́ǫ́jí* to complete that set. Some of those songs include the Returning Home Songs, the Mother Earth Songs, and the Women's Songs (FM).

In contrast to the Hogan Songs, the Twelve Word Songs are related to a definite rite: that of passing the corn pollen. Frank said:

> When you are singing the Twelve Word Song, when you still have two words to mention, you hand out pollen in two sacks, one to the men and one to the women. Everybody takes a pinch. In regular *Hózhǫ́ǫ́jí*, you have a different procedure; the patient takes a pinch, puts it in her mouth four times, and sprinkles it outward. Here, that's omitted.

In both Marie's and Lena's Kinaaldá, corn pollen was passed during the singing of both Twelve Word Songs, and, as Frank said, the pouches were started after the tenth verse, directly before the mention of Corn Pollen Boy.

When questioned about the content of the pollen prayers, Frank referred to the praying that followed the final Twelve Word Song and said:

> You pray for yourself and your children in your own language, in whatever way you want to pray. The people pray if they want an income of some kind or if someone in the house is sick. If your man is angry at you, you pray he will get over that and make it up to you.

In Chinle, the two Twelve Word Songs used in Kinaaldá were sung practically in complete unison. Gone were the numerous individual variations so prevalent in the Hogan Songs and other songs of the night. Now all the singers joined together and presented a unified version of both these songs. The reason for this may be the one suggested by Frank: "The singing of those songs is well established all over the reservation." Perhaps the two Twelve Word Songs used in Kinaaldá are standard Kinaaldá ones. Perhaps these songs have special restrictions of flexibility; maybe in their execution individual variation is not tolerated. Interestingly enough, in discussing the Twelve Word Song of the Blessing Way which is used in the War Ceremony when the rattle stick is deposited, Father Berard Haile says:

> The song is so well known that the natives recognize it immediately although there are numerous other songs of twelve words which are never recognized as such but are designated by

other names. Omissions or alterations are not allowed in the 12-Word Song.[70]

The Twelve Word Songs are distinct from the other songs musically and textually, and because of this and the limited number of versions of them, they are easily recognized. Texts and transcriptions of both songs follow.

Twelve Word Song No. 1

FRANK MITCHELL

Marie Shirley's Kinaaldá, 1963

Now he has come upon the Earth,
    ((In blessedness, now he has come upon long life,
    In blessedness, now he has come upon everlasting beauty,
    Blessedness is before, blessedness is behind,
    It is blessed, it is said.

    He came upon it,
    He came upon blessedness, he came upon blessedness.))

Now he has come upon Sky Darkness,
    ((In blessedness, now he has come upon long life,
    In blessedness, now he has come upon everlasting beauty,
    Blessedness is behind, blessedness is before,
    It is blessed, it is said.

    He came upon it,
    He came upon blessedness, he came upon blessedness.))

Now he has come upon Mountain Woman,
    ((the next six lines as in verse 1))

Now he has come upon Water Woman,
    ((the next six lines as in verse 2))

Now he has come upon Darkness,
    ((as in verse 1))

Now he has come upon Dawn,
    ((as in verse 2))

Now he has come upon Talking God,
    ((as in verse 1))

Now he has come upon Hogan God,
    ((as in verse 2))

---

[70]Haile, "Origin Legend of the Navaho Enemy Way," p. 291.

Now he has come upon White Corn,
　　((as in verse 1))

Now he has come upon Yellow Corn,
　　((as in verse 2))

Now he has come upon Corn Pollen Boy,
　　((as in verse 1))

Now he has come upon Corn Beetle Girl,
　　((as in verse 2))

　　　Blessedness is behind, blessedness is before,
　　　Blessedness is below, blessedness is above,
　　　Blessedness is extended all around,
　　　　as far as the horizons, it is said.

Twelve Word Song No. 2
FRANK MITCHELL
Marie Shirley's Kinaaldá, 1963

　　　It has come upon me, blessing has come upon me,
　　　The people, the ones who are my relatives, are blessed,
　　　The people, the ones who are my relatives, are blessed;

　　　It has come upon me, blessing has come upon me,
　　　The people, the ones who are my relatives, are blessed,
　　　The people, the ones who are my relatives, are blessed.

Now Darkness is coming up,
　　　((Behind it is blessedness and long life,
　　　Before it is blessedness and everlasting beauty,
　　　Before it, it is blessed,
　　　Behind it, it is blessed.))

Following it, Dawn is coming up,
　　　((Behind it is blessedness and long life,
　　　Before it is blessedness and everlasting beauty,
　　　Behind it, it is blessed,
　　　Before it, it is blessed.

　　　It has come upon me, blessing has come upon me,
　　　The people, the ones who are my relatives, are blessed,
　　　The people, the ones who are my relatives, are blessed.))

Following it, the Earth is coming up,
　　　((the next four lines as in verse 1))

Following it, the Sun is coming up,
　　　((the next seven lines as in verse 2))

Following it, Talking God is coming up,
((as in verse 1))

Following it, Hogan God is coming up,
((as in verse 2))

Following it, the Boy-returning-home-with-a-single-turquoise is
coming up,
((as in verse 1))

Following it, the Girl-returning-home-with-a-single-corn-kernel
is coming up,
((as in verse 2))

Following it, White Corn Boy is coming up,
((as in verse 1))

Following it, Yellow Corn Girl is coming up,
((as in verse 2))

Following it, Corn Pollen Boy is coming up,
((as in verse 1))

Following it, Corn Beetle Girl is coming up,
((next *two* lines as in verse 2; then:))
Behind it, it is blessed,
Before it, it is blessed,
Below it, it is blessed,
Above it, it is blessed,
Everything all around it is blessed.

It has come upon me, blessing has come upon me,
The people, the ones who are my relatives are blessed,
It is said, it is said.[71]

Twelve Word Song No. 1
FRANK MITCHELL
Ceremonial Recording, 1963

heye   neye   yaŋa   nii   ya - ei - ye   yike - ya   holạ'a   nai - ye

---

[71]It is interesting to note that in discussing the Twelve Word formulas found in the Twelve Word Song, Reichard (*Navaho Religion* I, 273) lists the twelve words as: "Earth, Sky, Mountain Woman, Water Woman, Talking God, *xa·ctc'é·óghan*, Boy-carrying-single-corn-kernel, Girl-carrying-single-turquoise, White-corn-boy, Yellow-corn-girl, Pollen Boy, and Cornbeetle Girl." She is quoting from Edward Sapir and Harry Joijer, *Navaho Texts* (Iowa City: Linguistic Society of America, 1942), pp. 257, 523, 225n, where the order is uncertain.

1.

nii ya - ei - ye yike - ya holą - 'a neiye ni-i ya'ei

ne'i yaŋa ho-lągha

neye ka nohotsan niiye ke - ya hozhǫ ni ka sa'a naghei

yeiyei ke - ya hozho niya bik'e hozho nei yi-ke - ya

hozho neya tsi - yijį howazho waneya ke - yeshdę

howo - zhǫ gola - ghana - ne

nii ya ei - ye yike - ya hozho neiye nii ya ei - ye yi-ke - ya

hozho neya ke - yi ei nei - yaŋa holagha

Verse 2

ⓐ *neye ka yadihil niiye keya*
ⓒ *keyeshde*
ⓓ *tsijijį*

ⓔ

Verse 3

   (a)   *neye ka dzilyisdzan niiye keya*
   (e)   as in verse 2

Verse 4

   (a)   *neye ka tui'esdzan niiye keya*
   (b)

   (c)   *keyeshde*
   (d)   *tsiyijį*
   (e)   as in verse 2
   (f)   *neye ei*

Verse 5

   (a)   *neye ka chadihił niiye keya*
   (b)   as in verse 4
   (e)   as in verse 2
   (f)   as in verse 4

Verse 6

   (a)   *neye ka haiyolkal deya keya*
   (b)   as in verse 4
   (c)   *keyeshde*
   (d)   *tsiyijį*
   (e)   as in verse 2
   (f)   as in verse 4

Verse 7

   (a)   *neye hashcheyaltii yeyi keya*
   (b)   as in verse 4
   (e)   as in verse 2
   (f)   as in verse 4

Verse 8

   (a)   *neye hashchehoghan niiya keya*
   (b)   as in verse 4
   (c)   *keyeshde*
   (d)   *tsiyijį*
   (e)   as in verse 2
   (f)   as in verse 4

Verse 9

(a) *neye nada'aɫgai yeyi keya*
(b) as in verse 4
(e) as in verse 2
(f) as in verse 4

Verse 10

(a) *neye nada'aɫsoi yeyi keya*
(b) as in verse 4
(c) *keyeshde*
(d) *tsiyiji̜*
(e) as in verse 2
(f) as in verse 4

Verse 11

(a) *neye ka tadidii niiya keya*
(b) as in verse 4
(e) as in verse 2
(f) as in verse 4

Verse 12

(a) *neye ka'eniltan niiya keya*
(b) as in verse 4
(c) *keyeshde*
(d) until the end:

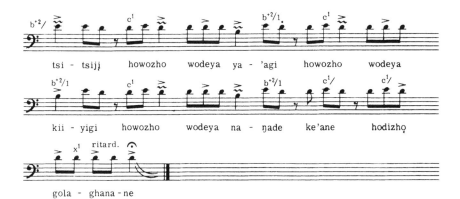

Twelve Word Song No. 2
FRANK MITCHELL
Ceremonial Recording, 1963

heye neye yą yaŋa kee yee yowa keye ya hazhowa

dine shikee yo - wa na'agheiyi ya hazhowa

dine shikee yowa zhowa he - ye aŋa heye eiye holaghei

neya ka hachal ałii - łiyei haiye gałi - ge hozhoni

bikesh deye ka sa'a naghei - ye neye ga-łige hozhoni

bikesh deye ka bike hozho - niye neye ga-łi-ge hozhowo

bitsi - ji hozhowo bikeshde hozhowo neye ei - ye

naŋa heye eiye holaghei

Verse 2

neye bikesh deya haiyol kali - ye

ⓑ *bikeshde*
ⓒ *bitsiji*
ⓓ *naŋa heye eiye*; then return to the opening chorus and sing between the *−*, leaving out the repeat.

Verse 3

A pitch rise of a whole step occurs during verse 2:

ⓐ

neye bikesh deya noho - tsoi - ye

Verse 4

ⓐ

neye bikesh deya ka johona - 'ei ye

ⓑ *bikeshde*
ⓒ *bitsiji*
ⓓ as in verse 2

Verse 5

ⓐ

neye bikesh deye ka hashcheya-lii - ye

Verse 6

ⓐ

neye bikesh deya ka hashche hogha-niye

ⓑ *bikeshde*
ⓒ *bitsiji*
ⓓ as in verse 2

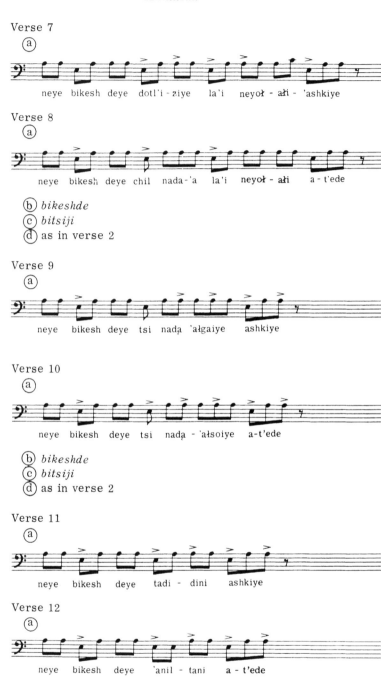

Verse 7

ⓐ

neye bikesh deye dotl'i - ziye la'i neyoł - ałi - 'ashkiye

Verse 8

ⓐ

neye bikesh deye chil nada-'a la'i neyoł - ałi a - t'ede

ⓑ *bikeshde*
ⓒ *bitsiji*
ⓓ as in verse 2

Verse 9

ⓐ

neye bikesh deye tsi nadạ 'ałgaiye ashkiye

Verse 10

ⓐ

neye bikesh deye tsi nadạ - 'ałsoiye a-t'ede

ⓑ *bikeshde*
ⓒ *bitsiji*
ⓓ as in verse 2

Verse 11

ⓐ

neye bikesh deye tadi - dini ashkiye

Verse 12

ⓐ

neye bikesh deye 'anil - tani a - t'ede

ⓑ follow what is below to the end.

bikeshde hozhowo bitsiji hozhowo biyagha hozho

bi-ki-gi hozhowo binade hozhowo ta'altso hozhowo

neye ei ye nana heye eiye

kee yee yowa keye ya hazhowa

dine shikee yo - wa na'a-gheiyi ya hazhowa

dine shikee yowa zhowa he - ye ana heye ne gola - ghana ne

The First Twelve Word Song

Range and Structure

In all instances, Twelve Word Song No. 1 is character-ized by a chorus beginning on a tone which is neither the tonic nor the final of the piece. The over-all range is a tenth, with the choruses being done within a fifth and the verses within a ninth. Structurally, the song is as follows: introduction, opening chorus, eleven verses each followed by a reduced chorus, twelfth verse followed by a slightly altered reduced chorus, and then a terminal formula. Internally, the song is highly integrated:

Introduction	x
Opening Chorus	a b a^1 b a/1 c
Verses 1−11	d a/2 b^+ a/3
	b^{+1} a/3 b^{+2} c^1 b^{+2}/c^2 c^{2+}
Reduced chorus:	a^2 b^{+2}/a^2 b^{+2} c^1

Verse 12   d a/2 b$^+$ a/3
                            b^{+1} a/3 b^{+2} c^1 b^{+2}/

Altered reduced
          chorus: c^1 b^{+2}/ c^1 b^{+2}/1 c^1/c^1
Concluding Formula   x^1

(From Frank Mitchell's First Twelve Word Song,
Marie Shirley's Kinaaldá)

Formulas

Certain figures are found regularly at key structural points.
For example:

Introduction

heye   neye   yaŋa

The End of the Opening Chorus

ne'i   yaŋa   holá̧ ⁻ gha

The Burden of the Verses

ne - yi ke - ya

A Fragment in the Verses

tsi - yiji   howazho   wa-neya

In songs where melodic lines are constantly changing and where
the song as a whole exists in many different versions, such un-
varying figures may be termed formulas. In a song such as the
Twelve Word Song, however, the whole song is unchanging. The
twelve verses are all sung to the same music, and everyone sings
a single version of the entire song. For present purposes such a
phenomenon has been termed a ''formula song.''

A Comparison of Four Versions of the First Twelve Word Song

The comparative material available for the first Twelve Word Song suggests that there is indeed a standard version of this song, one that surpasses regional boundaries. In Lena Shirley's Kinaaldá, the first Twelve Word Song was sung as it was performed in Marie's ceremony, except that the tonic was a minor third lower and a few of the intervals in the opening chorus were wider than before. This latter was to be expected since, with the lower tonic, Frank was not obliged to contract the higher skips in order to remain in a comfortable vocal range. Given three or four understandable interval differences, then, the first Twelve Word Song in Lena's Kinaaldá is almost Marie's song transposed down a minor third. Once again, the ceremonial singing was unusually unified.

Anne Keith's tapes include the first several verses of Willie Marianito's first Twelve Word Song, which was sung between the two sets of Hogan Songs before the singing was opened to the people. The opening chorus has a few notes that differ from Frank's version, but it soon settles into an exact duplication of the Mitchell first Twelve Word Song. Here again, the ceremonial singing is unified to the point where much of it is actually in unison. While the song is not complete (due to a change in tape reels during its latter half), the amount that is recorded is so close to Frank Mitchell's version that one might expect the rest of the song to be equally similar.

The other available version of the first Twelve Word Song is that recorded by Blue Mule. Certain variations are evident when his version is compared with Frank's. The tonal system in Blue Mule's is wider, including nine rather than six tones. The skips are restricted to intervals of a third and fourth, and grace notes are used. The major difference, however, is the fact that Blue Mule's version has only eight verses. The verses that are Nos. 5 to 8 in Frank Mitchell's song are omitted. According to Chic Sandoval, Blue Mule never sings this song with eight verses for ceremonies; instead, he uses all twelve. Since he did it with eight in the solo recording session and since many of Blue Mule's songs from this session seem either incomplete or confused in their textual ordering, there is a possibility that the omissions and variations were intentional.

With all the differences, though, the skeleton of Blue Mule's song is identical with Frank Mitchell's second Twelve Word Song. This is seen by comparing Frank's song with the Blue Mule version shown below.

Twelve Word Song No. 1

BLUE MULE

Solo Recording, 1963

neye ne ye ye yaŋa k'e yei yowa k'eye ya hozhowa

dine shike yu wa na-ŋa-ghai ya hozhowo

dine shikeya hozhola ei ye naŋa heye eiye holaghei

neye ka hachal-a-łii-łiye haiye gałi-ke hozhowo

bikesh deye ka sa'a naghe-i-ye haiyi gałi-ke hozhowo

bikesh deya ka bi-ke hozho-niye haiyi gałi-ke hozhowo

bitsi-ji hozho bikeshde hozhowo neye ei ye

naŋa   heye   eiye   holaghei

Verse 2

ⓐ

neye   bikesh   deye   haiyo - kaliye

ⓑ all the B flats that occurred from this point on in the first verse now become *c* naturals.

ⓒ *bikeshde hozho*

ⓓ *bitsiji hozhowo*

ⓔ *naŋa heye eiye*: then return to the opening chorus, and sing between the *−*, leaving out the repeat.

ⓕ

Verse 3

ⓐ

neye   bikesh   deye   naho - tso-i-ye

ⓑ all the original B flats now become *d* naturals.

Verse 4

ⓐ

neye   bikesh   deye   ka   joho - na - 'ei - ye

ⓑ as in verse 2

ⓒ as in verse 2

ⓓ as in verse 2

ⓔ as in verse 2

ⓕ as in verse 2

ⓖ

Verse 5

ⓐ

neye bikesh deye ka hashcheyal-ti - i - ye

ⓑ all the original B flats now become *c* naturals

Verse 6

ⓐ

neye bikesh deye ka hashcheho-gha -ni -yi

Verse 7

ⓐ

neye bikesh deye do-tł'i - ziyi ta'ai naiyo -'a-ła 'ashkiye

ⓑ all the original B flats now become *d* naturals

Verse 8

ⓐ

neye bikesh deye chil nadą -'i ta'i naiyo -'ała 'a - t'ede

ⓑ all the original B flats now become *c* naturals
ⓒ - ⓖ as in verse 2

Verse 9

ⓐ

neye bikesh deye dą - 'ałgaiye 'ashkiye

ⓑ all the original B flats now become *d* naturals

Verse 10

ⓐ

neye bikesh   deye dą-'ałtsoiye 'a -t'e-de

ⓑ all the original B flats now become *d* naturals
ⓒ - ⓖ as in verse 2

Verse 11

ⓐ

neye bikesh deye   tadi - dini 'ashkiye

ⓑ all the original B flats now become *c* naturals
ⓔ

nąna   heye ei   yeye

Verse 12

ⓐ

neye bikesh deye   enil - tani 'a-t'e-de

ⓑ all the original B flats now become *c* naturals
ⓒ - ⓕ as in verse 2
ⓖ

dine shikeya hozhola ei   ye   nąna heye e-- golaghana ne

The differences between the songs can be summarized by saying
that Blue Mule's uses more notes and is more decorated, but more
restricted in interval usage and shorter in length. Chic's statement that Blue Mule can and does sing the song as Frank does
when in a ceremonial situation should be remembered.

The Second Twelve Word Song

While related to Twelve Word Song No. 1 in some ways, the second of these songs must be considered as a separate entity. Its origin, position in the ceremony, and function are more clearly established than those of its predecessor, and in general, informants are more apt to verbalize about it rather than the first song.

The second Twelve Word Song is evidently more special than the first. This is the song that comes at the end of the Blessing Way and is sung at the end of other ceremonies. Its corrective powers and ability to bestow extensive blessing are greater than those of its predecessor. All this is emphasized by the fact that the people are expected to come into the hogan while it is sung, and, as in the opening Hogan Songs, no one may leave until the song is completed.

> When she runs east and returns, she enters the hogan sunwise. While she's out, the performer prepares a basket with white clay with which to anoint her. After the girl has returned from her race, then everybody is supposed to come back into the hogan, especially those people who have been singing. It's especially important for them to come back in. Then comes the Twelve Word Song. The singing of that song is well established all over the reservation. The Hogan Songs are used to start Kinaaldá and the Twelve Word Song to end the ceremony. During this time, no one can leave (FM).[72]

Differences between the First and Second Twelve Word Songs

Ranges, Tonal Systems, Skips, and Note Types

In discussing the second Twelve Word Song, no specific statement can be made about over-all range or complexity of tonal systems, for the three available versions range from an octave to a thirteenth and use between six and eight tones. Skips are restricted, though, to thirds, fourths, or fifths, in contrast to thirds, fourths, and eighths found in the first Twelve Word Song. The

---

[72]In saying this, FM contradicted some of his earlier and later statements and joined other informants who said that the last song in the Kinaaldá is the Twelve Word Song that precedes the distribution of the corncake.

note types are also more restricted than before, being limited to quarters and eighths.

Tonics

The tonics are now settled. In two of the three available versions, the starting, ending, and tonic tonal levels are identical. Only in one version (the second Twelve Word Song as sung for Marie's Kinaaldá) is there evidence of a difference between the starting level and the other two—a difference which occurred in *all* the versions of the first Twelve Word Song.

Structure

The first and second Twelve Word Songs can also be differentiated in structure. The second one is planned as follows: introduction; opening chorus which is repeated; verses 1–11, wherein the even-numbered verses are followed by reduced choruses (the opening chorus without repeats); verse 12 (an extension of earlier verses); and a final chorus (the reduced chorus changed to include the ending formula). The general outline shows that the structural differences between the first and second Twelve Word Songs are located in the choruses. The opening chorus and the reduced choruses which follow the verses in the second song are longer than their counterparts in the first. The reduced choruses are also placed differently, so as to occur only half as often. Finally, the second Twelve Word Song has a final chorus, whereas the first lacks one altogether.

Texts

The texts of the two kinds of Twelve Word Songs also differ. The Sun, the Boy-returning-home-with-a-single-turquoise, and the Girl-returning-home-with-a-single-corn-kernel are three characters who are unique in the second Twelve Word Song. They replace Sky Darkness, Mountain Woman, and Water Woman, but not respectively. In the second song, the blessedness established in the first is extended past the single subjective "he" to include "the people, the ones who are my relatives."

Similarities between the First and Second Twelve Word Songs

The degree of similarity between the two Twelve Word Songs must not be overlooked. Both songs are formula songs; the three versions of the second song compare even more closely than did the four of the first song. Now Blue Mule only "omits" the extension of the twelfth verse and the terminal, downward slide. Both Twelve Word Songs are sung with outstanding unity in ceremonial situations. Twelve words are important in each, nine of which are common to both songs. Finally, on a general level the structure of the songs can be considered similar.

Comparisons between the Twelve Word Songs and Other Kinaaldá Songs

The two Twelve Word Songs can be distinguished from other Kinaaldá songs in many ways. Not much information is available concerning their origin. Their ceremonial position seems to be both free and determined in the case of the first song and determined in the case of the second. As songs, however, they are definitely correlated with a specific rite and as such are the first fixed songs in the puberty ceremony to be truly "fixed." Then, too, they have a definite function: that of neutralizing earlier ceremonial errors.

The Twelve Word Songs are musically special in several ways. Their corrective function implies a correlated formalism. Such is indeed the case, for the Twelve Word Songs are formula songs. The verses unfold according to a common musical pattern, and the songs exist in "standard versions." People from several geographical regions tend to sing the Twelve Word Songs in the same version in both ceremonial and solo singing. Hence, when they are performed ceremonially, they are sung in complete unison. The Twelve Word Songs further differ from other Kinaaldá songs in that when they are performed, they are sung as individual, single songs, rather than in sets of four or in larger cyclical groupings. Then, too, they are known by the number twelve; it is the numerical concept, a multiple of the much-used Navaho four, rather than the deities or natural forces described in the songs which recalls these songs to singers' minds.

The Dawn Songs

> He came upon beauty,
> He came upon beauty.

Below the east, he came upon beauty,
> He came upon Dawn Boy,
Below the south, he came upon beauty,
> He came upon Sunbeam Girl,
Below the west, he came upon beauty,
> He came upon Evening Twilight Boy,
Below the north, he came upon beauty,
> He came upon Dipper Girl.

> He came upon beauty,
> He came upon beauty, it is said.

> (From Song No. 4. FRANK MITCHELL.
> Marie Shirley's Kinaaldá, 1963)

Myths and other accounts verify the fact that the free singing ends as the dawn begins. At this point, which is established by
clock time, watching the sky through the hogan's smoke hole, and
general consensus of opinion, the singing is turned over to the
main singer once again. He sings the Dawn Songs, *Yołkááł bighiin,*
the third kind of fixed songs to be used during the all-night singing.

Origin

The only reference to the mythological origin of the Kinaaldá
Dawn Songs is found in the 1963 Mitchell myth, where Frank mentioned the two boys who returned to the earth and sang these songs
for the first time at the second Kinaaldá of the First Girl to be
Born on Earth (*supra,* p. 15).

Informants mentioned these songs frequently.[73] Of particular interest to the author were two references found in *Dezba*
and *Spider Woman,* Navaho fiction by Gladys Reichard.

> To those outside, snugly wrapped in their blankets, the hours
> were only moments, and it seemed that they had only dropped to
> sleep when they were all awakened as if to a prearranged signal.
> The east was gray but not light, but it was not the sun which had
> aroused them. Nor was it a horse or a goat tramping curiously

---

[73]It is probable that one of the several rare aesthetic statements collected concerns these
songs. JF said, "Toward morning, they sing really pretty songs." Anne Keith, Field Notes, June
22, 1963.

and noisily near their beds. The signal was the change in the character of the songs. For many hours the songs had continued, varied in words and somewhat in melody and tone, but withal similar in style. But with the dawn the rattles beat excitedly,[74] the tone and rhythm quickened, a sound of great rejoicing burst from the hogan to greet the dawn as the girl prepared to go to meet it.[75]

I am aroused at dawn by a general bustle and by the changed and energetic character of the songs. The chorus has started with the dawn songs.[76]

Function

The Blessing Way has two kinds of Dawn Songs: a group of four which is used during Kinaaldá and Blessing Ways for a medicine bundle or a pregnant woman, and another group of eight which are used at other times. When used in Blessing Ways, the Dawn Songs have no function other than to greet the new day. In a Kinaaldá, on the other hand, they accompany the purification rite of washing the girl's jewelry and hair.[77] According to Frank, the singing of the four Dawn Songs is timed to correspond with the washing.

> [About daybreak] the singing is terminated, and the whole thing is turned back to the leader. He asks the person who managed the girl to set out the basket with the yucca root in it. A beautiful woman comes and pounds the root; she shreds it and then pours water into the basket to make foam for the girl to bathe her hair.
>
> The main singer gives instructions, and according to them the woman makes the soapsuds. The girl is not anointed with the soapsuds. She just kneels and washes her hair. The woman helps her. She sees that the girl has a good shampoo. The leader says, "Well, we have four songs to sing here; we'll just use our own judgment and go according to the washing. Don't rush." When the four songs are finished, the girl is ready to run.[78]

---

[74]The use of rattles is highly unlikely. No one else mentions them, and they should not occur in Blessing Way music.

[75]Gladys Reichard, *Dezba: Woman of the Desert* (New York: J. J. Augustin Publisher, 1939), p. 53.

[76]Gladys Reichard, *Spider Woman* (New York: Macmillan, 1934), p. 104.

[77]The Dawn Songs are separate from the Washing Songs, *Tanagishígíí*, in the Blessing Way proper. None of the examples of either of these song types available in the Wesleyan collection at this time seem similar to the Kinaaldá Dawn Songs.

[78]McAllester, Field Notes, July 19–20, 1961, p. 5b.

The leader sings the Dawn Songs as soon as the dawn starts to come. You know this by watching the sky and your watch. ... Now anyone who has a song to sing sings out until the dawn. Then the main singer finishes out with the *Yołkááł bighiin*, Dawn Songs. People there know when it is dawn, and they stop and let him sing. ... There are only four songs that make up these Dawn Songs. During the first two the main singer sees to the fixing of the soapweed in the basket to be used for washing the girl's hair. Then she [the ideal woman] washes all the girl's jewelry, beads, bracelets, and rings. She does not wash her hair tie. After that, the girl washes her own hair in the same water. During the last two of the four songs, she finishes washing her hair. When the singer sings the last song, she's just about through. As soon as he stops singing, she wrings her hair out and begins to run with it wet.

The lady helps her wash her hair. During the first two songs, she prepares the soapweed. The main singer sings the last two songs while she washes her jewelry and her hair. He sings according to the time of the hair wash (FM, 1963).

Confusion in Terminology

Not all informants and reports considered the Dawn Songs to be equivalent to the Washing Songs. In *Dezba*, Reichard places the washing rite at the beginning of the final night and has it accompanied by "Washing Songs."

The singers sang many groups of songs, each series devoted to the narrative of the adolescent rite of Changing Woman. Among the first of the songs were those telling of her purification by shampooing her hair in yucca suds. A group was sung as Dezba put the core of soapweed into the water and, rolling it between her palms, created foam which increased as she agitated the root and water.

The start of another group of songs was the signal for Gray Girl to put her head in the basket. They were continued as her mother helped her to shampoo and rinse her hair.[79]

Frank himself gave contradictory information about the Dawn Songs. In 1961, he told McAllester that the first four songs used when the hair was washed were called *Yikai yiin*, Dawn Songs. "The second four are the *Jaadesin*, Running Songs. Together, these are the eight Dawn Songs of the last night."[80] While

[79]Reichard, *Dezba*, p. 53.
[80]McAllester, Field Notes. July 19–20, 1961, p. 6.

working on the texts of Marie's Kinaaldá in 1963, Frank told the author the Second Twelve Word Song was "the Dawn Song." Later that same day, he said the four songs in question were a set of "Washing Songs," but the third in the set was "The Song of the Birth of Dawn, *Yikai yischį yisin*." Finally, in that same session, he called all four songs "the Dawn Songs," as he had done in his 1963 preceremonial procedural description.

Mention of these songs in the published literature can be found only in Goddard and in Wyman and Bailey. In the myth recorded by Goddard, it says: "There are six songs all alike which are called dawn songs."[81] Wyman and Bailey refer to only one song used during the washing rite, namely "The Soapweed Song."[82] Nine other writers mention the rite, but not the accompanying music. At least two informants, Edna Sterns[83] and Marie Shirley, reported that the singing stopped before the washing.

Timing the Dawn Songs with the Actual Dawn

The Navaho experience dawn in many stages. The language distinguishes between "leaning toward dawn," "first light (twilight)," "a faint light in the east," "gray dawn," "dawn," "daylight," "full daylight," and "sunrise."[84] Hence, it is not surprising that the Dawn Songs are started by the main singer only after much discussion about the color of the sky. Remarks from Marie Shirley's Kinaaldá show how in one instance these songs were begun.

(After the last free song, Group IX.)

[Several people]: It's dawn (faint light in the east, but still dark: *hayółkááł*).[85]

---

[81]Pliny Goddard, "Navaho Texts," *Anthropological Papers of the American Museum of Natural History*, XXXIV, Part I (1933), p. 152.

[82]Leland Wyman and Flora Bailey, "Navaho Girl's Puberty Rites," *New Mexico Anthropologist*, XXV, No. 1 (January–March, 1943), p. 9.

[83]Anne Keith, Field Notes, July 19, 1963.

[84]For additional linguistic information, see Haile, *A Stem Vocabulary*, II, 77–78; Franciscan Fathers, pp. 36, 38–39; and Robert Young and William Morgan, *The Navaho Language* (Salt Lake City, Utah: Deseret Book Company, 1958), p. 109.

[85]The interpreter, CS, translated all the terms as "dawn." The author has listened to the ceremonial tapes again and has included in parentheses the literal translation of the Navaho words the various people actually used.

FRANK: We'd better wait until there's more light before she runs her race.

ISABELLE: It is getting too late; it is getting daylight (it is daylight: *naneinłkáa*).

FRANK: Let us sing one more song.

DINÉ ŁBÁHÍ: It is getting too late; it is getting too light (it is becoming day: *yiilkah*) (*supra*, p. 55).

FRANK: Well, go ahead and prepare the soap. Who is going to fix the soapsuds? Are you turning the singing back to me now?

[Several]: Yes, it is dawn (it has become dawn: *yiską*).

FRANK: Prepare your soapsuds carefully. Go ahead.

(*Dawn Songs started.*)

Source Material

In addition to the text of the Kinaaldá Dawn Song which is available in Goddard's "Navaho Texts," the texts and music for eight more are available for study. Four are from Marie's ceremony and four from Lena's. The first song of the group from Marie's can be found on pp. 248–250. Blue Mule mentioned that four Dawn Songs were sung for the washing of the girl's hair, but they were not included in the group of nineteen songs he had agreed to record. Totsoni Mark was unable to record more than the Combing and Racing Songs from the first and last days and the Talking God Hogan Songs. The Dawn Songs that Willie Marianito sang for Carla Begay's Kinaaldá were not recorded, due to an exhaustion of the tape supply.

Note Types, Skips, and Ornamentation

The Kinaaldá Dawn Songs share many characteristics, while simultaneously being unique and individualistic. Note types include quarters, eighths, dotted eighths, and sixteenths, and skips cover intervals of a third and fourth and sometimes a fifth or sixth. Occasional downward slides in the choruses provide the only ornamentation.

Tonics, Ranges, and Tonal Systems

The tonic center is a *g* in all except the second Dawn Song in Marie's Kinaaldá, where it rises to *a♭* and then to *a♮*, and in the fourth song in the same ceremony, where it rises from *g* to *a* within the course of the song. The songs cover an octave or a ninth in range, with verses having either a sixth or an octave range and choruses a fifth, sixth, or octave. The tonal systems include five, six, or seven scale degrees, and the first, fourth, fifth, and sixth degrees are the most important.

Tempi

In Reichard's fictionalized accounts, the Dawn Songs can be recognized by "a quickening in tone and rhythm" and an "energetic character." A look at these songs shows that the basic rhythmic unit is the eighth note common to other Navaho songs. While the rhythmic unit does not quicken, the tempo does. Whereas the Hogan Songs are at M.M. ♪ = 138−160 and the free singing at M.M. ♪ = 144−138, these Dawn Songs are sung so that a ♪ = 168− 176. As such, they are the fastest songs in the Kinaaldá singing to this point.

Formulas

Both musical and textual formulas are found in the Dawn Songs. The contourally flat introductory *heye neye yaŋa*, the *hola-ghei* leading into the verses, and the final *golaghanane* have all been seen before. Interestingly enough, the ♫♫♪ figure which characterizes the finals of Frank Mitchell's Talking God Hogan Songs is used once again for the *golaghanane*.

Structure

Musically, the verses are most often sung to the melody of the first verse of each song. Structurally, the songs are uncomplicated. The choruses and verses are integrated quite thoroughly, and the songs develop according to an over-all scheme of:

Introduction	X
Opening Chorus	AA
Verse and Burden	BC
	BC
	BC
	BC

Final Chorus   A
Concluding Formula   X'

The Dawn Songs as a Set

The songs were sung in sequence, with only two interruptions in which Frank gave instructions. After Song No. 2, washing instructions were given, and after No. 4 the girl was told how to make the turn in her subsequent racing. As a set, the four Dawn Songs are musically related through formulas, specifics of the melodic line, actual melodic phrases, and structure. Yet they are distinct from one another in phrase lengths, beat patterns, contours, and musical conceptions of some of the textual formulas, as well as in melodic material. Hence, while they are a set, the related songs cannot be reduced to a single entity.

Texts

Textually, the songs are both related and unrelated. All the Dawn Songs have four verses, and all focus on one set of ideas— the appearance of four deities; Dawn Boy in the east, Sunbeam Girl in the south, Evening Twilight Boy in the west, and Dipper Girl in the north. McAllester asked Frank Mitchell in 1961 if the words of the Dawn Songs told how to do the washing. He replied:

> No, they are just a set of Dawn Songs. The songs merely name the Dawn People in the east, Sunbeam Girl in the south, Evening Twilight Boy in the west, and Night Girl in the north. In the direction of the east, two boys appeared. They were the ones that were recognized as Dawn Boys; from the south came the Sunbeam Girls; two boys appeared in the west; they were the Evening Twilight Boys; in the north, the Night Darkness Girls appeared. That's the story on that.[86]

The texts of the four Dawn Songs appear on pp. 245–247. In addition to the actual poetry in them, the author was particularly interested in two more examples of possible meanings for "vocables."

---

[86]McAllester, Field Notes, July 19–20, 1961, p. 8b.

```
heye neye yaŋa    ei-ei neiyila yik'eeya
                        ni       yik'eeya
                  it said he came upon it
```

```
ei-ei neiyila yik'eeya yi      ei-ei yik'eeya holaghei
    ni       yik'eeya              yik'eeya
  it said he came upon it         he came upon it
```

```
              He came upon it, it is said
              He came upon it, it is said
              He came upon it.
```

(Chorus of Song No. 2)

According to Frank Mitchell, the *ei-ei* sounds are not meaningless syllables, but cries imitating the voice of a baby. These recall other sounds that Frank identified as calls of the gods in his Chief Hogan Songs.

In the third song, the chorus consists of:

```
kaŋa seiye deya    diyeye yelaŋa    yikeyi yaŋa
     saidi         dighiin          yik'eeya              (etc.)
    ‾‾‾‾           holy             he has come upon it
```

Frank said that *seiye* is really *saidi*, a word that now has no known meaning. Such information suggests the possibility that some Navaho vocables were meaningful words at one time--words that became "tones" or "meaningless syllables" in the songs only after their linguistic origins had been forgotten.[87]

Comparisons of Available Dawn Song Sets

The second set of Dawn Songs, those from Lena's Kinaaldá, varied only slightly from Marie's in their musical details. Sometimes contours were slightly changed, sections were shortened by a few beats, and verses were more integrated by new phrase repetition. Textually, various vocables as well as a few words changed. However, both the musical and textual changes were minute.

---

[87]Reichard was skeptical: "There are references to 'archaic' words in Navaho myth and ritual, based upon an unfounded assumption." *Navaho Religion*, I, 267.

Distinguishing Characteristics

The closeness of the two ceremonial versions distinguishes these songs from most of the other ones compared thus far. So do other qualities. The Dawn Songs are clear in structure. Once heard, they are readily identified. Although grouped in sets which are small in comparison with the Hogan Song groupings, the songs are very interesting musically, being both interrelated and individualistic. The Dawn Songs are the first of the fixed songs to be associated with a major rite. Unlike the pollen-blessing which accompanies the last two verses of the Twelve Word Songs, the washing rite extends throughout the four Dawn Songs.

Dawn Song No. 1

FRANK MITCHELL

Marie Shirley's Kinaaldá, 1963

heye neye yaŋa
His child, now he has come upon it, he has come upon it,
Now he has come upon it, he has come upon it,
Now he has come upon it.

His child, now he has come upon it, he has come upon it,
Now he has come upon it, he has come upon it,
Now he has come upon it, *holaghei.*

Below the east, now he has come upon it,
    Now he has come upon Dawn Boy,
    His child, now he has come upon it,
    Where it is lying, now he has come upon it.
    Now he talks to it,
    Since he talks to it now, now it listens to him,
    Since it listens to him now, it obeys him,
    Blessedness comes out of his mouth, now he has come upon it,
    Now the child of long life and everlasting beauty,
                    now he has come upon it.

His child, now he has come upon it, *holaghei.*

Below the south, now he has come upon it
    Now he has come upon Sunbeam Girl,
    His child, now he has come upon it,

Where it is lying, now he has come upon it.
Now he talks to it,
Since he talks to it now, now it listens to him,
Since it listens to him now, it obeys him,
Blessedness comes out of his mouth, now he has come upon it,
Now the child of long life and everlasting beauty,
                              now he has come upon it.

His child, now he has come upon it, *holaghei*.

Below the west, now he has come upon it,
Now he has come upon Evening Twilight Boy,
His child, now he has come upon it,
Where it is lying, now he has come upon it.
Now he talks to it,
Since he talks to it now, now it listens to him,
Since it listens to him now, it obeys him,
Blessedness comes out of his mouth, now he has come upon it,
Now the child of long life and everlasting beauty,
                              now he has come upon it.

His child, now he has come upon it, *holaghei*.

Below the north, now he has come upon it,
Now he has come upon Dipper Girl,
His child, now he has come upon it,
Where it is lying, now he has come upon it.
Now he talks to it,
Since he talks to it now, now it listens to him,
Since it listens to him now, it obeys him,
Blessedness comes out of his mouth, now he has come upon it,
Now the child of long life and everlasting beauty,
                              now he has come upon it.

His child, now he has come upon it,
His child, now he has come upon it,
He has come upon it, he has come upon it,
He has come upon it, he has come upon it, it is said.

Dawn Song No. 2

FRANK MITCHELL

Marie Shirley's Kinaaldá, 1963

heye neye yaŋa
It said he came upon it,
It said he came upon it,
He came upon it, *holaghei*.

The rest of the song is identical with Dawn Song No. 1, except that the verb "has come" of Song No. 1 is now replaced by "came."

Dawn Song No. 3

FRANK MITCHELL

Marie Shirley's Kinaaldá, 1963

heye neye yaŋa
He has come upon holiness,
He has come upon it,
He has come upon holiness, *holaghei.*

The rest of the song is identical with Dawn Song No. 1, except that the chorus which is used between verses reads:

He has come upon holiness
He has come upon it, *holaghei.*

and the final chorus reads:

He has come upon holiness,
He has come upon holiness,
He has come upon holiness, it is said.

Dawn Song No. 4

FRANK MITCHELL

Marie Shirley's Kinaaldá, 1963

heye neye yaŋa
He came upon beauty,
He came upon beauty,
He came upon beauty, *holaghei.*

The rest of the song is identical with Dawn Song No. 1, except for three changes: the verb "has come" of Song No. 1 is now replaced by "came"; the chorus between verses reads:

He came upon it,
He came upon beauty, *holaghei.*

and the final chorus reads:

He came upon beauty,
He came upon beauty,
He came upon beauty,
He came upon beauty, it is said.

Dawn Song No. 1

FRANK MITCHELL

Ceremonial Recording, 1963

heye neye yaŋa   biya - zhaiyi lowo kaiyi keya naŋa

keya yeyina   kaiyi keya yaŋa keye keeyiya

neye kaiye yaiye yaŋa   yaŋa heye yaye yaŋa holaghei

neye ha-'i'-ashi biya - zhaiyila   kaiyi keeye yaŋa

haiyolkaldo ashki yeyina   kaiyi keeye yaŋa

biya nisi laŋa de kaiyi keeye yaŋa ka yikeeyi yaŋago

kayi chiiyeltiyish kayi chiiyal - tiyishgo ka nabiyi - saŋa

ka na - biyi - sanago   yeyi yino seya bi - zade hozho - nago

ka yikeeye yaŋa ka sa'a naghei ka bike hozhoni

biya - zhaiyila   kaiyi keye yaŋa biya - zhiyila

neye   ka yikeeya   yaŋa   holaghei

Verse 2 opens with different words:

neye sha-'da-'ashi   biya - zhaiyila   kaiyi   keeye   yaŋa

sha bitł'ola   at'ee - deyina   kaiyi keeye yaŋa ...(etc. verse 1)

There are also changes at ⓐ and ⓑ :

biza - de lana   kayi   keeya   yaŋa   holaghei

Verse 3 opens with new words:

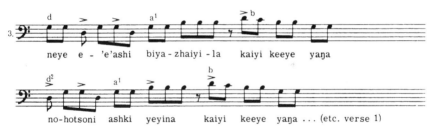

neye   e - 'e'ashi   biya - zhaiyi - la   kaiyi keeye   yaŋa

no-hotsoni   ashki   yeyina   kaiyi   keeye   yaŋa ... (etc. verse 1)

There is another change at ⓐ ; ⓑ stays as it was in verse
1.

bizade

Verse 4 opens with its own words:

neye   no - hokosi   biya - zhaiyila   kaiyi   keeye   yaŋa

nohokosi at'e - de - yi - la kaiyi keeye yaŋa ... (etc. verse 1)

The (a) phrase is done as in verse 1; (b) changes again, and then there is a final chorus:

bizade neye keyi yaŋa biyazhaiyi lowo

keyi keye yaŋa keye keyila kaiyi keya yaŋa

neye keyina neye keyi yą golaghana ne

The Racing Songs

> Her child, the sounds have faded into the distance,
> the sounds have faded into the distance.

Child of the west, the sounds have faded into the distance,
Turquoise Girl, the sounds have faded into the distance,
Her turquoise shoes, the sounds have faded into the distance,
Surrounded by Earth People,
the sounds have faded into the distance,
Mountains of jewels encircling her,
the sounds have faded into the distance,
All kinds of vegetation follow her in one direction as she runs,
the sounds have faded into the distance,
Now the sound of small speckled yellow birds is being heard
above her,
the sounds have faded into the distance,
Behind her, night has now passed on,
the sounds have faded into the distance,
Before her, night has now passed on,
the sounds have faded into the distance,
Behind her, it is blessed,
the sounds have faded into the distance,

Before her, it is blessed,
> the sounds have faded into the distance,
Now the girl can endure much without tiring,
> the sounds have faded into the distance,

> Her child, the sounds have faded into the distance,
> the sounds have faded into the distance.

> (From Song No. 2, used on the final morning;
> BLUE MULE, Solo Recording, 1963)

When the Dawn Songs have been completed, the girl makes her final run. The race on the last morning is accompanied by singing, as it is on the first day of the ceremony, if music is being used at that time.

Origin, Numbers, and Titles

Both the mythological accounts and informant interviews contain many references to these Racing Songs, or *Jaadesin*. There is no set number of songs for the race, however. From one to six songs were mentioned in regions where songs accompany the racing on the first day, and from two to four were given as the number of songs which accompany the girl's final dawn run on the fifth morning.

There is no reference in the myths to what deity was responsible for these songs or when and where the songs originated. The only suggestions about this came from Frank Mitchell and Totsoni Mark in answer to specific questions. Frank said that the Racing Songs originated before the Kinaaldá, being first sung by Talking God for Changing Woman as she ran her daily morning races while she was growing up. Changing Woman instructed the people to incorporate these songs, originally sung by her guardian, into the Kinaaldá when it was started. Totsoni Mark distinguished the set of songs used for races on the first day from those used for the final dawn run. He only knew about the origin of the latter.

> The songs for the last morning race are songs that pertain to the *Haskiin deskahi* and *Adestini*. The *Haskiin deskahi bighiin* and

Ádéstíní bighiin are used for her morning race on the last morning. They come from the story of the two heroes. These heroes
were sent to invite medicine men to the first Corral Dance that
was ever held. One went to the White Mountain Apache; the other
went to the Jicarilla Apache. They both came back. The one that
went to the Jicarilla brought back a roasted corn ear. The other
brought back a yucca fruit to show that he had been to the White
Mountain Apache. While they were gone, their grandmother sang
these songs. These songs were used because they were fleet-
footed; they had been practicing for a long time (*supra*, p. 402).

The songs are known by a variety of terms, including the
Footrace Song, the Legs Song, the Race Song, Young Women's
Racing Song, the Big Song, and the Racing Songs. Some informants, especially young girls who had just had their Kinaaldá, made
only general references to the music: "They were singing after
me in the hogan" (ES).[88]

Timing

Frank's comments suggested that the singing of these
songs is timed according to the racing.

> After the girl and those running with her leave, the main singer
> sings at least three of these songs. The time when the fourth one
> is started depends on how far she runs. If it is far, he does not
> start singing until he hears them yelling on return. When they are
> close, he starts the fourth. ... He will still be singing the fourth
> one when she comes in, goes around the fire, and goes to her place.
> The girl never tells him how far she will run. She is instructed
> in the beginning that she is to make her first run and turn around
> at a certain point (not designated, however). This is told to her by
> her mother or someone; hence, she knows to run the race and in-
> crease each one. She makes up her own mind about the turning
> point.[89]

> If the distance is great, the singer will take his time singing the
> songs. If it is short, though, he will rush through them. ... Each
> song has a set of words. The main singer uses his own judgment
> about how long he should sing. You can shorten these songs by
> leaving out some of the words. There might be snow on the ground
> which would make it hard for her to run too far. You cannot omit
> any of these four songs; you have to use all four.[90]

---

[88]Keith, Field Notes, July 19, 1963.
[89]Johnson, Field Notes, July 18 and July 4, 1963.
[90]McAllester, Field Notes, July 19–20, 1961, pp. 7b, 8a.

Other data have shown, however, that not all singers time their Racing Songs. From the Pinedale region, several girls reported being required to wait outside the hogan until the songs were finished before re-entering after their races. Others mentioned returning and being required to run a second time because the singing had not yet been completed.

The Shout

Singing is not the only sound that accompanies the race of the final morning, for throughout the ceremony, whenever the girl runs, she and her companions give special shouts while they are racing. The shout starts high and has a strong downward glissando. It is done on *yoo*. When asked about the shout, Frank said, "When you hear the Kinaaldá yell, it is just like hearing something over the radio. The yell is intended for Changing Woman, the Sun, and Talking God. You yell so these three hear you. The yell is special for Kinaaldá."

Available Recordings, Texts, and Transcriptions

A total of twenty-two Racing Songs are available for study: four from each of the Kinaaldá Frank sang, five from Blue Mule (one for the first day and four for the last morning), two from Baanzizba, six (illustrative fragments) from Totsoni Mark, and one transcription done by Dr. George Herzog from the cylinders of Wheelwright's *Creation Chants*. As mentioned previously, the particular cylinders containing the Kinaaldá recordings Mary Wheelwright obtained from Tł'aáh are not presently available; the texts are, however. Then, too, there are four texts of Racing Songs in Haile's "Blessingway" (Version I) and one in Goddard's "Navaho Texts." Texts will be found on pp. 262–276 for four of the eight Mitchell Racing Songs, the five Blue Mule ones, and the four Tł'aáh songs. Pages 276–289 contain transcriptions of the first of the four Racing Songs that Frank used in Marie's Kinaaldá, two of Blue Mule's Racing Songs (the one used on the first day and the first of the four used on the final morning, and finally the transcription done by Herzog, which is of the first Tł'aáh Racing Song.

Timing

As is true with the Dawn Songs, the Racing Songs accompany a specific major rite and are timed in certain regions according to the execution of that rite. But, in contrast, they are highly variable in textual content. Perhaps the variation is inevitable, since, unlike the washing rite, the racing is done out of the singer's sight and the timing must be done in accordance with knowledge of the distance of the girl's earlier runs and aural cues—the Kinaaldá shouts of the runners.

Distinguishing Characteristic

Musically, the Racing Songs are quite unlike the Dawn Songs. Once acquainted with them, one could not fail to identify them, since, with one exception, musically they can be considered to be *one* song.

Ranges, Ornaments, and Tonal Systems

The songs usually have a range of an octave, with the choruses being sung within a fifth and verses within a sixth. Ornaments are restricted to downward slides on the final tone, and skips emphasize thirds, fourths, and fifths, as is usual in Navaho music. Tonal systems generally include six scale degrees: the first, second, third, fourth, fifth, and its octave.

Verse Numbers and Structures

Verse numbers vary and thus cannot be used as identifying features in the Racing Songs. The structural plan and formulas, however, are consistent, and both serve as elements distinguishing these from other Kinaaldá songs.

The eight songs from Mitchell, five from Blue Mule, two from Baanzizba, and one from Tl'aáh are all structured as follows:

Introduction.
Opening Chorus with inner repetition of ideas.
From twelve to forty verses consisting of three segments which
    are patterned over any given time sequence as follows:

```
1 - 2    3
1   2    3
1 - 1  2 3
1 - 2    3
1   2    3
1 - 2    3 ⁹¹
```

Final chorus with inner repeat.
Closing formula.

Formulas

Four formulas occur in twenty-one of the twenty-two songs.
The opening is the flat

heye neye yaŋa;

it has been seen many times before and is not an identifying feature. The opening chorus does not close with the familiar *holaghei*; instead, it follows the musical phrase:

using the verb appropriate to the particular song and filling in
with the vocables *aŋa yeye*. For example, *deyisą́ aŋa yeye* (FM-
MS Song No. 1). This phrase terminates the opening chorus and
links it with the first verse, in addition to rounding out each verse;
it functions, therefore, as a burden. Another formula appears in
the second segment of the verses; it is Frank's phrase:

which is sometimes sung as

by Blue Mule and Baańzizba and at least once as

by Tł'aáh. The final formula is in the closing

---

⁹¹The hyphen indicates segments that are joined instead of being separated by a rest.

idea. This is a musical formula to which the particular verb associated with the given song is attached. As in the formula at the end of the opening chorus, spaces are filled with the *ana yeye* vocables. While retaining the final downward slide associated with other terminating formulas, the one associated with the Racing Songs differs from all others studied so far in rhythmic pattern, contour, and text.

One song is available, however, which does not fit the above-mentioned formulas. This is the Racing Song that Blue Mule said was used on the first day. While this song (pp. 279– 284) has a structure comparable to the one described above for Racing Songs, its second and third formulas differ from those mentioned above, and it has no fourth or terminating formula.

The Possibility of Two Types of Racing Songs

Blue Mule's first-day Racing Song suggests that there may be two kinds of Racing Songs in regions that use these songs on the first day of the puberty ceremony as well as on the last. It is probable that these two song types share structural details, but are musically distinguishable from each other as well as from other song groups. In the literature that mentions the use of songs on the first day, there are only two references to the use of Racing Songs; these are Blue Mule's and Totsoni Mark's. The Racing Songs recorded by the latter singer are too fragmentary to determine many significant structural characteristics. Thus, at this point, more first-day Racing Songs need to be collected and compared with their final-morning counterparts.

The Amount of Activity in the Songs

Note Types

Knowing that these songs accompanied a rite whose major emphasis is movement, the author was interested in seeing if the songs were musically more active than those in other groups. It was found that in several ways they were. In the Racing Songs, while the emphasized note types are still the quarter and eighth, sixteenth notes are used more frequently than in other song types previously studied.

Contours and Tempi

The contours do not fluctuate so much in these songs as in some of the other types, and thus melodic lines do not reflect the emphasis on movement. The tempi do, however. In discussing the Dawn Songs, it was mentioned that they were sung at M.M. ♪ = 168–176 and that they were the fastest songs in the ceremony to that point. But the Racing Songs can be sung even faster. While in Marie's Kinaaldá, Frank sang them at M.M. ♪ = 160–168, in Lena's he did them at M.M. ♪ = 176–184. Blue Mule's and Baañzizba's Racing Songs were sung at M.M. ♪ = 180–184, the ♪ = 184 being used most consistently.

Texts

The idea of motion reflected in note types and tempi is clearly established in the texts. While twenty-one of these twenty-two songs may be seen as a *single* song musically, textually all must be categorized as dealing with one of two verbs: "to run" or "to go." Of the texts using the latter verb, the majority emphasize four forms: "the sound is going off," "the sound has gone off," "the sound is returning," and "the sound has returned."

Variation

Even when classified as songs associated with one verb in four forms, each Racing Song remains textually unique. A high degree of variability is evident in the texts, for the words are never sung the same way twice, even by a single singer. Texts are shortened or lengthened, according to the timing of the running. These additions or omissions, another way of providing constant change and consequently, movement, are not seen as mistakes; in listening to the tapes out of their recording context, neither Blue Mule nor Frank Mitchell corrected the variables.

Surprisingly enough, the changes seem to be in the hands of the majority group. In Lena's Kinaaldá, especially, Frank was frequently outvoted and overridden in his choice of the form of the texts that were used in these songs. At times, he kept his version going simultaneously with the others for quite a while before he dropped out. At one point he remarked, "Maybe the others don't agree with what we're singing, but that's the way we were taught, and we go according to the way we were taught; we don't add anything."

Frank insisted that there are only four Racing Songs. However, he ordered the words of the four songs quite differently at Lena's ceremony. Thus, what actually seems to exist are four basic verbal progressions on which the singer may elaborate, drawing from a reservoir of defined Racing Song verses, but creating his own songs textually, according to temporal demands.[92]

Poetry

To the author, the Racing Songs are some of the most beautiful of Navaho poetry. The texts are full of images which are immediately appealing. Some of these include: "the breeze coming from her as she runs is beautiful," "the white shell stands erect all about her," "now comely servants follow her in one direction as she runs," and the girl "surrounded by Dawn People," "in the midst of dawn," "with mountains of soft fabrics encircling her."

Textual Structure

The Racing Song texts, thirteen of which are included in pp. 262–276 are unique. Frank's and those from SC (in Haile's "Blessingway," Version I) are grouped around four verbs; "the

---

[92]A quote from *The Singer of Tales* seems apropos: "To the singer the song, which cannot be changed (since to change it would, in his mind, be to tell an untrue story or to falsify history) is the essence of the story itself. His idea of stability, to which he is deeply devoted, does not include the wording, which to him has never been fixed, nor the unessential parts of the story. He builds his performance, or song, in our sense, on the stable skelton of narrative, which is the song in his sense" (Lord, p. 99).

sound is going off," "the sound has gone off," "the sound is returning," and "the sound has returned." These texts alternately tell of White Shell Girl and Turquoise Girl. They follow this diagram:

Introduction.
Opening Chorus.
Undefined number of verses concerning the girl.
Four directional verses (six in the fourth song).
"Sacred words" (long life and everlasting beauty).
Final Chorus.
Concluding Formula.

The girl's attire is described, and then the surroundings which encircle her as she runs. Of special interest is the wishful quality of these texts, shown in the idea of all kinds of servants forming a procession which leads up to the girl and goes beyond, as the sounds of her running fade into the distance. Frank gave the following unsolicited explanation for two of his four Racing Songs: "These songs [Nos. 1 and 3] pertain to the servants of a wealthy person. They're wishful; you hope that the girl will come to that stage where she can acquire servants[93] to wait on her."

The songs vary in their burden content, but they are closely related in many of their textual ideas through repetition and alternation. Examples of the latter include:

Odd-Numbered Songs	Even-Numbered Songs
Child of White Shell Woman	Child of Changing Woman
White Shell	Turquoise
Child of the east	Child of the west
soft fabrics	jewels
jewels	soft fabrics
horses	sheep
sheep	horses
in the midst of . . .	birds playing in the tip of the head plume

The odd-numbered songs in Frank's Racing Song group are longer than the even-numbered ones. Progressions of female attire, directions in which dawn is passing, and directions of blessing are

[93]To the author's knowledge, servants are not a part of contemporary Navaho households. The idea quite possibly reflects the age of the song; trade in female slaves, especially Paiute ones, was common in the 1860's. See Ruth Underhill, *The Navajos* (Norman, Okla.. University of Oklahoma Press, 1956), pp. 79–81.

common to both. Characteristically, the final song expands the usual twofold directional blessing to the summary five, including "below," "above," and "all around" in addition to "behind" and "before."

Comparative Structures

During Lena's Kinaaldá, Frank sang these songs so that all four included the series of being "in the midst of" numerous processions of various kinds of wealth; these processions characterized only the odd-numbered songs in Marie's ceremony. The ideas of "in the midst of the earth," "gathered spring waters," and "yellow corn" were added, and alternations were revised to include "gathered rain waters" (odd-numbered songs), "gathered spring waters" (even-numbered songs), "white corn" (odd-numbered song), and "yellow corn" (even-numbered song). Some other verses were omitted, and the chorus words were repeated a different number of times in all cases.

Blue Mule's texts share many ideas with those of Frank, including a progression of female attire, processions of various kinds of wealth, a girl who is a child of directions and deities, and the use of the four verbs. However, there is one song, for the first day, based on an entirely new idea: "the breeze coming from her as she runs is beautiful." Other differences are found in the fact that Blue Mule's Racing Songs expand the female attire progression and view it in four ceremonial jewels; white shell, turquoise, abalone, and jet. The Racing Songs of the final morning also add a five-part sequence of various bird sounds which are heard around the girl.[94] Omitting the idea of "dawn is passing" in the first Racing Song of the final morning, Blue Mule's includes it per se in the third song, while changing it to "night has now passed on" in the second and fourth. The final blessing has a dual direction until the last song, where, as in Frank's, it becomes five-part. In none of Blue Mule's songs

---

[94]According to Totsoni Mark, the people who run with the kinaaldá during her daily races represent the birds which are mentioned in the Racing Songs as following the girl as she runs.

are the blessings followed by the well-known "sacred words": "now long life, now everlasting beauty." The Racing Song from the first day moves directly from the dual blessing into the chorus. The first three Racing Songs from the final morning interject a new and certainly appropriate idea—"now the girl can endure much without tiring"—before turning to a summary chorus. The fourth song replaces this idea with "her speech is blessed." Other variations exist as well. According to Chic Sandoval, this should not be the case: "All these songs should have the same words with only the jewels and the horses and sheep alternating."

Baañzizba's two Racing Songs are musically similar to Frank's first one. Textually, however, they are closer to Blue Mule's, using similar progressions with a few expansions (so White Shell Girl is in verse 4 instead of 1) and reductions (so as to omit verses 29 – 32 of Blue Mule's song).

Totsoni Mark's songs are musically almost identical with Frank's. The six Totsoni uses for the first day progress through the following verbs: *sidits'áá'* (the sound is going off); *'asolts'áá'* (the sound is traveling along); *naselts'áá'*, "the sound has reached its furthest distance"; *nasists'áá'* (the sound is returning); *daselts'áá'* (the sound is right next door); and *naselts'áá'* (the sound has returned). The four Racing Songs that Totsoni uses on the last day are identical textually with Frank Mitchell's. Totsoni said that the word in the Racing Songs which indicates the possessor of the girl can be varied to express the relation that exists between the main singer and the girl and her family: "If she happens to be your own child, you use *shiyáázhí* (my child). If she is someone else's child and he is present, you use *niyáázhí* (your child). If he is not present, you use *biyáázhí* (his child)."

The four Racing Song texts collected from Tł'aáh by Wheelwright are structured still differently. Four verbs define the songs, but here the progression is not one of moving out, moving further out, starting back, and completely returning, as in most of the previous songs. Instead, it is "she runs out," "she runs back," "they run out shouting," and "they run back shouting."

The race is performed twice in the song group, first by the girl and then by "they," probably the girl plus her companions. Only during the second one is the shouting mentioned. While the literature related to double races on the final morning does not mention such a differentiation, perhaps it does occur in some regions. The Wheelwright collection does not include field-work data concerning the use of Racing Songs on the first day or the execution of the actual racing on the last day. Indeed, a classification of these songs as either first-day or final-morning Racing Songs cannot be made at this time.

The texts differ from those of Frank and Blue Mule in more ways than just in the burden content and the direction of the movement progression. Those songs follow the structural plan outlined by McAllester and already described (chorus, first-part verses, middle chorus, second-part verses, and final chorus). As they are two-part, alternation occurs within each song, rather than between separate songs. For example, White Shell Girl becomes Turquoise Girl in the second part of Song No. 1.

The actual subject matter is more specifically defined and also more restricted. Only two of Tł'aáh's four songs concern the manner in which the girl is attired as she runs. The last two concentrate solely on the elements, natural and otherwise, which surround her as she runs out and back with her companions, shouting all the time.

It is not known whether these songs are a complete set of four or if there were others that Tł'aáh also used. The absence of a fivefold directional progression in the fourth song seems to suggest the latter. However, in most of Tł'aáh's Kinaaldá and Blessing Way Songs, the final blessing progression is only dual in its direction.

Racing Song No. 1

FRANK MITCHELL

Marie Shirley's Kinaaldá, 1963

heye neye yaŋa
Her child, the sounds are fading into the distance,
Her child, the sounds are fading into the distance,

Her child, the sounds are fading into the distance,
Her child, the sounds are fading into the distance.

Now the child of White Shell Woman,
         the sounds are fading into the distance,
White Shell Girl, the sounds are fading into the distance,
Her white shell shoes, the sounds are fading into the distance,
Her white shell leggings, the sounds are fading into the distance,
Her white shell clothes, the sounds are fading into the distance,
Now, a perfect White Shell having been placed on her forehead,
         the sounds are fading into the distance,
Her white shell head plume, the sounds are fading into the distance.

The child of the east, the sounds are fading into the distance,
In the midst of dawn, the sounds are fading into the distance,
In the midst of white corn, the sounds are fading into the distance,
In the midst of all kinds of soft fabrics,
         the sounds are fading into the distance,
In the midst of gathered rain waters,
         the sounds are fading into the distance,
All kinds of soft fabrics lead up to her and go beyond,
         the sounds are fading into the distance,
All kinds of jewels lead up to her and go beyond,
         the sounds are fading into the distance,
All kinds of horses lead up to her and go beyond,
         the sounds are fading into the distance,
All kinds of sheep lead up to her and go beyond,
         the sounds are fading into the distance,
All kinds of wild game lead up to her and go beyond,
         the sounds are fading into the distance,
All kinds of servants lead up to her and go beyond,
         the sounds are fading into the distance.

Before her, dawn is passing,
         the sounds are fading into the distance,
Behind her, dawn is passing,
         the sounds are fading into the distance,
Before her, it is blessed,
         the sounds are fading into the distance,
Behind her, it is blessed,
         the sounds are fading into the distance,
Now the child of long life and everlasting beauty,
         the sounds are fading into the distance.

Her child, the sounds are fading into the distance,
Her child, the sounds are fading into the distance.

Racing Song No. 2
FRANK MITCHELL
Marie Shirley's Kinaaldá, 1963

heye yeye yaŋa
Her child, the sounds have faded into the distance,
  the sounds have faded into the distance,
Her child, the sounds have faded into the distance,
  the sounds have faded into the distance,
The sounds have faded into the distance.

Turquoise Girl, the sounds have faded into the distance,
Her turquoise shoes, the sounds have faded into the distance,
Her turquoise clothes, the sounds have faded into the distance,
Her turquoise face, the sounds have faded into the distance,
Now, a perfect turquoise having been placed on her forehead,
  the sounds have faded into the distance,
Her turquoise head plume, the sounds have faded into the distance,
Now at its tip there are small blue female birds, truly beautiful;
  it is shining at its tip,
  the sounds have faded into the distance,
They call as they are playing; their voices are beautiful,
  the sounds have faded into the distance.

Behind her, dawn is passing,
  the sounds have faded into the distance,
Before her, dawn is passing,
  the sounds have faded into the distance,
Behind her, it is blessed,
  the sounds have faded into the distance,
Before her, it is blessed,
  the sounds have faded into the distance,
Now the child of long life and everlasting beauty,
  the sounds have faded into the distance.

  Her child, the sounds have faded into the distance,
   the sounds have faded into the distance,
  Her child, the sounds have faded into the distance,
  Her child, the sounds have faded into the distance.

Racing Song No. 3
FRANK MITCHELL
Marie Shirley's Kinaaldá, 1963

heye yeye yaŋa
Her child, the sounds are returning,
  the sounds are returning,
Her child, the sounds are returning,

Her child, the sounds are returning,
    the sounds are returning,
Her child, the sounds are returning.

The child of White Shell Woman, the sounds are returning,
White Shell Girl, the sounds are returning,
Her white shell shoes, the sounds are returning,
Her white shell clothes, the sounds are returning,
Her white shell face, the sounds are returning,
Now, a perfect white shell having been placed on her forehead,
    the sounds are returning,
Her white shell head plume, the sounds are returning,
Now at its tip there are small blue male birds, truly beautiful;
    it is shining at its tip,
    the sounds are returning,
They call as they are playing; their voices are beautiful,
    the sounds are returning.

Before her, dawn is passing,
    the sounds are returning,
Behind her, dawn is passing,
    the sounds are returning,
Before her, it is blessed,
    the sounds are returning,
Behind her, it is blessed,
    the sounds are returning.

The child of the east, the sounds are returning,
In the midst of dawn, the sounds are returning,
In the midst of white corn, the sounds are returning,
In the midst of all kinds of soft fabrics, the sounds are returning,
In the midst of gathered rain waters, the sounds are returning,
In the midst of corn pollen, the sounds are returning,
All kinds of soft fabrics lead up to her and go beyond,
    the sounds are returning,
All kinds of jewels lead up to her and go beyond,
    the sounds are returning,
All kinds of sheep lead up to her and go beyond,
    the sounds are returning,
All kinds of wild game lead up to her and go beyond,
    the sounds are returning,
All kinds of servants lead up to her and go beyond,
    the sounds are returning.

Before her, dawn is passing, the sounds are returning,
Behind her, dawn is passing, the sounds are returning,
Before her, it is blessed, the sounds are returning,
Behind her, it is blessed, the sounds are returning,

Now the child of long life and everlasting beauty,
    the sounds are returning.

Her child, the sounds are returning,
Her child, the sounds are returning,
Her child, the sounds are returning,
Her child, the sounds are returning.

Racing Song No. 4
FRANK MITCHELL
Marie Shirley's Kinaaldá, 1963

heye yeye yaŋa
Her child, the sounds have returned,
Her child, the sounds have returned,
Her child, the sounds have returned,
Her child, the sounds have returned.

Now the child of Changing Woman, the sounds have returned,
Turquoise Girl, the sounds have returned,
The child of the west, the sounds have returned,
Her turquoise shoes, the sounds have returned,
Her turquoise leggings, the sounds have returned,
Her turquoise clothes, the sounds have returned,
Now, a perfect turquoise having been placed on her forehead,
    the sounds have returned,
Her turquoise head plume, the sounds have returned,
Now at its tip there are small blue female birds, truly beautiful;
    it is shining at its tip,
    the sounds have returned,
They call as they are playing; their voices are beautiful,
    the sounds have returned.

Behind her, dawn is passing,
    the sounds have returned,
Before her, dawn is passing,
    the sounds have returned,
Behind her, it is blessed,
    the sounds have returned,
Before her, it is blessed,
    the sounds have returned,
Below her, it is blessed,
    the sounds have returned,
Above her, it is blessed,
    the sounds have returned,
All around her, everything is blessed,
    the sounds have returned,
Now the child of long life and everlasting beauty,
    the sounds have returned.

Her child, the sounds have returned,
Her child, the sounds have returned,
Her child, the sounds have returned,
Her child, the sounds have returned.

Racing Song No. 1 (First Day)
BLUE MULE
Solo Recording, 1963

heye neye yaya
The breeze coming from her as she runs,
The breeze coming from her as she runs,
The breeze coming from her as she runs is beautiful;

The breeze coming from her as she runs,
The breeze coming from her as she runs,
The breeze coming from her as she runs is beautiful.

Black Jewel Girl,
  the breeze coming from her as she runs is beautiful,
Her black jewel moccasins,
  the breeze coming from her as she runs is beautiful,
Her dark-seamed, black jewel moccasins,
  the breeze coming from her as she runs is beautiful,
Her black jewel shoestrings,
  the breeze coming from her as she runs is beautiful,
Her black jewel leggings,
  the breeze coming from her as she runs is beautiful,
Her black jewel garters,
  the breeze coming from her as she runs is beautiful,
Her black jewel skirt,
  the breeze coming from her as she runs is beautiful,
Her black jewel skirt sash,
  the breeze coming from her as she runs is beautiful,
Her black jewel clothes,
  the breeze coming from her as she runs is beautiful,
Her black jewel arm band,
  the breeze coming from her as she runs is beautiful,
Her black jewel bracelet,
  the breeze coming from her as she runs is beautiful,
Her black jewel collar,
  the breeze coming from her as she runs is beautiful,
A black jewel rock crystal, now she has put it on,
  the breeze coming from her as she runs is beautiful,
Her black jewel ear pendant, now she has put it on her forehead,
  the breeze coming from her as she runs is beautiful,
A perfect black jewel, now she has put it on her forehead,

the breeze coming from her as she runs is beautiful,
Her black jewel head plume, now she has put it on,
    the breeze coming from her as she runs is beautiful,

All kinds of horses lead up to her and go beyond,
    the breeze coming from her as she runs is beautiful,
All kinds of sheep lead up to her and go beyond,
    the breeze coming from her as she runs is beautiful,
All kinds of wild game lead up to her and go beyond,
    the breeze coming from her as she runs is beautiful,
All kinds of vegetation lead up to her and go beyond,
    the breeze coming from her as she runs is beautiful,

Comely servants lead up to her and go beyond,
    the breeze coming from her as she runs is beautiful,
All kinds of jewels lead up to her and go beyond,
    the breeze coming from her as she runs is beautiful,
All kinds of soft fabrics lead up to her and go beyond,
    the breeze coming from her as she runs is beautiful,
In long life, in everlasting beauty,
    the breeze coming from her as she runs is beautiful,
Being with her, it extends as far as the horizons,
    increasing without a blemish,
    the breeze coming from her as she runs is beautiful.

Before, behind, it is blessed,
    the breeze coming from her as she runs is beautiful.

    The breeze coming from her as she runs,
    The breeze coming from her as she runs,
    The breeze coming from her as she runs is beautiful.

Racing Song No. 1 (*Final Morning*)
BLUE MULE
Solo Recording, 1963

heye neye yaŋa
Her child, she starts off shouting, she starts off shouting,
Her child, she starts off shouting.

Child of the east, she starts off shouting,
White Shell Girl, she starts off shouting,
Her white shell moccasins, she starts off shouting,
Her dark-seamed, white shell moccasins, she starts off shouting,
Her white shell shoestrings, she starts off shouting,
Her white shell leggings, she starts off shouting,
Her white shell garters, she starts off shouting,
Her white shell skirt sash, she starts off shouting,

Her white shell skirt, she starts off shouting,
Her white shell skirt sash, she starts off shouting,
Her white shell clothes, she starts off shouting,
Her white shell arm band, she starts off shouting,
Her white shell collar, she starts off shouting,
Her white shell ear pendant, she starts off shouting,
A perfect white shell, now she has put it on her forehead,
                  she starts off shouting.

Child of the east, she starts off shouting,
Surrounded by Dawn People, she starts off shouting,
Mountains of soft fabrics encircling her, she starts off shouting,
All kinds of horses follow her in one direction as she runs,
                  she starts off shouting,
All kinds of sheep follow her in one direction as she runs,
                  she starts off shouting,
All kinds of vegetation follow her in one direction as she runs,
                  she starts off shouting,
Now comely servants follow her in one direction as she runs,
                  she starts off shouting,
All kinds of soft fabrics follow her in one direction as she runs,
                  she starts off shouting,
All kinds of jewels follow her in one direction as she runs,
                  she starts off shouting.

Now the sound of small dark-colored birds is being heard
                  before her,
                  she starts off shouting,
Now the sound of blue small birds is being heard behind her,
                  she starts off shouting,
The sound of Corn Beetle is being heard below her,
                  she starts off shouting,
Now the sound of small speckled yellow birds
                  is being heard above her,
                  she starts off shouting,
The sound of all kinds of small birds is being heard all around her,
                  she starts off shouting.

Before her, it is blessed,
                  she starts off shouting,
Behind her, it is blessed,
                  she starts off shouting,
Now the girl can endure much without tiring,
                  she starts off shouting.

        Her child, she starts off shouting,
                she starts off shouting,
        Her child, she starts off shouting.

Racing Song No. 2 (Final Morning)
BLUE MULE
Solo Recording, 1963

heye neye yaŋa
Her child, the sounds have faded into the distance,
    the sounds have faded into the distance,
Her child, the sounds have faded into the distance.

Child of the west, the sounds have faded into the distance,
Turquoise Girl, the sounds have faded into the distance,
Her turquoise moccasins, the sounds have faded into the distance,
Her dark-seamed, turquoise moccasins,
    the sounds have faded into the distance,
Her turquoise shoestrings, the sounds have faded into the distance,
Her turquoise leggings, the sounds have faded into the distance,
Her turquoise dark sash, the sounds have faded into the distance,
Her turquoise garters, the sounds have faded into the distance,
Her turquoise skirt, the sounds have faded into the distance,
Her turquoise skirt sash, the sounds have faded into the distance,
Her turquoise clothes, the sounds have faded into the distance,
Her turquoise arm band, the sounds have faded into the distance,
Her turquoise bracelet, the sounds have faded into the distance,
Her turquoise collar, the sounds have faded into the distance,
A perfect turquoise, now she has put it on her forehead,
    the sounds have faded into the distance,
Her turquoise head plume, the sounds have faded into the distance,

Child of the west, the sounds have faded into the distance,
Surrounded by Earth People,
    the sounds have faded into the distance,
Mountains of jewels encircling her,
    the sounds have faded into the distance,
All kinds of sheep follow her in one direction as she runs,
    the sounds have faded into the distance,
All kinds of horses follow her in one direction as she runs,
    the sounds have faded into the distance,
All kinds of vegetation follow her in one direction as she runs,
    the sounds have faded into the distance,
Now comely servants follow her in one direction as she runs,
    the sounds have faded into the distance,
All kinds of jewels follow her in one direction as she runs,
    the sounds have faded into the distance,
All kinds of soft fabrics follow her in one direction as she runs,
    the sounds have faded into the distance.

Now the sound of blue small birds is being heard behind her,
    the sounds have faded into the distance,

Now the sound of small dark-colored birds
        is being heard before her,
        the sounds have faded into the distance,
The sound of Corn Beetle is being heard below her,
        the sounds have faded into the distance,
Now the sound of small speckled yellow birds is being heard
        above her,
        the sounds have faded into the distance,
The sound of all kinds of small birds is being heard all around her,
        the sounds have faded into the distance.

Behind her, night has now passed on,
        the sounds have faded into the distance,
Before her, night has now passed on,
        the sounds have faded into the distance,
Behind her, it is blessed,
        the sounds have faded into the distance,
Before her, it is blessed,
        the sounds have faded into the distance,
Now the girl can endure much without tiring,
        the sounds have faded into the distance,

    Her child, the sounds have faded into the distance,
        the sounds have faded into the distance,
    Her child, the sounds have faded into the distance.

Racing Song No. 3 (Final Morning)
BLUE MULE
Solo Recording, 1963

    heye neye yana
    Her child, the sounds are returning
        the sounds are returning
    Her child, the sounds are returning.

Abalone Girl, the sounds are returning,
Child of the east, the sounds are returning,
Abalone Girl, the sounds are returning,
Her abalone moccasins, the sounds are returning,
Her abalone shoestrings, the sounds are returning,
Her abalone leggings, the sounds are returning,
Her abalone dark sash, the sounds are returning,
Her abalone garters, the sounds are returning,
Her abalone skirt, the sounds are returning,
Her abalone skirt sash, the sounds are returning,
Her abalone clothes, the sounds are returning,

Her abalone arm band, the sounds are returning,
Her abalone bracelet, the sounds are returning,
Her abalone ear pendant, the sounds are returning,
A perfect abalone, now she has put it on her forehead,
                the sounds are returning,
Her abalone head plume, the sounds are returning,

Child of the south, the sounds are returning,
Now surrounded by Blue Afterglow People,
                the sounds are returning,
Mountains of soft fabrics encircling her,
                the sounds are returning,

Now the sound of small dark-colored birds is being heard
                before her,
                the sounds are returning,
Now the sound of blue small birds is being heard behind her,
                the sounds are returning,
The sound of Corn Beetle is being heard below her,
                the sounds are returning,
Now the sound of small speckled yellow birds
                is being heard above her,
                the sounds are returning,
The sounds of all kinds of small birds is being heard
                all around her,
                the sounds are returning.

Before her, dawn is passing, the sounds are returning,
Behind her, dawn is passing, the sounds are returning,
Before her, it is blessed, the sounds are returning,
Behind her, it is blessed, the sounds are returning,
Now the girl can endure much without tiring,
                the sounds are returning.

        Her child, the sounds are returning,
                the sounds are returning,
        Her child, the sounds are returning.

        Racing Song No. 4 (Final Morning)
                BLUE MULE
            Solo Recording, 1963

    heye neye yana
    Her child, the sounds have returned,
                the sounds have returned,
    Her child, the sounds have returned;

Her child, the sounds have returned,
the sounds have returned,
Her child, the sounds have returned.

Black Jewel Girl, the sounds have returned,
Her black jewel moccasins, the sounds have returned,
Her dark-seamed, black jewel moccasins,
the sounds have returned,
Her black jewel shoestrings, the sounds have returned,
Her black jewel leggings, the sounds have returned,
Her black jewel skirt sash, the sounds have returned,
Her black jewel garters, the sounds have returned,
Her black jewel skirt, the sounds have returned,
Her black jewel skirt sash, the sounds have returned,
Her black jewel clothes, the sounds have returned,
Her black jewel arm band, the sounds have returned,
Her black jewel bracelet, the sounds have returned,
Her black jewel collar, the sounds have returned,
Her black jewel ear pendant, the sounds have returned,
A perfect black jewel, now she has put it on her forehead,
the sounds have returned,
Her black jewel head plume, the sounds have returned.

Child of the north, the sounds have returned,
Surrounded by Dipper People, the sounds have returned,
Mountains of jewels encircling her, the sounds have returned,
All kinds of sheep follow her in one direction as she runs,
the sounds have returned,
All kinds of horses follow her in one direction as she runs,
the sounds have returned,
All kinds of vegetation follow her in one direction as she runs,
the sounds have returned,
Now comely servants follow her in one direction as she runs,
the sounds have returned,
All kinds of jewels follow her in one direction as she runs,
the sounds have returned,
All kinds of soft fabrics follow her in one direction as she runs,
the sounds have returned,
With her, it spreads out, with her, it increases without a blemish,
the sounds have returned.

Now the sound of blue small birds is being heard behind her,
the sounds have returned,
Now the sound of small dark-colored birds
is being heard before her,
the sounds have returned,
The sound of Corn Beetle is being heard below her,

the sounds have returned,
Now the sound of small speckled yellow birds
is being heard above her,
the sounds have returned,
The sounds of all kinds of small birds
is being heard all around her,
the sounds have returned,
Now the girl can endure much without tiring,
the sounds have returned,
Behind her, night has now passed on,
the sounds have returned,
Before her, night has now passed on,
the sounds have returned,
Now a girl of long life and everlasting beauty,
the sounds have returned.

Behind her, it is blessed, the sounds have returned,
Before her, it is blessed, the sounds have returned,
Below her, it is blessed, the sounds have returned,
Above her, it is blessed, the sounds have returned,
All around her, everything is blessed, the sounds have returned,
Her speech is blessed, the sounds have returned.

Her child, the sounds have returned,
the sounds have returned,
Her child, the sounds have returned.

Racing Song No. 1
TŁ'AÁH
Solo Recording, 1929
(WHEELWRIGHT, Creation Chant MS, pp. 211–214)

My little one, she runs out
My little one, she runs out
My little one, she runs out
My little one, she runs out

The White Shell Girl, she runs out
Having shoes of white shell, she runs out
Having leggings of white shell, she runs out
Having a shirt of white shell, she runs out
Having a feather of white shell, she runs out
The sacred words, your girl, she runs out
Before her, all is beautiful, she runs out
Behind her, all is beautiful, she runs out

My little one, she runs out
My little one, she runs out
My little one, she runs out
My little one, she runs out

The Turquoise Girl, she runs out
Having shoes of turquoise, she runs out
Having leggings of turquoise, she runs out
Having a shirt of turquoise, she runs out
Having a feather of turquoise, she runs out
The sacred words, your girl, she runs out
Behind her, all is beautiful, she runs out
Before her, all is beautiful, she runs out

My little one, she runs out
My little one, she runs out
My little one, she runs out
My little one, she runs out

Racing Song No. 2
TŁ'AÁH
Solo Recording, 1929
(WHEELWRIGHT, Creation Chant MS, p. 214)

"This song has exactly the same words as the preceding except that the word 'she runs out' of the initial, medial, and final chorus and which appears at the end of each line is replaced by 'she runs back.' "

Racing Song No. 3
TŁ'AÁH
Solo Recording, 1929
(WHEELWRIGHT, Creation Chant MS, pp. 215–217)

My little one, they run out shouting, they run out shouting
My little one, they run out shouting
My little one, they run out shouting, they run out shouting
My little one, they run out shouting

The White Shell Girl, they run out shouting
From under the East, they run out shouting
Before her, the wind blows the trees, they run out shouting
Behind her, the wind blows the plants, they run out shouting
The white shell stands erect all about her, they run out shouting

The sacred words, your girl, they run out shouting
Before her, all is beautiful, they run out shouting
Behind her, all is beautiful, they run out shouting

My little one, they run out shouting, they run out shouting
My little one, they run out shouting
My little one, they run out shouting, they run out shouting
My little one, they run out shouting

The Turquoise Girl, they run out shouting
From under the West, they run out shouting
Behind her, the wind blows the plants, they run out shouting
Before her, the wind blows the trees, they run out shouting
The turquoise stands erect all around her, they run out shouting
The sacred words, your girl, they run out shouting
Behind her, all is beautiful, they run out shouting
Before her, all is beautiful, they run out shouting

My little one, they run out shouting, they run out shouting
My little one, they run out shouting
My little one, they run out shouting, they run out shouting
My little one, they run out shouting

Racing Song No. 4
TŁ'AÁH
Solo Recording, 1929
(WHEELWRIGHT, Creation Chant MS, p. 217)

"This song is exactly the same as the preceding except that the word 'They run out shouting' is replaced by 'they run back shouting.'"

Racing Song No. 1
FRANK MITCHELL
Ceremonial Recording, 1963

heye neye yaŋa   biya-zhaiyi-laŋa   tsidesą   aŋa   yeye

biyazhaiyi   la - tside-są   aŋa   yeye

11. yodi iltas ei ye bitani - gowo tsidesą aŋa yeye

12. to'o lanashchiniye bitani - gowo tsidesą aŋa yeye

13. ta-di - diniye bitani - gowo tsidesą aŋa yeye

14. yodi iltas eiye yeye yodi iltas ei ye

(Pitch rise begins here
moves tonic up a half-
step by verse 20.)

ka bidahas - leiyi - gowo tsidesą aŋa yeye

15. nitłiz iltas ei ye ka bidahas - leiyi - gowo tsidesą aŋa yeye

16. lį iltanas ei ye ka bidahas - leiyi - gowo tsidesą aŋa yeye

17. dibe iltas ei ye ka bidahas - leiyi - gowo tsidesą aŋa yeye

18. dinichi - iltaŋas ei ye ka bidahas - leiyigowo tsidesą aŋa yeye

19. yisna iltas ei ye ka bidahas - leiyigowo tsidesą aŋa yeye

20. bi - tsiji yolkałnegowo tsidesą aŋa yeye

Racing Song No. 1 (First Day)

BLUE MULE

Solo Recording, 1963

19. dinichị iłtaŋas ą a yai-yi-na bida hazlą ya-go-wi-na

biyaiye yo li yaiye ye nizhowo

20. na-ni-ce iltaŋ-as ą a yai-yi-na bida hazlą ya-go-wi-na

biyaiye yo li yaiye ye nizhowo

21. yisna nizho wo ne-yi-naŋa bida hazlą ya-go-wi-na

biyaiye yo li yaiye ye nizhowo

22. nitłiz iltas ą a yai yi naŋe bida hazlą ya-go-wi-na

biyaiye yo li yaiye ye nizhowo

23. yodi iltas ą a yai yi naŋe bida hazlą ya-go-wi-na

biyaiye yo li yaiye ye nizhowo

24. sa'a nagha - iŋa ą yeye bike hozhoni nili neeyi-go

biyaiye yo li yaiye ye nizhowo

25. bii'il k'e'ai yil zheiye yishgowo doni - dineshi nili nee yi -go

biyaiye yo li yaiye ye nizhowo

26. tsitsi keeshde hozhoni nili ne yi - go

biyaiye yo li yaiye ye nizhowo

biyaiye yo laiye biyaiye yolai

ritard. - - - - - - - - - - - - -

biyaiye yo lį yaiye ye niyowe

Racing Song No. 1 (Last Morning)
BLUE MULE
Solo Recording, 1963

heye neye yaŋa biyazhaiyi nane tsidi saŋa tsidi sá̧ aŋa yeye

biyazhaiyi   laŋa   tsidi-zą   aŋa   yeye

1. ha'i - 'ashi   yeye   biya. - zhaiyila   tsedi   są   aŋa   yeye

2. yolgaiye   et-'eyi   deya   tsedi   są   aŋa   ye

3. yolgaiye   bike   yi-go-wa   tsedi   są   aŋa   yeye

4. yolgaiyeye   bi-ke   banas-chiini-go   hedesą   aŋa   yeye

5. yolgai   yeye   bik'e tł'ol la-go   tsedisą   aŋa   yeye

6. yolgai   ye'aŋ   yolgai   bis tł'ehyi-go   tsedisą   aŋa   yeye

7. yolgai   yeye   bijaz   nezhi-go   tsedisą   aŋa   yeye

8. yolgai   yeye   bitsis   la-da-go   tsedisą   aŋa   yeye

9. yolgai   yeye   bikal   k'ali - go   tsedisą   aŋa   yeye

10. yolgai yeye bizis ląda - go   tsedisą   aŋa   yeye

11. yolgaiye bi'e   de-go   tsedisą   aŋa   yeye

12. yolgai yeye bigaz nezhi-go   tsedisą   aŋa   yeye

13. yolgai yeye biyał bą ya-go   tsedisą   aŋa   yeye

14. yolgai yeye bijah tł'oh la   go   tsedisą   aŋa   yeye

15. yolgai yeye hada-t'ehiye   ka bitaz - isą   nigo   tsedisą   aŋa yeye

16. ha'i 'ashiye   biyaŋ-a - de   tsedisą   aŋa   yeye

17. haiyolkal di-ne-ye   binazlai - yi - go   tsedisą   aŋa   yeye

18. haiyol-kali   ye   bitah   ha-go   tsedisą   aŋa   yeye

19. yoɖi dzili   ye   bi   na-gha-de   tsedisą   aŋa   yeye

20. łi'iltaŋas   ei   ye   ka bihi-nilai - yi - go   tsedisą   aŋa   yeye

21. dibe iltas ei ye ka bihi-nilai- yi - go tsedisạ ạna yeye

22. nanice 'iltaŋas ei ye ka biihi - nilai-yigo tsedisạ ạna yeye

23. ka yisna nizhoniye ka biihinilai - yigo tsedisạ ạna yeye

24. yeheyai yeye yodi iltas ei ye ka biihi - nilai - yi- go

tsedisạ ạna yeye

25. nitliz iltas ei ye ka biihi -nilai - yigo tsedi - sạ ạna yeye

26. heye heye ka'ayash diɫhiɫ- iye bitsi tistsol tsị la-go

tsedi - sạ ạna yeye

27. ka 'ayash dotɫi - ziye bikeshde tsoltsị la- go tsedisạ ạna yeye

28. enil - ta -ni-ye bi-yagi tsoltsị lago tsedisạ ạna yeye

29. ka'ayash chozh ghaliye bi-ki-gi tsoltsị lago tsedisạ ạna yeye

30. ayash iltas ei ye bi-na-de tsoltsį la-go tsedisą aŋa yeye

31. bitsi-jį hozho- ni - go tsedisą aŋa yeye

32. bikeshdę hozho - ni - go tsedisą aŋa yeye

33. ka dotsi diidashii ne - 'ete - yi-de tsedisą aŋa yeye

biya-zhaiyi laŋa tsedi - saŋa tsedisą́ aŋa yeye

ritard. - - - - - - - - -

biya - shiyi - la tsedi są aŋa ye

Racing Song—TŁ'AÁH—Herzog Transcription
Song from the First Puberty Ceremony
Navaho Emergence Myths
P.R. 140*

ai neiye yaŋa ciya je la - ŋa ei sol dzaza

ei sol dzaŋa ciya je laŋa ei sol dzaŋ xa - ŋa-ye-ye

---

*This is the transcription of the original cylinder No. 140, song No. 25a, of Mary Wheel-wright's Songs of the Creation Chants. The Navaho and English texts of this song are on pp. 215-17 of the MS on file at Wesleyan University.

Second Twelve Word Song

After the last Racing Song has been finished and the girl has returned to her ceremonial place, the singer calls for everyone to come into the hogan. Then the second Twelve Word Song (already discussed *supra*) is sung. After the corn pollen has been passed and people have prayed, the girl goes out to the pit where the *alkaan* has been cooking. The distribution of the corncake and a meal follow: the singing does not resume for several hours. When it does, it begins with another group of fixed songs, the Combing Songs.

The Combing Songs

Now she is dressing up her child,
Now she is dressing up her child.

Now the child of White Shell Woman, now she is dressing her up,
In the center of the White Shell house, now she is dressing her up,
Her white shell shoes, now she is dressing her up,
Her white shell leggings, now she is dressing her up,

She is decorated with soft fabrics, now she is dressing her up,
She is decorated with jewels, now she is dressing her up.

Before her, it is blessed,
Behind her, it is blessed,
Now with long life and everlasting beauty,
　　now she is dressing her up.

　　Now she is dressing up her child,
　　Now she is dressing up her child, it is said.

(From Song No. 1; FRANK MITCHELL;
Marie Shirley's Kinaaldá, 1963)

Although rarely mentioned in mythological accounts, references to the Combing Songs, *Kinaaldá Béé'ézhóó'ígíí bighiin*, were
often found in informants' reports of Kinaaldá proceedings. Some
just said there was singing while the girl's hair was brushed;
others were more specific, mentioning one Soft Good Song, two
Combing Songs, or four Songs for Fixing Up the Girl.

Origin and Function

According to Frank Mitchell and Slim Curly (Haile's informant for "Blessingway," Version I), the Combing Songs originated at the first Kinaaldá. The function of these songs seems to
be to relate the manner in which Changing Woman was attired at
the first puberty ceremony. Although they are called Combing
Songs by most informants and are sung during the combing rite,
their texts are only concerned with the dressing and the decorating of the girl.

Differences in Usage and Number

As mentioned earlier, the Combing Songs, like the Rac-
ing Songs, are used at different times in different regions. In
Lukachukai and Ramah, Combing Songs (called Songs for Fixing
Up the Girl in these places) are the first ones sung during a
Kinaaldá; they are used during the first day as the girl is cere-
monially prepared. Then, too, in these regions and in all others,
the songs are used during the combing rites of the last morning.
Informants gave numbers from one to ten when discussing the

total number of songs sung during the combing on the first day. On the last day, however, the use of four Combing Songs was consistently reported.

Source Material

Blue Mule sang four songs, from which he reportedly chooses two or three to sing during the first morning's rites, depending on the timing of the event. Of these four, three were Songs for Fixing Up the Girl; the fourth, although it should have been the same kind in order to complete the set (according to CS), was a Racing Song which has already been discussed. Totsoni Mark sang fragments of two from a group of ten which may be used for the first morning's combing. Thus five complete and/or partial songs for the first day's combing rite are available for study in addition to eight from the final-morning combing: two from Marie's Kinaaldá, two from Lena's, and four from Blue Mule's solo recordings. The two Combing Songs that Frank Mitchell sang for Marie's Kinaaldá and two of Blue Mule's Songs for Fixing Up the Girl (the first from both the first and last day) are included on pp. 300−311. Texts available for study include those above, two from Haile's "Blessingway," Version I, and one from Goddard's "Navaho Texts." The texts for the songs transcribed on pp. 300−311 are given on pp. 296−299.

Kinds of Combing Songs

A comparative study of the twelve available Combing Songs revealed that at least four different kinds exist. The two used by Frank are essentially one song; Blue Mule's three for the first day are likewise one song musically, as are the four he sang for the combing done on the final morning. Totsoni's two fragments represent the fourth song type.

Shared Characteristics

All the Combing Songs have eight characteristics in common. They extend over a total range of a seventh or an octave

and begin with the well-known ♫ ♫ ♫ formula.   Most use a
_{heye nene yana}
limited tonal system of five or six tones in which the first, third,
and fifth scale degrees are the most important. All emphasize the
third and fourth as the important skip intervals; most use only a
downward slide for ornamentation and quarter notes, eighths, and
sixteenths as note types.   Tempi range between M.M. $\flat$ = 160 and
176. The songs are structured as follows:

Introduction	x
Opening Chorus	a b a^1 b^1 a^2 b^2
Verse 1	c a^3 b^3
Verse 2	c^1 a^4 b^3
Verse 3	c^2 a^4 b^3
etc.	(verse numbers range from seventeen to twenty-six)
Final Chorus	a^5 b^{1+} a^6 b^2/1
Concluding Formula	x^1

They use all the formulas found in the Talking God Hogan Songs,
including the dotted, retarding final figure, ♩♩♩♩ .

Differences

Many differences exist, however, among the sets.   Each
of Blue Mule's first-day songs contains twenty-six verses.   Each
verse is divided into three musical segments, and as the song un-
folds, the first and second segments expand.   The second segment
manages to become a partial burden musically by always ending
with the

phrase. The third segment is a complete burden; surprisingly
enough, it is *flat* in contour.

As is true with all the Combing Songs, textually, these
first-day Combing Songs are not one song. After the first song,
the text of which is on pp. 298–299, Blue Mule sang a song with
the chorus of:

She is decorating her child,
She is decorating her child,
She is decorating her child,
Beauty, with beauty, she is decorating her.

The subsequent verses emphasize turquoise, rather than white shell, and order the progression differently than in the first song. The third song begins:

> She has decorated her child,
> She has decorated her child,
> She has decorated her child,
> Beauty, with beauty, she has decorated her.

The verses concentrate on abalone; the order is more similar to Song No. 1 than No. 2, but not exactly identical. The odd-even-numbered alternation of "horses," "sheep," "soft fabrics," "jewels," "before," and "behind" now becomes obvious. According to Chic Sandoval, after the third song there should have been a fourth one about jet. Furthermore, "Blue Mule should have sung eight songs: four songs in the present tense and then four in the past tense. All four shells should be mentioned with the same tense. You change to the past tense if the girl is finished before the song is."

Combing Songs Used on the Last Morning

Blue Mule

Blue Mule's songs for the last morning are four in number, which he designated as songs for Fixing Up the Girl. The songs are structurally similar to those of the first day. However, now the over-all range is a seventh, rather than an octave, and both the opening and final choruses cover the entire range. Verse numbers vary: twenty-three, nineteen, eighteen, and nineteen. The formulas change, except for the opening one. The beginning chorus is linked with the first verse by a *holaghei* in 50 per cent of the songs; the others use a melodically moving phrase:

ai   ye   golaneiye

The burden which is musically the same in all four songs, is no longer flat:

The final ending is in two versions; both use a retarding final slide, but one is contourally flat and the other is not. The vocable expression of the verb *ni* (it is said) is either *ei yeye holane* or *ai yeye olane* rather than the usual *golaghanane*.

Textually, these songs are obviously different from those of the first day. Blue Mule arranged his set so it progressed through the four sacred jewels mentioned above, alternating the same verses in odd-even-numbered songs. But, while so doing, he constantly varied the total number of ideas in his songs so that no two progressed in the same manner, even with alternation being taken into account. In Blue Mule's songs, the actions which are stressed are "gazing upon the decorated one," "thinking about her," and "being happy."

Frank Mitchell

Four of Frank's Combing Songs are available for study. Those from Lena's Kinaaldá are essentially the songs from Marie's ceremony, although the verse numbers vary. Furthermore, the two from Marie's Kinaaldá are essentially a single song; thus, musically anyway, it is possible to speak of one Combing Song in cases where Frank was the singer. This song is characterized by a total range of an octave and choruses that have ranges of sevenths, if not octaves. The tonal system is six-part. Formulas are partially comparable to those in the first-day songs of Blue Mule; Frank used the *holaghei* link and the terminating *golaghanane*. The latter was sung, however, to an undotted figure,

The second segment of these songs is a partial musical burden, and the third is a complete one, although it is not flat in contour as the third segments are in Blue Mule's first-day songs.

Textually, the songs recall those Blue Mule used for the first day. Frank's verbs in the two songs were the present and past tense of "she is decorating her with it."[95] Many of the verses were likewise similar. Blue Mule's first-day songs are longer than Frank's Combing Songs.

In Marie's Kinaaldá, Frank sang the Combing Songs so that the first song had seventeen verses and the second, ten. Upon listening to the tapes after the ceremony, however, he corrected the second song, giving it a total of seventeen verses in the manner shown on pp. 297. In Lena's Kinaaldá, he sang the same songs so that each contained twenty-three verses. The familiar procession of various kinds of wealth "leading up and going beyond" the girl are added after the girl has been prepared with "soft fabrics" or "jewels" and before everything becomes "blessed behind her" or "before her." As in the case of the first ceremony, the first and second Combing Songs in the second are textually similar, with jewel changes and the alternation order of soft fabrics and horses and sheep pairs being taken into consideration.

Reasons for Variability

There is enough proof in these songs to say that the Combing Songs are another set which may vary in text and thus in duration. The fact that once again the singing must be correlated with a rite has explained this variability up to now. Here, however, it seems that something else—something the author has yet to identify with absolute certainty—is also a controlling factor. In Lena's Kinaaldá, the combing rite proceeded in the same manner as Marie's and lasted the same amount of clock time. Still, the songs were longer in Lena's. Tempi may explain everything, since Lena's songs were at M.M. ♪ = 168, in contrast to Marie's, which were done at M.M. ♪ = 160. However, other explanations also seem possible. In Lena's ceremony, the break between the distribution of the cake and the combing rite was longer; therefore, when Frank

---

[95]It is interesting that Songs Nos. 3 and 4 of Set II of the three sets that follow FM's Chief Hogan Songs use the same verbs: "is decorating" and "has decorated." The word order in these songs, however, is such that the first-day songs of BM are closer to the songs of the dressing up of the chief than FM's Combing Songs are.

began the Combing Songs, he was much more rested. It is also possible that he made the songs longer to appease the people and, perhaps, the deities for the longer rest period which had occurred before the final rites. When questioned about the difference, Frank could or would not recognize it, insisting, as usual, that there was only one way of singing these songs.

Combing Song No. 1
FRANK MITCHELL
Marie Shirley's Kinaaldá, 1963

> *heye neye yaŋa*
> Now she is dressing up her child,
> Now she is dressing up her child,
> Now she is dressing up her child, *holaghei*.
> Now the child of White Shell Woman,
>   now she is dressing her up,
> In the center of the White Shell house,
>   now she is dressing her up,
> On the even white shell floor covering,
>   now she is dressing her up,
> On the smooth floor covering of soft fabrics,
>   now she is dressing her up,
> White Shell Girl, now she is dressing her up,
> Her white shell shoes, now she is dressing her up,
> Her white shell leggings, now she is dressing her up,
> Her white shell clothes, now she is dressing her up,
> Now, a perfect white shell having been placed on her forehead,
>   now she is dressing her up,
> Her white shell head plume, now she is dressing her up,
> Now at its tip there are small blue male birds, truly beautiful;
>   it is shining at its tip,
>   now she is dressing her up,
> They call as they are playing; their voices are beautiful;
>   now she is dressing her up,
> She is decorated with soft fabrics, now
>   now she is dressing her up,
> She is decorated with jewels,
>   now she is dressing her up.
>
> Before her, it is blessed; now she is dressing her up,
> Behind her, it is blessed; now she is dressing her up,

Now with long life and everlasting beauty,
  now she is dressing her up.

  Now she is dressing up her child,
  Now she is dressing up her child, it is said.

Combing Song No. 2
FRANK MITCHELL
Marie Shirley's Kinaaldá, 1963

heye neye yana
Now she has dressed up her child,
Now she has dressed up her child,
Now she has dressed up her child, *holaghei*.

Now the child of Changing Woman,
  now she has dressed her up,
In the center of the Turquoise house,
  now she has dressed her up,
On the even turquoise floor covering,
  now she has dressed her up,
On the smooth floor covering of jewels,
  now she has dressed her up,
Turquoise Girl, now she has dressed her up,
[Her turquoise shoes, now she has dressed her up,
Her turquoise leggings, now she has dressed her up,
Her turquoise clothes, now she has dressed her up,
Now a perfect turquoise having been placed on her forehead,
  now she has dressed her up
Her turquoise head plume, now she has dressed her up,
Now at its tip there are small blue female birds,
  truly beautiful;
  it is shining at its tip,
  now she has dressed her up,
They call as they are playing; their voices are beautiful,
  now she has dressed her up,]
She is decorated with jewels, now she has dressed her up,
She is decorated with soft fabrics, now she has dressed her up.

Behind her, it is blessed; now she has dressed her up,
Before her, it is blessed; now she has dressed her up,
Now the girl of long life and everlasting beauty,
  now she has dressed her up.

  Now she has dressed up her child,
  Now she has dressed up her child, it is said.

Combing Song No. 1 (First Day)
BLUE MULE
Solo Recording, 1963

heye neye yaŋa
Her child, she is decorating her, she is decorating her,
Her child, her child, she is decorating her, *holaghei*.

White Shell Girl, she is decorating her,
With her white shell moccasins, she is decorating her,
With her dark-seamed, white shell moccasins,
        she is decorating her,
With her white shell shoestrings, she is decorating her,
With her white shell leggings, she is decorating her,
With her white shell garters, she is decorating her,
With her white shell dark sash, she is decorating her,
With her white shell skirt, she is decorating her,
With her white shell skirt sash, she is decorating her,
With her white shell clothes, she is decorating her,
With her white shell arm band, she is decorating her,
With her white shell bracelet, she is decorating her
She has put a perfect white shell in place,
        she is decorating her with it,
With her white shell ear pendant, she is decorating her,
A perfect white shell, now she has put it on her forehead,
        she is decorating her with it,
With her white shell head plume, she is decorating her.

Now with all kinds of horses following her in a line,
        she is decorating her,
Now with all kinds of sheep following her in a line,
        she is decorating her,
Now with all kinds of vegetation following her in a line,
        she is decorating her,
Now with comely servants following her in a line,
        she is decorating her,
Now with all kinds of soft fabrics following her in a line,
        she is decorating her,
Now with all kinds of jewels following her in a line,
        she is decorating her,
With her, it spreads out, with her it increases without a blemish,
        she is decorating her,
Now the girl of long life and everlasting beauty,
        she is decorating her with these things.

Before her, it is blessed; now she is decorating her,
Behind her, it is blessed; now she is decorating her

Her child, she is decorating her, she is decorating her,
Her child, she is decorating her, she is decorating her,
Her child, her child, she is decorating her, it is said.

Combing Song No. 1 (Last Morning)
BLUE MULE
Solo Recording, 1963

heye neye yaŋa
These things gaze on me
These things gaze on me,
These things gaze on me, it is said.

White Shell Girl, they gaze on her,
Her white shell moccasins, they gaze on her,
Her dark-seamed, white shell moccasins, they gaze on her,
Her white shell shoestrings, they gaze on her,
Her white shell leggings, they gaze on her,
Her white shell garters, they gaze on her,
Her white shell skirt, it gazes on her,
Her white shell skirt sash, it gazes on her,
Her white shell clothes, they gaze on her,
Her white shell arm band, it gazes on her,
Her white shell bracelet, it gazes on her,
Her white shell ear pendant, it gazes on her,
Her white shell head plume, it gazes on her.

With all kinds of horses following her in a line, they gaze on her,
With all kinds of sheep following her in a line, they gaze on her,
With all kinds of vegetation following her in a line,
        they gaze on her,
Now with comely servants following her in a line,
        they gaze on her,
With all kinds of soft fabrics following her in a line,
        they gaze on her,
With all kinds of jewels following her in a line,
        they gaze on her,
With her, it spreads out; with her, it increases without a blemish,
        it gazes on her,
Now the girl of long life and everlasting beauty,
        they gaze on her.

Before her, it is beautiful; they gaze on her,
Behind her, it is beautiful; they gaze on her.

These things gaze on her,
These things gaze on her, it is said.

Combing Song No. 1
FRANK MITCHELL
Ceremonial Recording, 1963

heye neye yaŋa beya zheiyi laŋa ka hashdeeyi leyi she

biya neyi laŋa ka hashdeeyi leyi she biya - zhiyiye laŋa

ka hashdeeye leeye holaghei

1. neye kaiyolkai esdzane biya-zheyi-la ka hashdeeye leeye sheye

2. yolagaiye yeba-ghani ya'ał-ni-ye-she ka hasheye leeye sheye

3. yolgaiye behos-te-li tsi-ba-ka'ahgi ka hasheye leeye sheye

4. yodi behos-te-li tsi-bakahgi ka hasheye leeye sheye

5. yolgaiye et-'e-de ka hasheye leeye sheye

6. yolgaiye bike-go ka hasheye leeye sheye

7. yolgaiye bistlee-go ka hasheye leeye sheye

bikeshde hozho-ni-go ka hasheye leeye sheye

ka sa'a naghei ka bike hozho beye deyi - laŋa

ka hasheye leeye sheye

bi - yazhi yila ka hasheye leeye sheye bi - ya-zhi yila

laŋa ka hashdee yi-le gola - ghana ne

Combing Song No. 2
FRANK MITCHELL
Ceremonial Recording, 1963

heye neye yaŋa ka hashdeyi laŋa ka hashdeyi laŋa yeye

biya - zhiyi laŋa ka hashdeyi laŋa ye beye neyil yeye neye

ka hashdeyi laŋa holaghei

neye ka esdzanadleeshe biyazhai yila ka hashdeyi laŋa yeye

2. dotłi - ziyi ye baghani ya'ał -ni-i -ye ka hashdeyi laŋa yeye

3. dotłi - ziyi behos-te - li tsiba - kah - gi ka hashdeyi laŋa yeye

4. nitłiz behas-te-li tsiba - ka-ŋa-gi ka hashdeyi laŋa yeye

5. dotłi - zi 'et- 'e-yi-de ka hashdeyi laŋa yeye

6. nitłiz be - dol -yą-go ka hashdeyi laŋa yeye

7. yodi be - dol-yą-go ka hashdeyi laŋa yeye

8. bi-keshde ho-zho - go ka hashdeyi laŋa yeye

9. bit - si-ji ho-zho - go ka hashdeyi laŋa yeye

10. ka sa'a nagheiye ka bıke hozho ne'e te-yı-na

ka hashdeyi laŋa yeye

biyazhi yila   ka hashdeyi laŋa ye   biyazhai yila

ritard.

kaŋa   ha'ashdeyi - lą   gola - ghana ne

Song for Fixing Up the Girl on the First Day, No. 1
BLUE MULE
Solo Recording, 1963

heye neye yaŋa biyo   hazhai-ye   beye hajidi - la-i - esheye

beye ha-ji-di -laiye biyaa-zhi biyaa-zhi-i - yeye

ye beye ha-ji-di-laiye   holaghei

1. neye yołgaiye et 'eeyi - deya   beye ha-ji-di-laiye   sheye

2. yołgaiye bik'ee - yi go-o   beye ha-ji-di - laiye sheye

3. yołgai yeye bik'eh banashchinai- yi go-o

beye ha-ji-di - laiye sheye

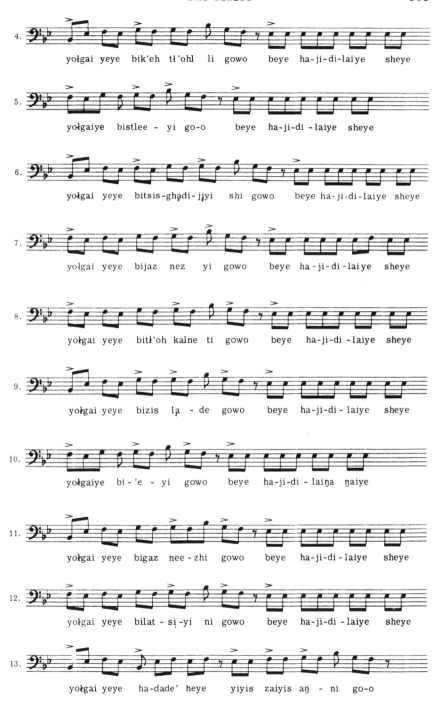

20. ka yisna nizhoniye ka bi-da-hazłaŋa yi gowo

beye ha-ji-di - laiye sheye

21. yo-di iltas ei - ye ka bi-da-hazłaŋa yi gowo

beye ha-ji - dilai sheye

22. nitłiz iltas ei - ye ka bi-da-hazłaŋa yi gowo

beye ha-ji-di - laiye sheye

23. diiyił k'e'ana diłjisgo bił doneh - dine - shi gowo

beye ha-ji-di - laiye sheye

24. k'a sa'a naghei ka bik'e hozhoni ne'et'ee - yi deye

beye ha-ji-di - laiye sheye

25. bi-tsi-jį̀ ho-zhǫ - ni gowo beye ha-ji-di -laiye sheye

26. bikeshde ho - zhǫ - ni go-o beye ha-ji-di laiŋe sheye

biyo wo-zhai-ye beye ha-ji-di - lai - yi sheye

beye ha-ji-di - laiye sheye

bi-yo wozhaiye beye ha-ji-di - la-i-yi sheye

beye ha-ji-di - laiye bi-ya-zhi bi-ya-zhi-i yeye

ritard. ----------

ye beye ha-ji-di - lai -- golag-haŋa ne

Song for Fixing Up the Girl on the Last Morning, No. 1
BLUE MULE
Solo Recording, 1963

heye neye yaŋa nei -lą 'aghei yeye la

beshi - kini geye sheye nei - la 'aghei yeye la

19. nitłiz iltas ei ye bebi-dahazlą aiyigo bebi-keni geya sheye

20. ka sa'a na biyił ke 'a'na diljisgo bił donidi - ne - deshigo

bebi-keni geya sheye

21. ka sa'a nagheiye ka bike hozho ne'et 'e yeyode

bebi - keni geya sheye

22. bitsijį hozho wolago bebi - keni geya sheye

23. bikeshde hozho wolago bebi - keni geya sheye

nila 'aghei yeye la bebi - keni geya sheye

ni lą ghei yeyila bebi - keni ge shi wowo

ei yeye hola ne

The Painting Songs[96]

> The red ocher of old age,
>> with the red ocher she nears you,
> The red ocher of old age,
>> with the red ocher she nears you.

Now the child of Changing Woman,
> with the red ocher she nears you.
In the center of the Turquoise house,
> with the red ocher she nears you,
Her turquoise clothes, with the red ocher she nears you,
The red ocher of Mountain Woman,
> with the red ocher she nears you,
Behind her it is blessed,
> with the red ocher she nears you,
Before her, it is blessed,
> with the red ocher she nears you,
Now the child of long life and everlasting beauty,
> with the red ocher she nears you,

> The red ocher of old age,
>> with the red ocher she nears you,
> The red ocher of old age,
>> with the red ocher she nears you, it is said.

(From The *Chííh* Song, FRANK MITCHELL, Solo Recording, 1963)

One other rite often occurs when the combing has been completed: the rite of painting the girl. As mentioned in Chapter II, there is regional variation in the material used in the painting as well as in the manner in which the painting is done.

Singing accompanies this rite, according to Frank Mitchell, Blue Mule, and other informants. The song or songs used correspond with the material being used; they are called either White Clay Songs (*Dleesh bighiin*) or Red Ocher Songs (*Chííh bighiin*).

Origin

Only one mythological account mentions songs in the original Kinaaldá painting rite. That account, from Wheelwright's

---

[96]The term "The Painting Songs" is the author's and is used purely for convenience. The Navaho speak of either White Clay or Red Ocher Songs.

Navajo Creation Myth, follows: "They told the Earth Spirit about this ceremony and he sent the white and red paint with which they painted her cheeks red, and they painted two small white stripes on each cheek. They sang of painting the maiden *Zhansheya-yanez-nuchee.*"[97]

Source Material

There are nine taped Painting Songs that are available for musical comparison: from Frank Mitchell, three versions of a single *Dleesh* Song and one *Chííh* Song; from Blue Mule, one *Chííh,* two *Dleesh* and *Chííh,* and two "neither *Dleesh* nor *Chííh*" Songs. On pp. 328—343 can be found one *Dleesh* and one *Chííh* Song by Frank Mitchell and one example each of Blue Mule's *Chííh, Dleesh* and *Chííh,* and "neither *Dleesh* nor *Chííh*" Songs. Textually, fourteen songs are available; in addition to those above, the Wheelwright Creation Chant manuscript includes one song for "white clay," one for "old clay," and one for "red ocher." A single text for a *Chííh* and a *Dleesh* song can also be found in Haile's "Blessingway," Version I. Texts for the songs given on pp. 328—343 appear on pp. 319—327, along with the two other versions of Frank's *Dleesh* Song and the three Wheelwright Painting Songs.

Function

Of the fourteen available Painting Song texts, only six are clear-cut in function. Tł'aáh's three and three of Blue Mule's five describe the painting of the girl. Frank Mitchell's four concentrate on the girl who "moves" with "white clay" or "red ocher," and those of Slim Curly (Haile, "Blessingway," Version I) discuss the "preparing" of the child of Changing Woman and White Shell Woman in both the present and past tenses. The remaining two of Blue Mule mention neither *dleesh* nor *chííh.*

---

[97]Wheelwright, *Navajo Creation Myth,* p. 76.

Number of Songs Used with Each Substance

According to Frank, people decide which substance, *dleesh* or *chííh*, is to be used in the painting. In 1961, he said he had two songs for the application of white clay, the songs being called *Kinaaldá beidleesh.*[98] On June 14, 1963, he gave the same information when describing Kinaaldá procedures. A few days later, however, he said, "If they use that red stuff, they sing two songs. They only sing one for *dleesh.*" In each Kinaaldá that Frank sang that summer, he used *dleesh* and only one *Dleesh* Song.[99] When he was asked to record the two *Chííh* Songs he had mentioned, he said that there was only one song for *dleesh* and one for *chííh*. A solo version of each was recorded.

When asked how many songs were used for painting, Blue Mule said, "The White Clay Song comes first; then the Red Ocher one; you anoint the girl with white clay first, and then red ocher. The words repeat, as they did in the first-day songs I sang for you. There are two of these songs. Red Ocher is used just for the face. You put it on in dabs on the girl's cheeks. Then white clay is put on." After this remark, he proceeded to sing five songs; the first mentioned neither substance; the second, *chííh*, the third, both *dleesh* and *chííh*; the fourth, neither; and the fifth, both. The songs of Slim Curly were given in sequence; the *chííh* song was followed by the *dleesh* one.

Similarities between Dleesh and Chííh Songs

Although the evidence is not conclusive, the material now available suggests that *Dleesh* and *Chííh* Songs are musically similar. Frank's songs show that *Dleesh* and *Chííh* Songs are similar, at least when sung by one singer. A comparison of different singers performing the same kind of song can be done only with Frank's and Blue Mule's *Chííh* Songs at present. Here definite similarities are found. Perhaps the *Dleesh* Songs of these two

---

[98]McAllester, Field Notes, July 19–20, 1961, p. 6b.
[99]Wyman and Bailey (p. 10) report a single *Dleesh bighiin.*

singers would likewise be comparable. For the present, anyway, the songs will be treated as a group.

Musical Characteristics

These Painting Songs have several important musical characteristics. While Frank's solo versions had a limited tonal system, both his ceremonial ones and Blue Mule's solo versions were based on systems of six to eight tones. As such, they have some of the widest systems to be found in the entire ceremony.

In the Painting Songs, there is more than the usual amount of emphasis on the I, III, V triad degrees. And yet, with it all, musical variations abound. No single tempo could be established for these songs. Blue Mule sang his at M.M. $\flat$ = 176 – 184[100] but Frank Mitchell, in both ceremonial and solo recordings, sang his much slower (M.M. $\flat$ = 152 – 168) with the emphasis on $\flat$ = 152 in Marie's ceremony and on $\flat$ = 160 in Lena's. The inner verse segments were always changing, and thus the contour charts contain more than the usual number of melodic-line diagrams. One cannot help being amazed at all the variations possible, even when there is a basic involvement of only three tones.

Unifying Elements

In spite of all this internal change, however, the songs are well unified. All use the opening *heye neye yaya*, chorus link *holaghei*, and the concluding *golaghanane*

formulas seen in other Kinaaldá songs. The Painting Songs are constructed with a limited number of basic phrase ideas. The opening choruses state all but one or two of these, and the verses build on them through constant variation. These verses contain three segments. The first one varies constantly, with the text controlling its over-all length. The speech tones seem to have no

---

[100]Note that BM's fastest tempo in singing the Painting Songs is equivalent to the speed of the fastest Racing Songs, the fastest songs in Kinaaldá.

effect on the melodic lines, which strongly emphasize the triad. The second segment is a partial burden musically; it always contains the figure

Blue Mule, Variant

in which the slide is done on a *gi* or *go*. The third segment is a musical and textual burden:

Blue Mule, Variant

ye'i   yine   dleeyi   sheye   yehasteyi   leye   sheye

Similarities between Painting and Combing Songs

Interestingly enough, the structural diagram[101] of the available Painting Songs is quite similar to that of the Combing Songs. (*supra*, p. 292).

Introduction	x
Opening Chorus	a b a^1 b^1 a^2 c
Verse 1	d d^1 a^2 b^2
Verse 2	d^2 a^3 b^2
Verse 3	d^2 a^3 b
Verse 4	d^3 a^3 b
etc.	Verse numbers range from fifteen to twenty-seven
Final Chorus	a^1 b c/ c/1
Concluding Formula	x^1

Further comparisons of these songs show that they share many melodic ideas as well as structural and developmental ones. Finding a significant number of common elements suggests the possibility that the Painting and Combing Songs belong to one musical cycle. It is possible that musical ideas can be shared by a number of songs, even though the texts cause the songs to be classified in separate categories.

The combing and painting rites have certain features in common which seem to provide at least partial explanations for the musical similarities in the accompanying songs. Both rites

---

[101]The diagrams of the *texts* (no music available) of Tł'aáh's songs contrast with this diagram.

are final-morning ones in which the girl receives physical attention from another person. And in both the object is to make the
girl beautiful and physically "one" with the deities portrayed in the
songs. For the Navaho, there seems to be a definite correlation
between physical and spiritual beauty.

Texts

The variation which is so evident in the internal development of the verses is even more obvious in the texts of the *Dleesh*
and *Chííh* Songs. A study of the texts obtained from Frank Mitchell, Blue Mule, Slim Curly, and Tł'aáh reveals that textually
there is no single *Dleesh* or *Chííh* Song. While all four singers
used similar deities in their songs and alternated similar pairs,
they projected the idea of the actual painting in four different ways.
Frank's songs were concerned with the attiring and protective encircling of the girl who, with either white clay or red ocher, "progresses near you." Blue Mule's fluctuated between the present
and past tense of the verb "to prepare." Progressing through four
of the sacred jewels, his songs emphasized a lengthier, more specific toe-to-head preparation of the girl. If there was any mention
at all of the substance with which the painting is done, it occurred
in only one or two verses. It is possible that Blue Mule mentioned
both white clay and red ocher in correspondence with the painting
procedures in the Lukachukai area. Slim Curly's texts used the
same verb as Blue Mule's, but did not go through a progression in
which the girl is attired. The texts of Tł'aáh's songs constantly
referred to the act of painting, mentioning the substance used in
the burden of each song. At least in the English version of these
songs, the painting itself is not a delicate operation; here, people
identified only as "they" *smear* the girl with white clay, old clay,
and finally red clay. Tł'aáh's Painting Songs differ from Frank
Mitchell's, Slim Curly's, and Blue Mule's in structure, too; they
consist of an opening chorus, verses, middle chorus, verses, and
a final chorus.

Verse Numbers

The available Painting Songs suggest that there is no set number of verses in either White Clay or Red Ocher Songs.

Chart 6 Substance	Frank Mitchell (MS's Kinaaldá) No. of verses	Frank Mitchell (LS's Kinaaldá) No. of verses	Frank Mitchell (Solo Recording) No. of verses	Blue Mule (Solo Recording) No. of verses	Tł'aáh (Solo Recording) No. of verses	Slim Curly (Solo Recording) No. of verses
Dleesh	15	27	18		14	15
Chííh			14	21	18	16
Old Clay					14	
Dleesh and *Chííh*				20 21		
Neither *Dleesh* nor *Chííh* but grouped with these songs				20 18		

Frank's *Dleesh* Songs beautifully exemplify the element of individual freedom and creativity which characterizes so much Navaho singing. Each of the three performances is textually different, despite Frank's continual insistence that there is only one *Dleesh* Song and only one way to sing it. As mentioned earlier, the texts of all three of these performances are on pp. 319–322.

Timing

The Painting Songs accompany a rite and in a sense are timed to correspond with it. In this instance, however, the timing is not so exact or strict as before. The woman painting the girl is instructed in the procedures before the song starts. Once the singing begins, she paints the girl at her own rate of speed; in no cases witnessed so far was it necessary for her to co-ordinate her actions with the songs which describe the painting progression. Hence, the lengthening or shortening of the *Dleesh* Song does not seem to be directly related to timing procedures. The circumstances of the night, the amount of rest the singer has had, and the amount of drinking which has been done, among others suggested in the discussion of the Combing Songs, are possible controlling factors.

Dleesh Song
FRANK MITCHELL
Lena Shirley's Kinaaldá, 1963

heye neye yaŋa
The white clay of old age,
    with the white clay she nears you,
The white of old age,
    with the white clay she nears you,
The white clay of old age,
    with the white clay she nears you, *holaghei.*

Now the child of White Shell Woman,
    with the white clay she nears you,
In the center of the White Shell house,
    with the white clay she nears you,
On the even white shell floor covering,
    with the white clay she nears you,
On the smooth floor covering of soft fabrics,
    with the white clay she nears you,
White Shell Girl, with the white clay she nears you,
Her white shell shoes,
    with the white clay she nears you,
Her white shell leggings,
    with the white clay she nears you,
Her white shell clothes,
    with the white clay she nears you,
Now a perfect white shell having been placed on her forehead,
    with the white clay she nears you,
Her white shell head plume,
    with the white clay she nears you,
Now at its tip there are (fabrics) small blue male birds,
        truly beautiful;
        it is shining at its tip,
    with the white clay she nears you,
They call as they are playing; their voices are beautiful,
    with the white clay she nears you,
The white clay of the earth,
    with the white clay she nears you,

Dressed in soft fabrics,
>with the white clay she nears you,
Dressed in jewels, with the white clay she nears you,

All kinds of soft fabrics lead up to her and go beyond,
>with the white clay she nears you,
All kinds of jewels lead up to her and go beyond,
>with the white clay she nears you,
All kinds of horses lead up to her and go beyond,
>with the white clay she nears you,
All kinds of sheep lead up to her and go beyond,
>with the white clay she nears you,
All kinds of wild game lead up to her and go beyond,
>with the white clay she nears you,
All kinds of servants lead up to her and go beyond,
>with the white clay she nears you.

Before her, it is blessed,
>with the white clay she nears you,
Behind her, it is blessed,
>with the white clay she nears you,
Below her, it is blessed,
>with the white clay she nears you,
Above her, it is blessed,
>with the white clay she nears you,
All around her, everything is blessed,
>with the white clay she nears you,
Now the child of long life and everlasting beauty,
>with the white clay she nears you.

>(Her child, with the white clay she nears you,
>Her child, with the white clay she nears you,
>>it is said.)

>With the white clay of old age,
>With the white clay she nears you,
>With the white clay of old age,
>With the white clay she nears you, it is said.

Dleesh Song

FRANK MITCHELL

Marie Shirley's Kinaaldá, 1963

heye neye yaŋa
The white clay of old age,
>with the white clay she nears you,
The white clay of old age,

with the white clay she nears you,
The white clay of old age,
with the white clay she nears you, *holaghei*.

Now the child of Changing Woman,
with the white clay she nears you,
In the center of the white shell house,
with the white clay she nears you,
On the even white shell floor covering,
with the white clay she nears you,
The white clay of the earth,
with the white clay she nears you,
Dressed in soft fabrics,
with the white clay she nears you,
Dressed in jewels,
with the white clay she nears you.

All kinds of soft fabrics lead up to her and go beyond,
with the white clay she nears you,
All kinds of jewels lead up to her and go beyond,
with the white clay she nears you,
All kinds of horses lead up to her and go beyond,
with the white clay she nears you,
All kinds of sheep lead up to her and go beyond,
with the white clay she nears you,
All kinds of wild game lead up to her and go beyond,
with the white clay she nears you,
All kinds of servants lead up to her and go beyond,
with the white clay she nears you.

Before her, it is blessed,
with the white clay she nears you,
Behind her, it is blessed,
with the white clay she nears you,
Now the child of long life and everlasting beauty,
with the white clay she nears you.

The white clay of old age,
with the white clay she nears you,
She has become its child, it is said.

Dleesh Song
FRANK MITCHELL
Solo Recording, 1963

heye neye yaŋa
The white clay of old age,

         with the white clay she nears you,
    The white clay of old age,
         with the white clay she nears you,
    The white clay of old age,
         with the white clay she nears you, *holaghei*.

Now White Shell Woman,
         with the white clay she nears you,
In the center of the White shell house,
         with the white clay she nears you,
On the even white shell floor covering,
         with the white clay she nears you,
On the smooth covering of soft fabrics,
         with the white clay she nears you,
White Shell Girl, with the white clay she nears you,
Her white shell shoes,
         with the white clay she nears you,
Her white shell leggings,
         with the white clay she nears you,
Her white shell clothes,
         with the white clay she nears you,
Now a perfect white shell having been placed on her forehead,
         with the white clay she nears you,
Her white shell head plume,
         with the white clay she nears you,
Now at its tip there are small blue male birds, truly beautiful;
         it is shining at its tip,
         with the white clay she nears you,
They call as they are playing; their voices are beautiful,
         with the white clay she nears you,
The white clay of the earth,
         with the white clay she nears you,
Dressed in soft fabrics,
         with the white clay she nears you,
Before her, it is blessed,
         with the white clay she nears you,
Behind her, it is blessed,
         with the white clay she nears you,
Now the child of long life and everlasting beauty,
         with the white clay she nears you.

    The white clay of old age,
         with the white clay she nears you,
    The white clay of old age,
         with the white clay she nears you, it is said.

Chííh Song

FRANK MITCHELL

Solo Recording, 1963

heye neye yaŋa
The red ocher of old age,
    with the red ocher she nears you,
The red ocher of old age,
    with the red ocher she nears you,
The red ocher of old age,
    with the red ocher she nears you, *holaghei*.

Now the child of Changing Woman,
    with the red ocher she nears you,
In the center of the turquoise house,
    with the red ocher she nears you,
On the even turquoise floor covering,
    with the red ocher she nears you,
On the smooth floor covering of jewels,
    with the red ocher she nears you,
Turquoise girl, with the red ocher she nears you,
Her turquoise shoes, with the red ocher she nears you,
Her turquoise leggings, with the red ocher she nears you
Her turquoise clothes, with the red ocher she nears you,
Now a perfect turquoise having been placed on her forehead,
    with the red ocher she nears you,
Her turquoise head plume,
    with the red ocher she nears you,
Now at its tip there are small blue female birds, truly beautiful;
    it is shining at its tip,
    with the red ocher she nears you,
They call as they are playing; their voices are beautiful,
    with the red ocher she nears you,
[The red ocher of Mountain Woman,
    with the red ocher she nears you,]
Dressed in jewels, with the red ocher she nears you,
Dressed in soft fabrics,
    with the red ocher she nears you.

Before her, it is blessed,
    with the red ocher she nears you,
Behind her, it is blessed,
    with the red ocher she nears you,
Now the child of long life and everlasting beauty,
    with the red ocher she nears you.

The red ocher of old age,
        with the red ocher she nears you,
The red ocher of old age,
        with the red ocher she nears you, it is said.

Chííh Song
BLUE MULE
Solo Recording, 1963

heye neye yaŋa
She has prepared her child,
She has prepared her child,
She has prepared her child, *holaghei*.

Turquoise Girl, she has prepared her,
With her turquoise shoestrings, she has prepared her,
With her dark seamed, turquoise moccasins, she has prepared her,
With her turquoise shoestrings, she has prepared her,
With her turquoise leggings, she has prepared her,
With her turquoise garters, she has prepared her,
With her turquoise skirt, she has prepared her,
With her turquoise skirt sash, she has prepared her,
With her turquoise clothes, she has prepared her,
With her turquoise bracelet, she has prepared her,
With her turquoise collar, she has prepared her,
Now the pollen of all kinds of jewels has been placed in her
        mouth for her speech,
        with it she has prepared her,
With her turquoise ear pendant,
        she has prepared her,
With her turquoise head plume, she has prepared her.

Changing Woman, she has prepared her,
With all kinds of jewels following her in one direction,
        she has prepared her,
With all kinds of soft fabrics following her in one direction,
        she has prepared her,
With the face of the red ocher of old age,
        she has prepared her,
Now the girl of long life and everlasting beauty,
        with these things she has prepared her,
All kinds of soft fabrics, all kinds of jewels,
        with her, spread out; with her, increase
                without a blemish;
        with these things, she has prepared her.

Behind her, it is blessed,
　　with these these things she has prepared her,
Before her, it is blessed,
　　with these things she has prepared her.

　　She has prepared her child,
　　She has prepared her child, it is said.

"Both Dleesh and Chííh" Song
BLUE MULE
Solo Recording, 1963

　　heye neye yaŋa
　　Now she has prepared her child,
　　Now she has prepared her child,
　　Now she has prepared her child, *holaghei*.

Turquoise Girl, now she has prepared her,
With her turquoise moccasins, now she has prepared her,
With her dark-seamed, turquoise moccasins,
　　　　now she has prepared her,
With her turquoise shoestrings, now she has prepared her,
With her turquoise leggings, now she has prepared her,
With her turquoise garters, now she has prepared her,
With her turquoise skirt, now she has prepared her,
With her turquoise skirt sash, now she has prepared her,
With her turquoise clothes, now she has prepared her,
With her turquoise arm bands, now she has prepared her,
With her turquoise bracelet, now she has prepared her,
With her turquoise collar, now she has prepared her,
With her turquoise ear pendant, now she has prepared her,
With her turquoise head plume, now she has prepared her.

Now with the white clay of old age, now she has prepared her,
Now with the red ocher of old age, now she has prepared her,

With all kinds of soft fabrics now following her in one direction,
　　　　now she has prepared her,
With all kinds of jewels now following her in one direction,
　　　　now she has prepared her.

(Before her) Behind her, it is blessed,
　　with these things, now she has prepared her,
Before her, it is blessed,
　　with these things, now she has prepared her.

　　Now she has prepared her child,
　　Now she has prepared her child, it is said.

"Neither Dleesh nor Chííh" Song
BLUE MULE
Solo Recording, 1963

heye neye yaŋa
She is preparing her child
She is preparing her child,
She is preparing her child, *holaghei*.

White Shell Girl, she is preparing her,
With her white shell moccasins, she is preparing her,
With her dark-seamed, white shell moccasins,
           she is preparing her,
With her white shell shoestrings, she is preparing her,
With her white shell leggings, she is preparing her,
With her white shell garters, she is preparing her,
With her white shell skirt, she is preparing her,
With her white shell skirt sash, she is preparing her,
With her white shell clothes, she is preparing her,
With her white shell arm band, she is preparing her,
With her white shell bracelet, she is preparing her,
Now the pollen of all kinds of soft fabrics has been placed in
           her mouth for her speech,
           with it she is preparing her,
With her white shell ear pendant, she is preparing her,
Now a perfect white shell having been placed on her forehead,
           with it she is preparing her,
With her white shell head plume, she is preparing her,

Now with all kinds of soft fabrics following her in one direction,
           she is preparing her,
Now with all kinds of jewels following her in one direction,
           she is preparing her,
Now the girl of long life and everlasting beauty,
           with these things she is preparing her.

Before her, it is blessed,
           with these things she is preparing her,
Behind her, it is blessed,
           with these things she is preparing her.

         She is preparing her child,
         She is preparing her child, it is said.

Painting Song No. 1

TŁ'AÁH

Solo Recording, 1929

(WHEELWRIGHT, Creation Chant MS, pp. 218–220)

They have smeared her with white clay,
They have smeared her with white clay,
They have smeared her with white clay,
They have smeared her with white clay,
They have smeared her with white clay.

The Changing Woman, they have smeared her with white clay;
The earth spirit, they have smeared her with white clay;
All sorts of soft goods have been laid down,
    they have smeared her with them,
All sorts of hard goods have been laid down,
    they have smeared her with them,
The sacred words: they have smeared her with white clay;
All being beautiful before her,
    they have smeared her with it,
All being beautiful behind her,
    they have smeared her with it,

They have smeared her with white clay,
They have smeared her with white clay,
They have smeared her with white clay.

The White Shell Woman, they have smeared her with white clay,
The mountain spirit, they have smeared her with white clay;
All sorts of hard goods have been laid down,
    they have smeared her with them,
All sorts of soft goods have been laid down,
    they have smeared her with them,
The sacred words: they have smeared her with white clay;
All being beautiful behind her,
    they have smeared her with it,
All being beautiful before her,
    they have smeared her with it,

They have smeared her with white clay,
They have smeared her with white clay,
They have smeared her with white clay,
They have smeared her with white clay,
They have smeared her with white clay,
They have smeared her with white clay.

Painting Song No. 2

TŁ'AÁH

Solo Recording, 1929

(WHEELWRIGHT, Creation Chant MS, pp. 220–221)

"This song is the same as the preceding except that the line 'they have smeared her with white clay' is replaced by "they have smeared her with old clay."

Painting Song No. 3

TŁ'AÁH

Solo Recording, 1929

(WHEELWRIGHT, Creation Chant MS, p. 221)

"This song is the same as...[Painting Song No. 1 in this series] except that the chorus line 'they have smeared her with white clay' is replaced by:
'they have smeared her with old red clay'
and between the last line (of the song) and the final chorus...is inserted the following:

"All being beautiful under her,
       they have smeared her with it,
"All being beautiful above her,
       they have smeared her with it,
"All being beautiful all around her,
       they have smeared her with it,
"Her voice being beautiful,
       they have smeared her with it."

White Clay Song

FRANK MITCHELL

Ceremonial Recording, 1963

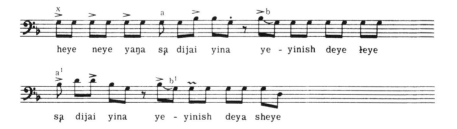

heye   neye   yaŋa   są dijai   yina   ye - yinish   deye   łeye

są   dijai   yina   ye - yinish   deya   sheye

9. yołgaiye hada - te'i'ye ka bita yisą - go ye - ninish deye jeye

10. yołgaiye beye be'e -tsos - go ye ye - ninish deye jeye

11. yodi be'a bilatah - gila ka ayash dotłiz - iye biką eiye

tsegha dini - zhoniye ka danana jiyigo ye - ninish deye jeye

12. bi - za - na hodleshgo biyine nizhǫ - go ye - ninishde jeye

13. noho - tsaniye bidleeshi ye - ninish deye jeye

14. yodi bedo - li - ą - go ye - ninish deye jeye

15. nitłiz bedo - li - ą - go ye - ninish deye jeye

16. yodi iltas ei ye ka bidahaz - lą - go ye - ninish deye jeye

17. nitłiz iltas ei ye ka bidahaz - lą - go ye - ninish deye jeye

ye - ninish de jeye

biyazhai yila ye - ninish deye je biya - zhaiye

laŋa yeiye ninish dleesh golaghana ne

Red Ocher Song

FRANK MITCHELL

Solo Recording, 1963

heye neye yaŋa są je chii-le ye - yinish chii jeye

są je chii-la ye - yinesh chiye je

są je chii ye laŋa yeye yinesh chini holaghei

neye ka esdzanadleeshe biyazhi yila ye - yinesh chiye jeye

dotłi - ziye yebaghan ya'alnii - gi ye - yinesh chiye jeye

Red Ocher Song

No. 2 in a Series of Five Painting Songs

BLUE MULE

Solo Recording, 1963

heye neye yaŋa biyazhi yilaŋa yehasteyi laŋa yeye

biyazhi yilaŋa yehasteyi laŋa yeye

biyazhi yila yehashteyi laŋa holaghei

1. niye dotłizi et'e - de ye hashteyi laŋa yeye

2. dotłi - zi bik'e-go ye hashteyi laŋa yeye

3. dotłi - ziye bike banashchi̧ - go ye hashteyi laŋa yeye

4. dotłi - ziye bik ' e tł 'olgo ye hashteyi laŋa yeye

5. dotłizi bistle - go ye hashteyi laŋa yeye

6. dotłiziye bijaz nez - go ye hashteyi laŋa yeye

22.

bit-siji   hozho - go   ye hashteyi laŋa   yeye

biya - zhi   laŋa   ye hashteyi laŋa   yeye

ritard.-------------------

biya-zhi   le   ye hashteyi la - golaghana   ne

Song That Mentions Both White Clay and Red Ocher
No. 3 in a Series of Five Painting Songs
BLUE MULE
Solo Recording, 1963

heye   neye   ye   yaŋa   biyazhai   yiłaŋa   ka hashteyi laŋa   yeye

biyazhai   yilaŋa   ka   hashteyi laŋa   yeye   biyazhai   yila

ka hashteyi   łaŋa   holaghei

1.   neye   dotłizi   et'e - de   hąhas-teyi   łaŋa   yeye

2.   dotłizi   bik'e - go   yehash - teyi   laŋa   yeye

3.   dotłizi   bis li   biye   bitsin   bike   banashchį - go

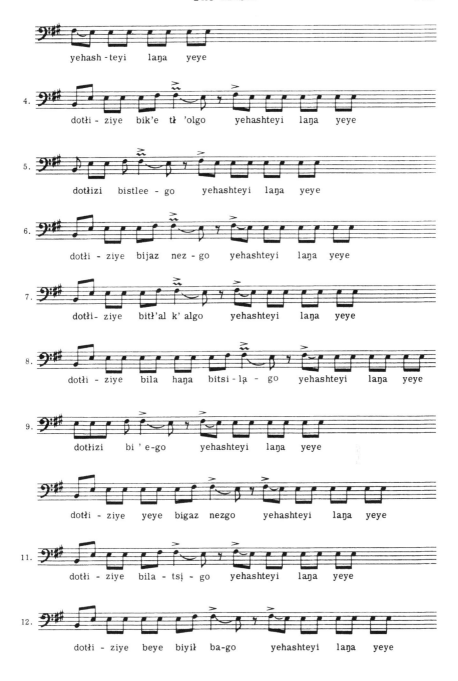

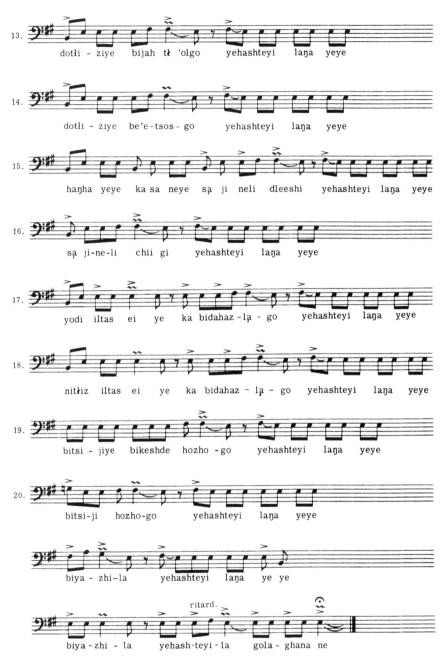

13. dotłi - ziye bijah tł 'olgo yehashteyi laŋa yeye

14. dotłi - ziye be'e-tsos-go yehashteyi laŋa yeye

15. haŋha yeye ka sa neye są ji neli dleeshi yehashteyi laŋa yeye

16. są ji-ne-li chii gi yehashteyi laŋa yeye

17. yodi iltas ei ye ka bidahaz-łą-go yehashteyi laŋa yeye

18. nitłiz iltas ei ye ka bidahaz - łą - go yehashteyi laŋa yeye

19. bitsi - jiye bikeshde hozho -go yehashteyi laŋa yeye

20. bitsi-ji hozho-go yehashteyi laŋa yeye

biya - zhi–la yehashteyi laŋa ye ye

ritard.

biya - zhi - la yehash-teyi - la gola - ghana ne

Song That Is Neither White Clay nor Red Ocher

No. 1 of a Series of Five Painting Songs

BLUE MULE

Solo Recording, 1963

heye neye yaŋa biyazhiyi laŋa ye - yehasteyi leye sheye

biyazhi yila ye-hashteyi leye sheye

biyazhi yila ye-hasteyi leye holaghei

1. neye yeye niyi yeye yołgaiye et 'eyide ye-hashteyi leye sheye

2. yołgaiye bike-yigo ye-hashteyi leye sheye

3. yołgai yeye bike banashchį - go ye-hashteyi leye sheye

4. yołgai yeye bik'e tł'ol - go ye-hashteyi leye sheye

5. yołgaiye bistle - go ye-hashteyi leye sheye

6. yołgai yeye yedi yaŋa be yołgaiye bijaz nez-go

Conclusion of the Singing

With the completion of the Painting Song, the Kinaaldá singing, at least in the Chinle area, is finished.   Only the outdoor
molding rite remains before the public part of the ceremony is
terminated.   Once that is complete, the girl goes back into the
hogan, signifying the official end of her puberty ceremony.   The
guests leave, and the girl begins her remaining four days of ceremonial quietness and contemplation.

Summary

The music in Kinaaldá is unaccompanied vocal music; it is
sung in a style which is characteristically Navaho in all respects
except for the absence of falsetto singing.   The songs are Blessing
Way Songs and are divided into groups or sets.   Certain songs or
song sets must be sung at specific times during the night by the
main singer; these are the "fixed songs."   During the rest of the
night other songs may be contributed by those present, in whatever
order they wish; these are the "free songs."   The fixed songs may
or may not accompany rites; the free ones do not.

The fixed songs have been examined in detail, and their
characteristics have been described and compared.   If singing accompanies the activities on the first day of the ceremony, the
Combing and Racing Songs are the first ones to be used in Kinaaldá.
Otherwise, the Hogan Songs which open the all-night singing are
the first fixed songs to be heard.

The Hogan Songs are of two types.   The Chief Hogan Songs
are used the first time a girl has a Kinaaldá; they describe the
building of the original hogan.   The Talking God Hogan Songs are
used for a second Kinaaldá.   They are different from the Chief
Hogan Songs in structure, music, and texts, which deal with the
movement of Changing Woman toward her home.   As a group, the
Hogan Songs are viewed as "special" songs by singers and informants alike.

Many different song groups comprise the free singing which follows the Hogan Songs. In the midst of these song sets, a fixed song, one of the two Twelve Word Songs used in Kinaaldá, is sung.

The Twelve Word Songs, the second of which is sung after the girl's final dawn race, are also regarded as special songs. Here, the songs themselves are believed to be imbued with special powers to rectify any mistakes made in the ceremonial affairs to that point. The songs are the first fixed ones to be definitely associated with a rite. Musically they are special because they are formula songs. A standard version of each exists, and for once, in the performance of these songs, individual variation is not allowed.

With the appearance of dawn, the free singing is gradually brought to a close and the main singer is reinstated as the controlling force. From this time on to the end of the ceremony, only fixed songs are used. The Dawn Songs or Washing Songs which are now sung are easily recognized by their structure. They are distinct not only because they are the first fixed songs to accompany a major rite but also because they are sung at faster tempi than any of the previous Kinaaldá songs.

Once the girl's hair and jewelry have been washed, it is time for her to make her last run to the east. There are four songs which accompany the running; evidently if music accompanies the ceremonial activities on the first day, from one to six Racing Songs are sung at that time. The Racing Songs used for the first and last days are of two different kinds. The ones used during the last morning, however, are essentially one song. As a group, the Racing Songs may be sung so as to be the fastest-moving songs in the Kinaaldá. The singing of these beautiful songs is timed according to aural cues, rather than visual ones.

The second Twelve Word Song is sung upon the girl's return; then the 'alkaan is distributed and a meal is eaten. The Combing Songs follow, while the girl's hair is brushed and tied once again with the ceremonial hair string. In certain regions,

Combing Songs accompany the same rite when it occurs on the first day. The Combing Songs cannot be reduced to a single song; however, they do have some features in common.

The girl is painted after her hair is brushed. In some regions the painting is done with only one substance, white clay or red ocher. In these places, the people choose the substance, and the main singer sings a Painting Song which corresponds with it. In other areas, both white clay and red ocher are used in the painting. Then it is possible that a Painting Song which mentions both *dleesh* and *chííh* will be used. The Painting Songs as a group are similar to the Combing Songs and for this and other reasons are not so easy to identify as some of the other Kinaaldá songs. With the completion of the chosen Painting Song, the Kinaaldá singing is terminated.

Only a certain amount of generalization is possible in regard to Kinaaldá music. Analysis, of course, shows that many of the songs, regardless of the group to which they belong, do share certain elements. For example, consider the widespread use of particular introductory and concluding formulas, specific tempi, structural schemata, textual ideas, and even specific burden motives. However, analysis also conclusively indicates the fallacy of trying to treat the singing connected with a puberty ceremony as a single item, "Kinaaldá music." Each set of songs must be viewed individually; the music, texts, and ceremonial context must all be studied. Neither the rendition of any given song nor the composition of any song set is ever exactly the same from one performance to the next. Change and fluidity prevail; in the songs of Kinaaldá a balance between individual creativity and traditional formalism is constantly being achieved and then redefined.

CHAPTER FOUR

The Kinaaldá in Its Cultural Context

IN addition to analyzing the myth, rites, and music that combine to constitute the Kinaaldá, the ceremony should be studied within its cultural context. The reasons for which the ceremony is held, the meaning Kinaaldá has for the Navaho, and the beliefs associated with all its rites should be investigated and determined.

Reasons for Kinaaldá

"For the Southwest Athabascans in general ... the girls' puberty ceremony is an integral part of the culture, indispensable for both the girl and the community."[1]

Of the questions discussed in this chapter, perhaps the most basic is why do the Navaho have Kinaaldá? What does it mean to a girl, her family, and the community in which she lives?

The data once again exemplify "the principle of many reasons" cited by Ladd as characteristic of Navaho philosophy. The myths suggest that the Kinaaldá originated to insure procreation. "It was performed at the instigation of First Man and First Woman

---

[1] Harold Driver, "Girls' Puberty Rites in Western North America," *University of California Anthropological Records*, VI, No. 2, Culture Element Distributions: XVI (1941), p. 34.

who were planning for the birth of future generations . . . 'to enable her [Changing Woman] to create a new race, and to transmit to this new race the power of generation.' ''[2]

According to Frank, ''The ceremony was started so women would be able to have children and the human race would be able to multiply. To do this, women had to have relations with men. The Kinaaldá was created to make it holy and effective, as the Holy People wanted it to be'' (*supra*, p. 11).

None of the informants stated that the puberty ceremony is held to insure that a girl will have many children. Frank Mitchell was the only one who implied it. ''She's eligible to be married after the second period. It's a girl's duty to reproduce children.'' There was general agreement, however, that the ''girl who has had the puberty rite is considered [eligible] for marriage.''[3]

Informants gave varied reasons for holding a Kinaaldá. Some of these reflected its inclusion as a subceremony in the Blessing Way Complex; they emphasized the prophylactic and ''good hope'' aspects of Kinaaldá. Virginia Wilson said the ceremony was held so that the girl ''could have anything she wanted: food, silver, anything she wanted in the future. You know that from the songs they sing.''[4] According to Lisa Jones, ''You have Kinaaldá so you don't grow old right away.''[5]

Other reasons were more humorous:

> Jane Tim had it because she bothers the boys all the time. When you bother boys too much you do your Kinaaldá right away.
> . . . The boys are supposed to come to your Kinaaldá so they know they're not supposed to bother you. That's what my auntie told me (JM).[6]

---

[2]Father Berard Haile, ''Origin Legend of the Navaho Enemy Way,'' *Yale University Publications in Anthropology*, XVII (1938), p. 251, n. 23.
[3]Dorothea Leighton and Clyde Kluckhohn, *Children of the People* (Cambridge, Mass.: Harvard University Press, 1947), p. 77.
[4]Anne Keith, Field Notes, June 26, 1963.
[5]*Ibid.*, July 19, 1963.
[6]*Ibid.*, August 16, 1963.

The most common reason cited was educational. The girl receives instructions during Kinaaldá. It is believed to equip her with the knowledge necessary to assume an adult role in the society. She is expected to "get out of her pants and into a skirt" (Ja.M)[7] and to begin acting like a lady and a grownup.

> That's what you're a girl for, to do your Kinaaldá. . . . I think you have to do more work. . . That's what they're ladies for, to work. When you do your Kinaaldá you begin to be a lady and have to do more work. My auntie told me. (JM).[8]

> If you do it for four days, you will get the habit of doing it all your life. If you put food before the people all the time and help around the house, you will be willing to do those things for people wherever you go. You know when you grow up, you have to learn some things. You get most of those things out of those four days. You learn those things you have to do as a woman, as a mother.
> They don't teach you anything about children, but they do teach you something about cooking and helping people—how to help people. You pick up these things and think about them; they just come to your head (Ja.M).[9]

If the Kinaaldá is not performed, the girl is usually regarded as not being fully educated.

> If you don't do Kinaaldá, you won't learn how to do anything (IY).[10]
> If you do not have the ceremony, you'll be a lot different from the other girls you know. They teach you about everything during that time, such as what you are not supposed to say to your kids. You get a lot out of those four days. You are not expected to be that way all at once. You have to practice it yourself; if you don't, you are lazy. You lie around and be lazy like me. I used to practice; this is the only summer I am doing this (Ja.M).[11]

The Kinaaldá is thought to have a lasting effect on the life of the girl. Many informants agreed with Reichard, who stated in

---

[7]*Ibid.*, July 9, 1963.

[8]*Ibid.*, August 16, 1963.

[9]*Ibid.*, July 9, 1963.

[10]*Ibid.*, July 28, 1963.

[11]Keith, Taped Interview, July, 1963. This agrees with Gladys Reichard's statement that "knowledge must be ripened by experience which takes time to acquire," in *Navaho Religion*, Bollingen Series XVIII (New York: Pantheon Books, 1950), I, 39. It also exemplifies generalizations made by Lucile Charles, "Growing Up Through Drama," *Journal of American Folklore*, LIX, No. 233 (July–Sept., 1946), p. 261. Furthermore, it agrees with data in Audrey Richards, *Chisungu* (New York: Grove Press, 1956) pp. 128–129.

Dezba that these four days determine the future of the girl.[12] "I'll be like that in my future life ... They tell me that a lot of that determines how you're going to be in your future life" (Aug.S).

In expressing these ideas, informants stressed two determinants. The first, the instructions which the girl receives, has been discussed. The second is the girl's actions per se. The Navaho believe that everything the girl says and does during the ceremony is indicative of the kind of person she will be in the future. The girl is believed to be highly susceptible during this time to a variety of influences, both physical and mental. As was true at her birth,[13] her body is again considered to be soft and capable of being reshaped by molding. It is almost as if the girl, in becoming a woman, has been physically and mentally reborn and is passing through several days in which both her body and her personality can be reshaped by the people around her, so as to correspond more closely with the cultural ideal.

Meaning of the Ceremony

From the moment that a woman in the household learns of the girl's pubescence, the girl is subject to regulations, requirements, and taboos. Usually, she is told what is expected of her by her mother, grandmother, or aunt. After that, everyone cooperates to insure that these expectations are fulfilled.

The regulations as well as the rationalizations behind them exemplify Ladd's "principle of many reasons," that is, multiple causation and multiple justification. They concern all the actions involved in Kinaaldá. By reviewing the regulations as well as the justifications for them, some insights as to their meaning for the Navaho emerge.

---

[12]Gladys Reichard, *Dezba: Woman of the Desert* (New York: J. J. Augustin, Publisher, 1939), p. 50.

[13]Leighton and Kluckhohn, p. 17.

General Restrictions

Timing

Ideally, the ceremony begins as soon as the girl has announced the onset of menstruation and is in process during her actual period. Postponements are possible, however. Whenever the ceremony is held, the dates for it should be arranged so as not to conflict with an eclipse, which has the power of "erasing any sing" (WM).[14] The Kinaaldá should also be scheduled so as not to interrupt any four-day waiting period a singer must observe before performing any ceremony after a death has occurred in the family, be it in the nuclear group or the clan.

Ceremonial Behavior within the Hogan

Once the ceremony has begun, the girl is expected to enter the hogan, circle the fire clockwise, and take her ceremonial position in the west, with the main singer on her right. Others must enter in the same manner and then sit so that the men are in the south and the women in the north.

Segregation Taboos

The segregation taboos are not so numerous as might be expected in view of the Navaho fear of the powers of menstruating women.[15] As was indicated (*supra*, p. 7), this is probably related to the fact that the dangers from the menstrual blood of the first two periods are counteracted by the Blessing Way Songs used in Kinaaldá.

---

[14]Keith, Field Notes, July 9, 1963. Frank and Rose Mitchell consciously avoided the eclipse which was scheduled for July 20, 1963, in arranging the dates for Lena Shirley's Kinaaldá. The *bijí* of a Kinaaldá which was in process in another area at that time was held on the third night, July 19, rather than on the usual fourth one, so the Kinaalda was completed before the eclipse began (VW). *Ibid.,* July 19, 1963.

[15]For discussions of the power of menstrual blood, see Leighton and Kluckhohn, p. 87; Reichard, *Navaho Religion,* I, 173; Franciscan Fathers, *An Ethnologic Dictionary of the Navaho Language* (St. Michaels, Ariz.: St. Michaels Press, 1910), p. 109; John Ladd, *The Structure of a Moral Code* (Cambridge, Mass.: Harvard University Press, 1957), p. 424; and Walter Dyk, *Son of Old Man Hat* (New York: Harcourt, Brace, 1938), pp. 13–14.

Whereas many North American Indian tribes treat the pubescent girl as if she were tainted, the Navaho honor the moment of her maturity. I have had no evidence that menstruation itself is considered corrupt; rather, its appearance is regarded as the fulfillment of a promise, the attainment of reproductive power.[16]

Frank Mitchell equated the first menstrual blood with "dew of vegetation."

When Changing Woman had her first period, they prepared her by using the dews of various plants. They put that into her body to enable her to produce offspring for the human race. On that account, today we believe that when a girl has her first period, there is nothing wrong with that. It is something sacred to us. Jewels in males and plant dew in females lead to conception.

It is our belief that *ch'il dahtoo'* is menstrual blood. A woman has the dew of vegetation which leads to the birth of children. On the other hand, the dew of jewels, *ntł'izh bidahtoo'*, is installed in a man to produce offspring. That is where the holy part comes in. So the girl's first period is not looked on as something dangerous. . . .

It is pretty hard to say when the second period will come. Sometimes quite a time passes between the first and second. It is all the work of nature who takes care of us. . . . After the first two, the blood starts to appear every so often. This blood is considered unsanitary.[17]

Only a few taboos related to blood were mentioned by Kinaaldá informants. Ja.M said that "you should not step on anything's blood" and that "you must take something red so your menstruation won't smell."

The women just told me you have to leave it alone. You must wash your hands every time. You can't let the little kids get into it. When you wash your hands or maybe your panties, you have to wash out the wash basin.[18]

RD said:

If you get even a bit of your blood on your hands, your hands get real hot and it really swells. Your back will get hunchbacked too. You must not watch butchering or touch sheep's blood, or you might dream about dead people and get sick. Neither singing nor the hospital can help this kind of sickness.[19]

---

[16]Reichard, *Navaho Religion*, I, 173.

[17]David McAllester, Field Notes, July 19–20, 1961, p. 7b. Portions of this material appear *supra*, p. 6 and p. 399.

[18]Anne Keith, Taped Interview, July, 1963.

[19]Keith, Field Notes, July 23, 1963.

There is also a taboo against telling the boys and men you have reached puberty and, in the case of the boys, why the Kinaaldá is being done. "You tell your mother, grandmother, sister, aunt, or cousin when it happens. You don't tell the men or boys" (MS).

> My brothers didn't know what the ceremony was about. They just knew that we were having that Navaho "cake dealy."[20] They will learn from their girl friends or in biology class. They didn't ask my ma because she told them to shut up, saying, "It's not for boys to know. You'll find out when you get married" (Ja.M).[21]

> My brother got there that Saturday night around one or two o'clock [a.m.] when the singing was going on. He just came in. He said he was wondering what the big fire was for. He didn't know that his sister was a kinaaldá (Aug.S).

Segregation taboos are not often reported. Only a few informants mentioned that the girl must eat by herself outside the hogan and stay alone when not actually participating in the ceremony. The Kinaaldá observed by the author showed no recognition of these restrictions.

Attitude of the Girl and Participants

The attitude of the girl is extremely important during the ceremony. It is believed that her adult personality will be determined by mannerisms and actions displayed during the Kinaaldá. Taboos in this area are numerous.

Tabooed Action	*Result if Taboo not Observed*
Being mean or grouchy.	Ugly adult personality.
Laughing.	Deep wrinkles will form around her mouth.
	Rest of her face will wrinkle in her youth.
	Her teeth will be bad.
	Her '*alkaan* will not cook properly.
	She will be a loud woman.
Ignoring what parents say during Kinaaldá.	Teeth will not last.

---

[20]Keith said that Ja.M. used this expression all the time; to her, the Kinaaldá was that "Navaho cake dealy."

[21]*Ibid.*, July 9, 1963.

Ignoring orders from others.	Future laziness and disregard for others.
Treating children badly.	She will be a mean mother capable of killing her children by slapping them.

At least one informant said that prepubescent female observers are not to laugh either, or they will have to do their Kinaaldá immediately.

Food Taboos

Throughout her Kinaaldá, the girl is subjected to specific food taboos. It is advisable that she only eat things made from corn; mush and bread made from corn meal are preferred. These must be made without salt or any additional flavoring. One informant said that for the breakfast on the final morning, a corn-hominy mixture must be eaten.

The taboos and the consequences resulting from a breach of them are listed below. Of these, the taboos on sweets and salt were most commonly mentioned by informants.

Tabooed Substance	*Result if Taboo not Observed*
Salt.	Weakness, unable to cook and weave. Laziness. Ugliness. Skin becomes wrinkled in youth. White stuff on your baby's nose when it is born.
Sweets.	Teeth will be bad. Teeth will fall right out. Be generally weak and unable to cook and weave. Skin becomes wrinkled in youth. Ugliness.
Meat.	Ugliness. Laziness.
All seasonings.	Skin becomes wrinkled in youth. Ugliness.
Canned fruit.	Be too weak to cook and weave.

Hot things.	Skin becomes wrinkled in youth.
	Sickness.
Candy.	Teeth fall out.
Corn pollen.	Teeth fall out.
Your own *'alkaan.*	Teeth fall out.
	Get old right away.
	Teeth ruined before you are old.
	Tooth trouble.
	Selfishness when you grow up (even if you just touch it).

Water Taboos

Beliefs associated with water in Kinaaldá have two dimensions; one of these involves restrictions concerning the use of water during the ceremony.

Restriction	*Result if Ignored*
Do not wash face for four days.	Causes rain.
	Causes ugliness.
Have no contact with water.	Causes rain.
Get no water on upper lip.	Causes mustache.
Boil all drinking water	Get "blood" from the water.
	Become unhappy, mean, lazy, and sick.

The other involves the association between Kinaaldá and rain. It is believed that if the girl looks at the sky, washes her face, or has any contact with water, it will bring rain. The amount of rain will vary proportionally with the number of Kinaaldá occurring in a given region: "When there are lots of Kinaaldá around, it rains often" (WM).[22] The association between Kinaaldá and rain has both positive and negative aspects. The rain that results if the girl looks at the sky and so forth may ruin the public celebration. On the other hand, it may be beneficial to crops: "When the cake is put in the pit, you pray, 'Let the corn grow fast; let the rain rain real hard.' It rains right away" (RD).[23]

---

[22]Keith, personal communication.
[23]Keith, Field Notes, July 23, 1963.

Sleep Taboos

The girl should sleep as little as possible during the ceremony. It is believed that she should go to bed late and get up early
in order to become a good worker and fortunate and to prevent her
from aging rapidly. The only occasion when these sleeping restrictions are relaxed is during the *bijị́*; then not only is it permissible for her to rest but she is encouraged to do so, since she
is not allowed to sleep during the final night. If she should, misfortune would result. Those keeping the vigil with her in the hogan
must also remain awake; should they fall asleep, they would cause
harm to the girl.[24] The girl may not sleep again until noon of the
last day.

When sleeping, the girl must lie on her back, not in a flexed
position. Should she violate this, misfortune and kyphosis might
result. She must sleep in her ceremonial place in the hogan on a
sheepskin covered by her own ceremonial blanket. She must lie
with her head near the hogan wall and her feet toward the fire.
Before retiring, she must remove all her jewelry and deposit it
preferably in a ceremonial basket. While no reason could be obtained for this restriction, it is probably related to the fact that
the basket symbolizes one or more of the jewels valued by the
Navaho.[25]

Action Taboos

The girl is forbidden to scratch her head or body with her
fingernails; if she does, her flesh will be scarred and her hair will
fall out. The Mitchells said this taboo was no longer in effect.
However, when Marie scratched her head during the final morning
of her Kinaaldá, Frank and several of the women stopped her immediately. Only one informant mentioned the possible use of a
wooden scratching stick.

---

[24]In practice, some relaxation of this requirement seems permissible, especially in the
case of small children and singers who have been drinking.

[25]Reichard, *Navaho Religion*, II, 523.

Restrictions Associated with Specific Rites

In addition to the general restrictions which become effective as soon as the girl has announced her menstruation, there are
other restrictions associated with the rites of the Kinaaldá. These
are discussed below, in the order in which they occur.

Hair-Combing

The hair-combing and tying that initiate a Kinaaldá are
done to make the girl resemble Changing Woman. "You tie her
hair up with unwounded buckskin and let it hang down her back in
a tail for four days, because that is the way *Esdzan nadle* began
it" (DS).[26]

According to informants, the hair string must be of unwounded buckskin, mountain lion skin, otter, beaver, deerskin, or
"special deerskin." Frank said that it is impossible to have all
these available; "you use whichever kind is at hand."

The brushing is an act of purification. According to Frank,
wearing the hair in a pony tail was formerly a hair style restricted
to Kinaaldá. Now, however, "all do it, even the gray-haired
ladies." The hair style includes a partial covering of the face
with the hair in some regions, to correspond with the regional
conception of Changing Woman's Kinaaldá. The hair may not be
curled and the girl may not wear make-up during the ceremony.
"If the girl follows these restrictions, she'll have natural beauty."
(JF).[27]

Dressing

The girl is ceremonially dressed and adorned with silver
and turquoise jewelry, belts, and sashes which belong to the family. According to Frank (*supra*, p. 12), this is done because White
Shell Woman did it at the original Kinaaldá. It is believed that the

---

[26] Flora Bailey, Field Notes, 1938.
[27] Keith, Field Notes, June 22, 1963.

wearing of jewels will bring wealth and success: the more the girl wears, the greater blessing for her and for the owners of the jewelry as well. As Driver says, "She impersonates [the] culture heroine in the hope that she will become as virtuous and success-ful."[28]

The wearing of jewelry and the ceremonial clothing is, how-ever, an inconvenience for many Navaho girls, especially when the Kinaaldá is held during the summer. Their elders, however, en-courage them to persevere and in so doing emphasize the endur-ance aspect of the dressing rite.

> I felt so uncomfortable in those things. But my mother told me that that was something that I would have to take, because in the future, I would meet something that would be more uncomfortable than wearing those hot clothes that I was uncomfortable in in that warm weather. So she said just to sweat it out so that...in the future I would be able to face anything hard that came up (Aug.S).

Lifting

The lifting of the children often follows the dressing rite. According to Wheelwright's *Navajo Creation Myth*, (1942, p. 77) Changing Woman did this to her attendants in order to thank them for their gifts at her first Kinaaldá. Other informants said, how-ever, that lifting made the recipients grow more rapidly. Frank added, "The reason for the lifting is that the girl is in condition to form the bodies of others. If they are small, she wants them to be taller and lifts them. If they are tall, she pushes them down so they will not grow out of shape."

Molding

Next, the girl is molded on a pile of blankets and other articles contributed by those present, who believe that in so doing these goods will soon be replaced by new ones. On the first day, the girl is molded inside the hogan "to make her consciously feel for her home. It is done to make her responsible as a housekeeper.

---

[28]Driver, p. 33.

On the last morning, it is done outside with her face to the hogan and body not far from the door so that whenever the girl is away, her mind will always be in her home'' (FM).

The molding is performed by an "ideal" woman, one who has physical strength, perfect health, beauty, energy, and ambition. She must have a good character and not be promiscuous or sadistic. She must be pleasant, friendly, and personable. If the girl desires riches, the woman should also be prosperous, prone to good fortune, and the owner of silver and other wealth. She must do the molding correctly. The ideal woman is believed to possess the power to reshape the girl and remake her in her own image and, indirectly, in that of Salt Woman, whom she personifies (FM). Most informants said that the molding makes the girl shapely and beautiful.

> The woman molds the girl to press her into a good figure and shape her body. At that time and period she is soft and can be pressed into certain forms. You shape her so she will have a good figure. If it is not done, she will probably have a belly like a nanny goat's. The present day has things such as beauty contests; there, girls are judged by the shape of their bodies. Just anyone can notice that in a crowd of people; you notice a perfect body right away. Others that are all out of shape also attract your eyes (FM).

In the myths, the molding was done to honor the Sun and the Moon or to make the girl resemble a perfect form of Changing Woman or her equivalents. Reichard says:

> Pressing is a common procedure meaning identification by absorption. . . . It is assumed that until a person has been made holy, he is not an image of the power he seeks to control, but after such a power takes him in hand, kneading, pressing, or massage will make him resemble the Holy People. Because Changing Woman was molded when she became mature, there is now a massaging rite in the Girl's Adolescent Ceremony.[29]

In addition to being a beautifying process, molding is also credited with influencing the girl's posture and stature. It can make her erect and prevent lumps and a humped back. It also

---

[29]Reichard, *Navaho Religion*, II, 584.

makes her strong and influences her height. If she is short, she
can be stretched at this time, and her hair and fingers can be
pulled so they will grow. If she is tall, she may be struck on the
top of the head and on the soles of the feet to inhibit further growth.
Molding also affects the girl's disposition. It can make her nice
and friendly. The specific act of hitting her mouth is often included so she will not be disagreeable, talkative, use profanity, or
argue with her mother.

Those watching the molding are required to catch the blankets when the girl throws them to their owners after the reshaping.
Not to do so brings "bad luck." Some specify that the goods must
be caught with the right hand in order for their owners to get new
ones. The people must thank the girl when receiving their goods,
since in effect they are receiving a gift from Changing Woman.
"You say 'thank you' for the returned blankets. Whenever there
is a kinaaldá, she symbolizes Changing Woman. That is why they
say 'thank you.' You hope for a new blanket soon in the future. In
white man's religion, they pray and ask for help. They get something and then they say 'thank you' " (FM).

Racing[30]

The racing, in the actual running, its frequency, the dis-
tances covered, and the fact that it is often done while the girl is
menstruating, introduces another endurance factor into the ceremony. The rationalization for the girl's run is in the myth of the
original Kinaaldá: "The First Woman went through all of this; we
are just following suit as we have been told to do" (FM).

The myths vary in the identity of both the participants in the
race and those benefiting from them. Informants, however, agreed
that the girl runs to improve her leg muscles, to prevent laziness,
to strengthen her body, to make her a good runner, to make her
strong, supple, and energetic, to insure that she will continue to
be lithe and active throughout womanhood, to insure bravery, and

---

[30]"Racing was originally done every day in Navaho life for endurance, so those running
would get toughened up and be able to stand anything. Otherwise, they would be lazy and not know
how to make a living for their children" (Aug.S).

to bring many sheep and horses in the future. "The racing is done to acquire a long life and a happy life. If the girl runs, she will enjoy beauty; she will be elevated, energetic, and not too lazy to do anything. The races are like a belagáana's exercises to strengthen his body and get himself into physical condition to endure much" (FM). All seemed to agree with Reichard's statement that "racing is a rite that seems to symbolize strength and fortitude."[31]

The race is surrounded by regulations and taboos. It must begin and end in the hogan. Normally, it is run toward the east. The girl may run as far as she wishes. She must turn sunwise when she returns. Frank said she should increase the distance of each race; "the further she runs, the longer she will live." She is to run the complete distance and not shorten her race or rest. If she falls, this is considered unlucky; it shows she lacks strength. She must not look back. If she does, "she'll get her next menstruation two weeks or a month from then; if she doesn't, it won't come until later, a year or two from that time" (MS).

People of any age may accompany the girl. The Navaho believe it is beneficial to participate. Some also consider it from the practical angle of exercise and pre-Kinaaldá training and practice: "The racing is open to everybody. It's mostly the teenagers who run. They're going to have their periods and they might as well practice" (FM).[32] "Racing builds energy. It's like an army taking a trip. It gives you muscles. You practice so you will be prepared if you want to run from an enemy later" (MS).

To run with the girl is to share her blessedness. Some attribute symbolic meanings to the participants: "The girl takes her last run toward the east, this time followed by many young children, symbolically attesting that she will be a kind mother, whom her children will always follow."[33]

[31]Reichard, Navaho Religion, II, 585.

[32]McAllester, Field Notes, July 19–20, 1961, p. 8a.

[33]Edward Curtis, The North American Indian, Vol. I, Apache, Jicarillas, Navajo (Cambridge, Mass.: The University Press, 1907), p. 125. Citing a race where six young men accompanied the girl, Gladys Reichard refutes Curtis, saying the race signifies sexual camaraderie, rather than predicts the character of motherhood. Social Life of the Navajo Indians, Columbia University Contributions to Anthropology, VII (New York: Columbia University Press, 1928), p. 138.

Those who accompany the girl enjoy the experience. Like her, however, they too are under certain restrictions. Formerly, the race was a contest; those who ran actually competed with the girl; if she could beat them, it was a sign of good fortune. At present, though, there is little competition. It is believed that only prepubescent girls may run ahead of the Kinaaldá. If others violate this taboo, they will become gray-haired and will die before the girl.

While running, all are supposed to give the Kinaaldá shout. This is done to attract the attention of Changing Woman, the Sun, and Talking God to the race. "You yell so the people from Heaven listen and hear you" (GK).

Corn-Grinding

Perhaps the greatest test that the girl endures is grinding corn. While being a practical means of preparing the corn needed for the 'alkaan it also serves to keep the girl occupied during the day. It is believed to insure that in the future the girl will be strong and industrious. It also makes her successful. The only restrictions connected with the grinding are that the girl be persistent and that others help her. The latter requirement sets a good example for the girl. It also brings blessing and success to the helpers.

The 'Alkaan

The baking of a sweetened corn bread in a pit oven is a feature of the Night, Flint, and Feather Chants as well as the Kinaaldá. It is baked as a mark of respect and as an offering to the Sun. Several Kinaaldá myths mention that the original 'alkaan was made for the Sun and the one at the second ceremony for the Moon.

There are many taboos associated with the corncake in addition to those mentioned earlier (which prevent the girl from eating her own 'alkaan.) In mixing the flour, both hands must be used. Corn pollen[34] and some mirage powder are mixed in the flour to make the cake rise. The water which is added must boil "for hours so it is really hot." Once the lumps have been removed by stirring, the batter is allowed "to ferment" (CS).

The fire pit cannot be dug by fire dancers or *jaashzhini* (*supra*, p. 38).

> These people (*jaashzhini*), those building fires at Squaw Dances, and the fire dancers who carry torches in the Mountain Chant cannot come near the fire pit or help with the digging. If they do, the cake may not cook; it may stay all mushy (CS).
>
> *Jaashzhini*, fire eaters, and the clown of the Yeibichai are forbidden to dig that hole. They are considered to be people who go wild all the time and who do not observe rules (FM).

In digging the pit, the loose dirt must be piled on the north side (RM). If the girl has had the "fire ceremony" performed for her, she is not allowed to do any ceremonial cooking; if she does, the cake will be ruined (CB).[35]

The cake batter is arranged in the pit according to ritual proscriptions. The bottom of the pit is first lined with cornhusks, tips clockwise. The girl places a husk cross in the bottom after the lining is complete. According to Frank, "The cross is the foundation of the cake and the completion of the top. Its physical shape is a custom and cannot be explained more thoroughly." As the batter, which is poured from the north, rises, the edges of the pit are similarly lined. After the batter has been poured, raisins are added and the cake is blessed with corn pollen by the girl and others, who pray. Next, the cake is covered with husks; finally, the other husk cross is added. Then newspaper, earth, and wood chips are added and the fire is started.

The man chosen to watch the fire during the night cannot be one who has participated in a fire dance; if he has, the cake will not bake. He must be dependable and must refrain from drinking.

---

[34]FM later denied that corn pollen was used at this point.

[35]Keith, Field Notes, July 4, 1963. In Chinle, when MS's cake did not bake properly, numerous explanations were given. They included such reasons as:the fire had not been controlled properly, corn meal had been used, and white people had been present at the ceremony.

While it is important that many people chop firewood, only one man watches the fire; "if many do, the cake will not come out well" (VW).[36]

All-Night Vigil

During the night of all-night singing, an endurance test in the form of sleeplessness is enacted. "The patient and ideally everyone in the hogan should remain awake; by paying attention to the song ceremony, one benefits from the entire performance even though one is present at this rite alone. Missing any part of the long series interrupts the flow of power, causing weakness."[37] As suggested by Ladd's "principle of general effects," the actions of all those present are intereffective.

A blanket hangs over the hogan door to signify that a ceremony is in process. Inside, various goods, having a symbolic value of their own,[38] are brought into view. The people feel that through the singing a blessing is evoked on the goods and those who own them. If the goods are thus blessed, it is believed that they will increase in kind and number in the near future. Goods are also displayed for aesthetic reasons. "When some people come to our house, they want to know that the house is neat. They also want to know what you have. Seeing these things makes them feel O.K. It makes it pretty inside" (RD)[39]

Other taboos in effect during the night concern the singing. These include procedures already delineated in Chapter III, such as opinions about the appropriateness of recording the ceremony, restrictions on movement until the Hogan Songs are complete, and the singing of certain songs at specific times of the night in prescribed ways.

---

[36]Keith, Field Notes, June 26, 1963.

[37]Reichard, *Navaho Religion*, I, 118–119.

[38] For example, the buckskins are symbols of life, and the baskets, symbols of the original jewels. Reichard, *Navaho Religion*, II, 506–613.

[39]Keith, Field Notes, July 23, 1963.

Washing

The washing rite occurs at dawn. In itself it is a purification procedure, or, as Reichard says, "a change from profane to sacred, from the strange and doubtful to the controlled."[40] Only a few restrictions are involved. The washing must be done in a ceremonial basket. A yucca root must be used. In Kinaaldá there is no specified way of cutting the root, as in other ceremonies. As Frank said:

> You just go and get a four-inch piece of yucca. You can use any implement you want to uncover the root. You just need to cut a piece of it. The only requirement is that the person who cuts it must remember the direction in which it was growing, because after the root is used, when it is deposited outside, you must know which is the tip end. This end must never face the hogan.
>
> I don't know why this is so. The woman who is doing the washing is told which end is which because she has to work with it so the tip end is up toward the smoke hole.

The jewelry must be replaced in the same order as before the washing. The water is emptied at the back of the hogan to bring good luck to the house.

Cake Distribution

Racing follows, as was previously described. Then the *'alkaan* is cut and distributed. In removing the cake from the pit, cuts are made from the east clockwise around the edge. There were differences of opinion about who should do the cutting. In any case, the first piece is given to the kinaaldá; she gives it to the singer of the Hogan Songs, to "the one she likes best," or to the grindstone. According to Frank, this is a time for fun. He said the piece belongs to the grindstone. If no person has been designated to receive it for the stone, the girl gives it to a favorite. This is considered an honor. It is believed that if the cake is not shared with everyone, the girl will be selfish. However, it must

---

[40]Reichard, *Navaho Religion*, I, 110.

be apportioned correctly, with the size of the pieces varying with the magnitude of the tasks performed by the helpers. The largest piece in the middle is known as the heart of the cake. This goes to the main singer; "if it doesn't, you just make yourself real selfish" (Ja.M).[41] "Willie should have gotten the heart, but he didn't which means that CB is going to be stingy when she grows up. That might not sound right, but it is" (Ja.M).[42] Before the middle portion is removed, pinches from the corners of the four pieces adjacent to it are buried in the center of the pit. This is done as an offering: "The cake belongs to the earth; these pieces are buried as a sacrifice to the earth and as an offering . . . That is done in order to be thankful for the harvest and for raising corn on the earth"(FM).[43]

Others who receive portions of the 'alkaan include those who helped grind, cook, chop wood, and sing and those who brought food.

Brushing and Painting

After the cake has been cut and a meal served, the girl's hair is brushed again. The same restrictions are in effect as on the first day. Next, she is painted. According to Frank, "The painting represents the original bath of Changing Woman. Originally the paint was not clay, but white shell. This is why she was called White Shell Woman." Wyman and Bailey note that the painting is done "so the Holy People will know you."[44] The painting affects age, rain, and height. The use of both *dleesh* and *chííh* is believed to prevent premature wrinkles. People rub the paint on their faces "to keep them young."[45] The *dleesh* must not touch the girl's hair, or it will turn gray early in life (FM).[46]

---

[41]Keith, Field Notes, July 9, 1963.

[42]*Ibid.*, July 4, 1963.

[43]McAllester, Field Notes, July 19–20, 1961, p. 6b.

[44]Leland Wyman and Flora Bailey, "Navaho Girl's Puberty Rite," *New Mexico Anthropologist*, XXV, No. 1 (January–March, 1943), p. 10.

[45]Reichard, *Social Life of the Navajo Indians*, 138.

[46]McAllester, Field Notes, July 19–20, 1961, p. 7a.

According to Wheelwright, if the girl's face is painted from the forehead down to the chin, this will bring rain. If the painting is done from the chin upward, it will aid plant growth.

Most informants added that if the cheeks are painted upward, the girl will be tall.[47] BT said the same result could be achieved by painting the heels upward;[48] ES said the cheeks should be painted with a cross if height were desired.[49]

When Frank was asked if the Navaho preferred height, he said:

> We have our feeling about the size of a person. If a man is tall and has heavy muscles, he looks tough. His clothes seem to fit him. A person like this is envied by others. One time I made this remark not thinking. "A short man regardless of how old he is, the girls are not afraid of him; they always play with him. But a tall man, the girls will dodge him." I'm tall myself, and maybe I was ridiculing myself. It's the same with horses, sheep, goats, and any other kind of four-footed animal. We like them to have a good size. We like things to be fat, even vegetation. We like to grow tall corn. . . . [50]
>
> Way back in the days before the large things came out, it was hard for a tall man or a tall woman to get into things. Now if you're tall, you don't have to worry about it. They even make hats that fit you (1963).

If the cheeks are painted downward, the girl will cease to grow. "I made a mistake and painted myself downward; that's why I'm so short. I can't even grow" (RD).[51] If a horizontal line is made across the cheeks, the girl will be broad.

Being painted is considered a blessing. The girl can share her blessing by painting those in the hogan who desire it. They indicate whether she is to apply the paint in an upward or downward direction. Frank Mitchell said, "If the person is a minor, the parents speak for him."[52]

---

[47] GK said that painting in an upward direction also makes you "grown-up."

[48] Leightons, Field Notes, April 6, 1940.

[49] Keith, Field Notes, July 19, 1963.

[50] McAllester, Field Notes, July 19-20, 1961, pp. 8b, 9a.

[51] Keith, Field Notes, July 23, 1963.

[52] FM later gave a contradictory statement: "They used to tell her, but now all the people get painted in an upward direction."

During the painting, individual prayers are said.

> While they were putting on this (dleesh) they said, "I want all kinds of jewelry, all kinds of good animals, all kinds of profit, I want it;" like they were praying (KCM).[53]

> This time is like a blessing. The girl takes things she has been blessed with and blesses everyone in the hogan. It's a blessing where you pray to get jewels and fabrics. If the people believe in it deeply, many times they will put their hands into the basket and rub them together and then go all over themselves while praying (FM).

Completion of the Kinaaldá

In some regions, the painting is followed by molding, the return of the goods, and the entrance of the girl into the hogan. This completes the public part of the ceremony.

In accord with the usual Navaho ceremonial practices, a four-day period of ceremonial quiet then begins. During this time, the girl continues some Kinaaldá activities, although in general the taboos are not in effect. Ideally she reflects on the ceremony and its teachings.

> It is a custom with our people to keep everything holy. A kinaaldá must abstain from ordinary chores and keep herself secluded from everything for four days after the ceremony. Then according to our customs she may go anywhere and do anything. During the four days she must sleep in her ceremonial place. The idea is that once she is decorated, she should stay that way until four days after the 'alkaan. Now, though, she can put away her ceremonial clothing but still she has to stay in seclusion ["and meditate" (CS)]. This is similar to white people's religion where you work for six days and rest on the seventh. The girl just has to keep quiet; she can change her clothes. In the old days, after the 'alkaan, the hair was done up into a pony tail, but not really bundled up in the usual way until four days after the 'alkaan. A kinaaldá is supposed to sleep in her place in the ceremonial hogan during these four days, as are patients in other ceremonies (FM).

> My father said that if you do this for four more days you will get into the habit more than some of them who just come and go. Those people just forget about everything. My father said medicine won't do any good unless you stay with it at least a night or two; but four is the best, he said. So that is what I did for four days after my 'alkaan (Ja.M).[54]

---

[53]Robert Rapoport, Autobiography of Kay Chee Martin (MS), 1948.

[54]Keith, Field Notes, July 9, 1963.

The Kinaaldá as an Exemplification of Navaho Religion

To the Navaho, the world is a dangerous place in which to live, for it is a mechanistic and materialistic world run by inexorable laws.[55] Nature is more powerful than man, and practically all the numerous deities are dualistic, being capable of harming as well as helping mankind. Man's only hope is to remain in harmony with the universe. This he attempts to accomplish through numerous ceremonials and prescribed formalism.

As Kluckhohn and Leighton point out, there is no Navaho word for religion: "Their world is still a whole. Every daily act is colored by their conception of supernatural forces, ever present and ever threatening."[56] Reichard says:

> To the Navaho, religion means ritual. The song, the myth, the material properties, the ritualistic acts, the rites that make up the ceremonies are held together by an elaborate system of symbolism, a sum total of numerous associations....
> ....Good then in Navaho dogma is control. Evil is that which is ritually not under control....
> ....One who knows how to keep things in order has the key to life's problems....
> ....One purpose of ritual is to extend the personality so as to bring it into harmonious relation with the powers of the universe.[57]

There is a conscious attempt during Kinaaldá to follow the order prescribed by the Holy People. The ceremony develops according to a definite sequence. The songs of the final night recapitulate the original puberty ceremony, and through the repetitions which are continuous in their structure, blessings accumulate, harmonious relations between the supernaturals and the naturals are assured, and security is achieved.

However, while possible evils are being combated through order and formalism, positive, beneficial effects are inherent. As part of the Blessing Way, the Kinaaldá emphasizes happiness, joy, and hope, elements which are as much part of the Navaho view of the world as are danger and evil.

---

[55]Paraphrase of Ladd, p. 207.

[56]Clyde Kluckhohn and Dorothea Leighton, *The Navaho* (Cambridge, Mass.: Harvard University Press, 1948), p. 122.

[57]Reichard, *Navaho Religion*, I, 3−4, 5, 14, 35.

Many of the major Navaho deities are introduced in Kinaaldá including Changing Woman, White Shell Woman, Salt Woman, Talking God, Hogan God, Corn Pollen Boy, Corn Beetle Girl, the Sun, the Moon, Mountain Woman, Water Woman, Corn Plant Woman, Wood Woman, First Man, and First Woman. Although most Navaho deities can harm as well as help mankind,[58] the songs and myths, as well as informants' comments, show that only their positive, beneficent aspects are stressed in Kinaaldá. Changing Woman, the main deity of the puberty ceremony, is one of the few gods in Navaho religion whose motives are solely good.

Actions Which Insure Blessing

Prayers

In contrast to the formal prayers used in major Navaho ceremonies, where the words of the medicine man are repeated by the patient, the prayers in the Kinaaldá are individual and personal. By using their own words with or without additional formulas from the songs, the Navaho ask for what they desire. While the effect of these prayers is not the compelling one attained through repetition,[59] they are, nevertheless, thought to be highly efficacious.

The first attempt to communicate with the supernaturals is the thanks offered when the girl returns the goods loaned to her for the molding on the first day. The girl has become Changing Woman through the efforts of the ideal woman, who represents Salt Woman. The goods have been contributed in order to bring blessing on them and their owners and to increase chances of getting new ones. When they are returned, thanks are in order. Frank said to Marie at this time, *"Ahyéhé shimásáníleehé"* (Thank you, my Changing Grandmother).

> You see, when she starts to distribute these robes she tosses them to their owners. They give thanks, calling her "my white shell mother" and saying, "May I prosper and may all things be

[58] *Ibid.*, pp. 63–70.

[59] See Gladys Reichard, *Prayer: The Compulsive Word*, Monographs of the American Ethnological Society, VII (New York: J. J. Augustin Publisher, 1944).

good to me." It's just like the priests who say grace when eating; they don't know where God is, but that's their belief.[60]

Wishes for blessing and new property are represented in the molding, in the display of goods in the hogan, and in the number of people who participate in the ceremony.

The first blessing of an object occurs on the day when the cake is put into the pit. The girl moves the husk crosses in the blessing manner before placing them in position in the pit. The cake is also blessed by the girl and whoever else wishes to do so; the blessing is made by sprinkling corn pollen on the cake in the proper manner. At this time what some informants call a communal prayer to the cake is made. Frank said:

> There are no special prayers while blessing the pit; you just pray. If you do not pray, then you just think or wish. You think about good vegetation, plenty, no hunger, hardships, or suffering, good luck, and good life. All the people bless the pit.

Other informants mentioned similar subjects for these prayers:

> My corn is going to grow; I will have a lot of sheep.[61]

> The prayer was for me to be real healthy (ES).[62]

> Let the corn grow fast. Let the rain rain real hard (RD).[63]

> You pray for the cake to cook and be good. The girl prays while going through the blessing of the cake about the cake and herself (GK).

The corn pollen that is offered throughout the ceremony constitutes a prayer. The hogan is marked in the ritual manner with pollen at the beginning of the final night's activities. This makes it a safe, holy, and sacred place, appropriate for a religious ceremonial at which gods will be present. The goods are also marked, and the people bless themselves.

"Each takes some pollen and puts it on his tongue and head and then swings it outward and upward to the sky, the earth, or the gods. You say a prayer in your own words during this" (FM).

---

[60] McAllester, Field Notes, July 19–20, 1961, p. 7a.
[61] Wyman and Bailey, p. 7, quoting from the field notes of Dr. W. W. Hill.
[62] Anne Keith, Field Notes, July 19, 1963.
[63] *Ibid.*, July 23, 1963 (*supra*, p. 355).

The prayer following the final Twelve Word Song was the most intense of the Kinaaldá prayers. When asked about it, Frank said, "You pray for yourself and your children in your own language in whatever way you want to pray. The people pray if they want income of some kind or if someone in the house is sick. If your man is angry at you, you pray he will get over that and make it up to you."

The songs constitute sung prayers. "She can have anything she wants: food and silver, anything she wants in the future. You know that from the songs they sing" (VW).[64] Frank (*supra*, p. 259) explained the wishful character of some of the songs. All the sequential progressions concern sheep, horses, jewels and fabrics, and other desirable things.

The painting of the girl and the subsequent painting of others is another time for prayers, as mentioned earlier (*supra*, p. 368).

Offerings

The first offering is made to the grindstone when the first piece of cake is cut. The second and final offering consists of burying four pinches of cake to feed the Earth and thank her for the abundant harvest.

In the Chinle Kinaaldá, at least, the last religious act duplicates the first; it is an appropriate "Thank you" to the girl who, representing Changing Woman, returns to their owners the newly blessed goods used during the final molding.

Symbolism in Kinaaldá

Navaho religion is characterized by a sense of balance. "The ritualistic teachings stress male and female as a basic form of symbolism; the notion is that only by pairing can any entity be complete."[65] The ideas of "like produces like" and the "part stands for the whole," two "laws of thought" quite basic to Navaho thinking, according to Kluckhohn and Leighton,[66] perhaps explain the general philosophy behind any and all of the symbolism.

---

[64]*Ibid.*, June 26, 1963 (*supra*, p. 348).

[65]Reichard, *Navaho Religion*, I, 29.

[66]Kluckhohn and Leighton, pp. 230–231.

In the Kinaaldá, the girl herself is a symbol, not only of the major Navaho deity, Changing Woman (and her counterparts: White Shell Woman, Turquoise Woman, and others[67]) and the concepts with which she is associated, such as Earth and Life, but also of the power of reproduction. Her coming of age is connected with new growth of plants and changes in environmental conditions.[68] As Reichard states, "Restoration to youth is the pattern of the earth, something for which the Navaho lives, for he reasons that what happens to the [Mother] earth may also happen to him."[69]

Perhaps one of the most important symbols in the ceremony is that of the sun. The sun is conceived as a circle and projected symbolically. The ceremonial hogan is seen as a circle when it is blessed with corn pollen. When people enter, it is in a sunwise direction. They seat themselves in a circle. The racing is done according to the position of the sun in the sky, and the girl turns sunwise when she returns home. The cake is circular, "so it will be like the sun" (GK), and is baked in a circular pit. The baking is timed according to the passage of the sun. "All the people watch the time; during the summer, the nights are short. You go according to the sun. You give it enough time to bake right. In the winter, you wait till later. Someone has to direct that time schedule. Women are inside and outside keeping track" (FM).[70] When done, it is cut in a sunwise direction. The center assumes anthropomorphic qualities attributed to the sun; it becomes a heart, and as a living thing, it may not be cut with a knife.

The sun is a symbol of life, creation, blessing, and power. According to Reichard, this suggests a sun cult, a monism wherein belief centers on universal harmony or destiny. "The sun is an

---

[67]According to Reichard, an aesthetic motive is represented here. "The notion of multiple selves is a convenient supernatural device for spanning the difference of space and necessity. It is an artifice that lends force to the power of repetition and recapitulation, and it is also a means of elaboration, of obtaining balance, symmetry, and contrast especially in plastic representation. Pairing is an illustration of a cultural compulsion. The reason that Whiteshell Woman and Turquoise Woman are doubles for Changing Woman is aesthetic as well as ritualistic." *Navaho Religion*, I, 249.

[68]McAllester, Field Notes from FM, July 19—20, 1961, p. 11b.

[69]Reichard, *Navaho Religion*, I, 21.

[70]McAllester, Field Notes, July 19—20, 1961, pp. 4a—b.

agent of that monism, a central deity who correlates the nether
and celestial worlds with this one, who exists to assist man to his
final destiny. Changing Woman may possibly be the female mani-
festation of Sun."[71] Disappearance of the sun, as in an eclipse,
initiates efforts to re-establish harmony. Taboos are in force
during this phenomenon.

According to Reichard, time and space are symbols of recapitulation.

> Among the primary mythical concepts are ideas about time and
> space. If something happened, once, it may happen again. If there
> is life and activity in this world, there must have been similar
> worlds elsewhere, below and above. Man and his experience must
> be identified with events in earlier—that is, mythological—times
> and in the lower worlds.[72]
>
> Time is relative, and, ritualistically speaking, past, present,
> and future are interchangeable.[73]

Thus, when a Kinaaldá is held, Changing Woman's first Kinaaldá
is symbolically re-enacted.

Symbolism is also involved in the colors used in the costume and painting of the girl. For example, white is associated
with a division between the sacred and profane, symbolizing a
change to holiness. It further implies day, newness, and hope.
The song texts mention other colors: birds are blue, dark-colored,
and "speckled yellow"; mocassins are dark-seamed; the jewels
mentioned are white shell, turquoise, abalone, rock crystal, and
black jewels; white clay and red ocher are paired with White Shell
Girl and Turquoise Girl; and corn is both white and yellow.[74]

Directional symbolism also is associated with Kinaaldá.
Application of ceremonial materials on the body follows specific
directions. Prescribed directional patterns are in force when entering the hogan, sitting, using corn pollen, racing, and handling
the yucca root. Reichard discusses the symbolic meanings of the
directions. For example, many things are "ritualistically dealt

---

[71]Reichard, *Navaho Religion*, I, 76.
[72]*Ibid.*, p. 13.
[73]*Ibid.*, p. 24.
[74]See *ibid.*, pp. 187–208 and 214–216 for a discussion of the symbolic meanings attached
to other colors and color pairs.

with from base to tip, because growth, and therefore life, is upward."[75]

The sexes in balance are symbolized in the song texts, the ceremonial behavior in the hogan, and the racing (according to Reichard). The balance is established in contrasting pairs.

Precious stones have symbolic implications. For example, turquoise is a "collective term for all the precious stones, wealth, or mixed offerings. Good fortune is attributed to this stone."[76] Both white shell and turquoise are emphasized in Kinaaldá.

The usual sacred numbers occur in Kinaaldá, as in other ceremonies. The number four is emphasized most strongly. Ideally, the Kinaaldá is a four-day ceremony. Many of its rites and songs include references to four or its multiples. There is also a special emphasis on the idea of "the first." As Reichard says: "So much importance is attached in both myth and practice to beginning an event or to the first time an act takes place as to make initiation a major symbol.... Apparently the first try has power because it signifies the purpose and predicts the outcome."[77] The importance of "the first" is shown in the contrasting attitudes toward the first and subsequent menstruations. The idea that the Kinaaldá is a time of rebirth is also widespread. The ceremony stresses the newness and the influential power of actions and attitudes expressed during its celebration.

Alternation characterizes the various rites and songs. According to Reichard, "The main function of alternation... is to prevent overdoing."[78] Likewise, "A conscious negation is as significant as other symbols. Prescription is almost impossible without restriction."[79]

The food used in Kinaaldá also has symbolic meaning. Corn, the symbol of food, fertility, and life itself, is of major

---

[75]*Ibid.*, p. 162. The discussion of direction symbolism is on pp. 161–170.
[76]*Ibid.*, p. 209.
[77]*Ibid.*, pp. 248–49.
[78]*Ibid.*, p. 180.
[79]*Ibid.*, p. 184.

importance. "Corn is more than human; it is divine; it [is] connected with the highest ethical ideals."[80] Food in general is a major symbol of each chant. It signifies plenty, "[indicating] the success of a ceremony, strength, endurance, and transformation."[81] The avoidance of certain foods is an act of purification.

Sound symbolism is also present. Reichard says that "one or more sounds are significant symbols of every ceremony."[82] A special shout characterizes Kinaaldá racing. The songs used during the ceremony contain references to sounds of the deities, of animals, or of acts associated with them. The Dawn or Washing Songs contain such ideas as "Since he talks to it now, now it listens to him. ... Blessedness comes out of his mouth." The Racing Songs mention other sounds: sounds of the running "fading into the distance" and then returning; sounds of "small blue male" and "female birds who call with beautiful voices as they are playing in the tip of the girl's head plume"; sounds of the "breeze coming from her as she runs"; and the sounds of the Corn Beetle and all kinds of small birds, including dark-colored ones, blue male and female ones, and "speckled yellow ones." The sounds of some of these birds are also present in the Combing Songs and the Painting Songs. In other Kinaaldá songs, some of the syllables previously thought to be meaningless have now been shown to be imitations of the sounds and calls associated with particular deities.[83]

The pollen applied in order to attain blessing represents control. It is an outstanding "symbol of life and protection, fructification, verification, and the continuity of life and safety."[84] "Matthews summarizes the meaning of pollen: 'Pollen is the emblem of peace, of happiness, of prosperity, and it is supposed to bring these blessings.'"[85]

---

[80]Reichard, *Navaho Religion*, II, p. 540.

[81]*Ibid.*, p. 557.

[82]*Ibid.*, p. 560.

[83]*Supra*, p. 118.

[84]Reichard, *Navaho Religion*, I, 250.

[85]*Ibid.*, p. 251, quoting from Washington Matthews, "The Night Chant, a Navaho Ceremony," *Memoirs of the American Museum of Natural History*, VI (May, 1902), 42.

Expression of the Navaho View of Life in the Kinaaldá

The Navaho conception of life is apparent in the Kinaaldá material. As Reichard states, a Navaho's life cycle is called "a walk through time."[86] Living in the present and doing so in harmony with the universe is of utmost importance. The life crises are significant events. Children are highly desirable as continuers of the race, and births are a source of joy. That the onset of puberty, which enables reproduction, is a happy event is well attested above. According to Reichard,[87] illness is an inevitable result of being out of harmony with the universe. Sickness results from failure to observe some of the numerous restrictions, excess in any activity, ignorance of ceremonial law or transgressing it, contact with the dead, being too weak to withstand the power of a chant, or sorcery. Only through the time-honored means of appropriate ceremonialism can sickness or disease be combated.[88]

Old age, while viewed as something to be avoided, is accepted when it comes. As Rose said, "There's nothing we can do about this business of age; you just have to take it as it comes." Many of the Kinaaldá taboos are directed at preventing premature age. Others, however, stress respect for elders. These latter teachings reflect the beliefs that the spiritual powers of the aged may be strong and communicable and that their powers for evil are to be feared.

As Reichard indicates, the Navaho have "little idea of personal immortality."[89] "One loses personal identity at death and becomes an indefinable part of the universal whole."[90] Kluckhohn and Leighton describe the Navaho afterworld:

> Existence in the hereafter appears to be only a shadowy and uninviting thing. The afterworld is a place like this earth, located to the north and below the earth's surface. It is approached by a trail

---

[86]Reichard, *Navaho Religion*, I, 37.

[87]*Ibid.*, paraphrase of material on pp. 80–81.

[88]Now this view is being extended to include a certain amount of recognition of the value of medical treatment.

[89]*Ibid.*, p. 33.

[90]*Ibid.*, p. 42.

down a hill or cliff, and there is a sandpile at the bottom. Deceased
kinfolk, who look as they did when last seen alive, come to guide
the dying to the afterworld during a journey that takes four days.
At the entrance to the afterworld, old guardians apply tests to see
if death has really occurred.[91]

As Reichard says:

> Normally the Navaho staves off death as long as possible, rely-
> ing upon religions formula to keep him safe. He admits that death
> is inevitable and is not nearly as afraid of it as he is of the dead. . . .
> . . . Indifference about the afterlife doubtless reflects the ethi-
> cal system, which holds that man suffers here on earth, if at all,
> but need not expect punishment after death; the individual spirit
> may be lost in the cosmos. Man can better his life here on earth
> by ceremonial control; he cannot change his ultimate destiny.[92]

Aesthetics

The Navaho have two words for "beautiful": *nizhóni* and *hózhǫ*. But each of these means more than "beautiful." *Nizhóni* can
be translated as "pretty," "clean," "nice," "fine," and "good";[93]
hózhǫ can mean "happiness," "pleasantness," "blessed," "well-
being," and "harmony."[94] The key to Navaho aesthetics lies in
these two words and in two others which are practically identical:
zhǫ, "beauty," and *shǫ*, "to be good."[95] The Navaho aesthetic is
actually a three-dimensional concept. In addition to the pure aesthetic of *l'art pour l'art*, or approaching beauty for beauty's sake,
it also pertains to what is moral and what is functional.

The Kinaaldá songs and the ceremony give insights about
what the Navaho consider to be "pretty" or "beautiful." The
twenty-fifth Talking God Hogan Song shows that the surface of
rocks, the sides of mountains, bushes and trees which have leaves,
and flowing springs are all considered "beautiful." In the Racing

---

[91]Kluckhohn and Leighton, p. 126.

[92]Reichard, *Navaho Religion*, I, 40–41.

[93]Robert Young and William Morgan, *The Navaho Language* (Salt Lake City, Utah: Deseret
Book Company, 1958), p. 170.

[94]Leon Wall and William Morgan, *Navajo-English Dictionary*, (Window Rock, Ariz.: Navajo
Agency, 1958), p. 36.

[95]Father Berard Haile, *A Stem Vocabulary of the Navaho Language* (St. Michaels, Ariz.:
St. Michaels Press, 1950, 1951), I, 278; II, 20, 139.

Songs, various birds and blowing breezes are said to be "beautiful."

People, as well as elements of nature, are "beautiful." The songs and myths mention various deities who are "beautifully clad"; they include Talking God, Hogan God, White Corn Boy, Yellow Corn Girl, Corn Pollen Boy, and Corn Beetle Girl. Comely servants appear in the various processions of desirable things which lead up to the girl and then go beyond her. The girl is also seen as being "beautiful"; the songs refer to the addition of various items of costume which make her progressively more beautiful. Finally, in the last line, she is called "the child of long life and everlasting beauty." It is obvious in reviewing the ceremonial restrictions that a beautiful girl to the Navaho is one who possesses a straight, humpless back, good posture, a good figure, "natural beauty," good teeth, long hair, and unscarred and unwrinkled skin.

Objects may be beautified. The twenty-fifth Talking God Hogan Song mentions prayer sticks which are "beautifully decorated" with various sacred jewels. RD (*supra*, p. 364) mentioned spreading various attractive things around the hogan to "make it pretty."

Sounds can also be beautiful. Many of the songs mention that as the birds in the tip of the girl's head plume are playing, they call and "their voices are beautiful." Comments relevant to musical aesthetics were offered freely by three Kinaaldá informants.

> We had a big crowd that night.... Everything went so nicely. I don't know how many people came to the Kinaaldá. The hogan was packed, and yet the people just sang so nicely. ...It was really nice. And they all kept together, and that's what makes it sound so pretty (Aug.S).
>
> Anyone can start the singing of a sacred song. Toward morning, they sing real pretty songs (JF).[96]
>
> [Describing the free singing:] There were nine men and five ladies who sang, and others were watching. The ladies sang and

---

[96] Keith, Field Notes, June 22, 1963.

then the men, so that it went back and forth like two choruses. They
sang a lot of special songs. The ladies sang about sheep, mountains, and water men. They were really pretty songs (RD).[97]

An element of perfection and holiness must be associated
with the object or person before the person or object can be considered "beautiful." In the last Chief Hogan Song, "the house
from which beauty radiates" is a house that has been "swept
clean." In other songs, the "beautiful" items are the "perfect"
jewels which are placed on the girl's forehead and the goods
"which extend to the horizon increasing without a blemish." In the
tenth Chief Hogan Song, the "house of everlasting beauty" is first
a "holy house" built with wood, soft fabrics, jewels, gathered rain
waters, and corn pollen. In the Dawn or Washing Song Group, the
song that mentions "beauty" in the chorus and burden is preceded
by one mentioning "holiness"; in Song No. 3, the main idea is that
"he has come upon holiness" below the east, south, west, and
north; Song No. 4 terminates the set with the idea that below the
four cardinal points "he came upon beauty."

What is beautiful is not only that which is aesthetically appealing on its own terms or that which is holy and perfect; it is
also that which serves a beneficent purpose, that which is functional. Valuable property is displayed in the hogan during a ceremony not only for purposes of decoration and show but also for its
symbolic value. The beautiful fabrics, blankets, and deerskins,
for example, are "soft goods" which collectively may symbolize
life.[98] Furthermore, the display of these goods enhances the possibility that they will increase in kind and number in the near
future.

In "Enemy Way Music," McAllester has shown that in the
realm of music the good and the beautiful are inseparable. As one
of his informants said, "It's songs like the Lightning Way and some
of the songs in the Blessing Way that are most beautiful. It's good
for the patient and makes him well. If it's worthwhile its beauti-

[97]*Ibid.*, July 23, 1963.
[98]Reichard, *Navaho Religion*, II, 530.

ful. You could never say skip dance songs are beautiful."[99] Such statements and similar ones which the author collected in the summer of 1964 indicate that at least some Navaho consider the Kinaaldá songs to be "pretty." Since these songs belong to the Blessing Way Ceremony, it is evident that a mixture of functionalism is implied in the aesthetic. The songs bring good fortune to those singing and hearing them. They assure the girl of good health, good luck, a happy home, abundant crops, jewelry, soft fabrics, sheep, horses, and other animals in her future life.

That the Navaho believe that "that which is beautiful is good" is evident in the rites of the Kinaaldá, as well as in the singing. For example, the girl is molded so she will be beautiful. Being beautiful in this case, however, implies more than having a good figure. It means the girl will be strong, ambitious, and capable of enduring much. The molding affects the girl's personality as well as her body. It implies that she will be friendly, unselfish, and cheerful; it means she will be a kind mother and a responsible housekeeper. A "beautiful" girl, therefore, is not only physically appealing; she is also "good" and "useful."

The Role of the Religious Practitioner

Many aspects of the role of the singer or religious practitioner in Navaho culture are reflected in the Kinaaldá. Within the predominantly matrilineal and matrilocal Navaho society, the singer, who is usually male, is generally highly respected as the possessor of esoteric knowledge. Characteristically, however, he is also feared, since there is always a possibility that he may use his special powers to harm others.

Once the singer has agreed[100] to perform a Kinaaldá, he has many duties.[101] Throughout the ceremony, he is responsible for

---

[99] David McAllester, "Enemy Way Music," *Papers of the Peabody Museum of American Archaeology and Ethnology, Harvard University*, Vol. XLI, No. 3 (1954), p. 71. A discussion of Navaho musical aesthetics is on pp. 71–75.

[100] The singer may refuse because he is busy or tired, because the payment offered to him is not acceptable, or because of existing eating and/or drinking conditions at the household involved.

[101] "Psychotherapy and Navaho Religion," by Dorothea and Alexander Leighton (*Psychiatry*, Vol. IV, No. 4 [November, 1941], pp. 515–523), is recommended to those interested in the psychological role of the singer and the effect of ceremonies.

the religious proceedings. He directs and controls the timing and is responsible for correct execution of the rites. He leads the fixed singing and insures that songs are rendered "correctly." Should this not be done, the Holy People who attend the ceremony would be angry, and the patient and others in the hogan would be harmed. According to Ladd's informant, Bidaga:

> If the singing is really doing well the Holy People will sure be happy. They listen to the song and they enjoy the song, and they listen outside. They stay outside all night till morning. Then they go away. The Holy People say it's really good singing, and let's go back home—so they go back home. If the singing is not very good, he always missing the song, missing the words, the Holy People will not listen and also will not happy. Oh so too bad for the singing—if he miss the words while singing.
> ...So the Holy People they outside, they listen. If this singing is going pretty good, when the patient go out [after the completion of the Hogan Songs]—they feel happy. If the Singer not doing well, the Holy People will say: It's too bad for all the people what's in there in the hogan. Not just for the patient but for all the people in there....
>
> . . . .
>
> The Holy People is, they say—any person make fun of the song, make laughing at the song. The man who does it that way to the Blessing Way song, that person is not going to live very long. Also make fun of the medicine man. That's the way it happens a lot around here. It seems to him that way. Indians, young people just get sick and they just dies.[102]

Throughout the ceremony, the singer is also responsible for maintaining good morale so the people will perform their duties cheerfully and remain attentive during the all-night singing.

While reports differ as to when the singers must arrive, they agree that the main singer should remain until the public Kinaaldá activities are completed. According to Frank Mitchell:

> Some singers stay there for singing, but not for the last blessing. If they want to leave early, before the last blessing outside, they can take their 'alkaan and go home. They can leave early if they want to get home to their wives. The main singer is the last one to leave. If the one who did the main singing wants to leave early, he can appoint a man there to do the painting of the girl if

---

[102]Ladd, pp. 374–376.

he knows that that man knows the song. Then he can leave. It looks better, however, to stay to the very end.

Frank said that the main singer in Kinaaldá is paid for his services with a large piece of 'alkaan. Other informants mentioned money, robes, blankets, grain, wine, shirts, bread from the store, cookies, and candy. Several said that he is not given material of any sort, a fact which differentiates Kinaaldá and Blessing Way payments. Others made no such distinction.

The singer, however, does not have absolute control over a Kinaaldá. The family giving the ceremony determines which procedures will be followed, where alternate forms are available. For example, according to some informants, the family decides whether songs will accompany the rites on the first day.

Furthermore, the singer is not regarded as infallible. Usually those who come to help with the singing are chanters themselves or at least know some version of the songs associated with the particular ceremony. They check the singer as well as assist, as it is important that the ceremony be executed "correctly." As has been shown,[103] definitions of correctness vary. Differences in procedures and songs are openly discussed. At times during the singing, the majority will override the main practitioner and render their versions of portions of the songs. It is not uncommon, therefore, for several versions to be sung simultaneously, with each individual insisting that his version is the "correct" one. This usually brings objections from the main singer, which may or may not be ignored,[104] depending on the composition of the chorus. In the Kinaaldá witnessed by the author, when a question of the proper version arose while women were singing with the men, the women ceased singing until agreement was reached and then rejoined the chorus.[105]

---

[103]See Charlotte Johnson, "Talking God's Hogan Songs" (MS), pp. 50–54.

[104]This seems to be more acceptable at certain times than at others.

[105]In the one case where a woman singer was leading, the singing was mainly of a solo nature. Any corrections shouted at her by the male singers were ignored by the woman (Bird Woman), who sang two songs at LS's Kinaaldá.

CHAPTER FIVE

The Future of the Kinaaldá

IT is well known that some Navaho myths and rituals have become obsolete within the last hundred years, "but to say that they became extinct because the last old man who knew them died is a very superficial explanation. Had they not lost their importance as conditions changed for the People, younger men would have taken the trouble to learn them."[1]

It seems unlikely, however, that this will be the case with the Kinaaldá. Navaho society is still preferentially matrilineal and matrilocal. The Blessing Way, to which the Kinaaldá belongs, is prophylactic rather than curative. Informants said that it is the best-understood Navaho ceremony and that it is conducted more frequently than any other on the reservation.

Change is inevitable in any culture, and there is abundant evidence for this among the Navaho. Some informants, when discussing Kinaaldá, insisted that the ceremony has not altered since the day it began. However, even these gave evidence of change in their descriptions of Kinaaldá procedure. The modifications recognized by most informants are in details of practice, rather than in basic function.[2] A list of them appears in Chart 7.

---

[1]Clyde Kluckhohn and Dorothea Leighton, *The Navaho* (Cambridge, Mass.: Harvard University Press, 1948), p. 166.

[2]Some changes are recognized in the myths. For example, at the first ceremony the girl received a new name, and then never again; she was originally painted with white shell, rather than *dleesh*.

CHART 7*

Item	Old Way	Present Way
1. Timing of the ceremony	Within a few days of puberty	Can be postponed due to school in some regions
2. Pony tail	Only used for Kinaaldá	Anyone can wear hair in this style
3. Hair string	Tied only with appropriate string	Rubber band put on first
4. Race	Competition	No competition
5. Grinding	Done to singing† Use only grinding stones	No singing Use corn grinders bought at the store as well
6. Taboos	Mentioned	Many not mentioned
7. Food taboos	Allow sugar	Not allow sugar
8. Cake	Ferment and sweeten by chewing sprouted wheat and spitting it into batter No sugar No raisins	No longer do this Add sugar Add raisins
9. Cake size	Small	Bigger than before
10. Measuring the pit	Horn implements used	Shovels used
11. Pit lining	A kind of plant	Cornhusks
12. Drinking	None	Much
13. Police	Not present	Presence requested
14. Cake-cutting	Wood or stone implements used	Knives used

---

*Informants also said that puberty formerly occurred when girls were fifteen to sixteen years old, but that it happened now between the ages of ten and fourteen.

†See Charlotte Johnson, "Navaho Corn Grinding Songs,"*Journal of the Society for Ethnomusicology*, VIII, No. 2 (May, 1964), pp. 101–120.

Item	Old Way	Present Way
15. Painting	Downward direction or whatever people wanted	Upward direction
16. Aftermath of ceremony	Four-day quiet	Quiet, but length of duration can be shortened
17. Clothing	Retain ceremonial dress during four-day quiet	Change clothes when public part of ceremony is over

The most frequently mentioned alteration was in the old method of chewing and spitting into the cake batter.

> The chewing and spitting into the batter is the only difference I know of. You chew and spit in order to sweeten the cake. This has been abandoned because of contagious diseases (FM).

> They used to grind some kind of wheat and put it in to sweeten it. Some people chewed wheat and spit it into the pan. I don't like that. I was asked at my Kinaaldá if it would be all right to let the people do that and I said, "No." Then they asked if I would do it myself and I said "No" again; no one was going to put those germs in there! (GK)

Almost as frequently mentioned in the comments of informants was relaxation of taboos.

> Now they don't pay attention to things like that at Kinaaldá. Girls eat candy and sweet stuff. It's no wonder that present-day girls begin to lose their teeth and that their teeth become decayed. Even coffee used to be drunk unsweetened. . . . There are many things that you were not supposed to do in the early days when you were in that condition. Nowadays, those things are no longer observed. They don't bother to tell the girls about those things anymore. They just tell them to go ahead and go about their business just as at any other time (RM).

> [After giving a list of taboos] These were the things done in the old days (MCS).

But in the Kinaaldá observed by the author, most of the earlier taboos were enforced. Only three instances of uncorrected "violations" were recorded. In Marie Shirley's ceremony, Augusta

Sandoval left the hogan before the Hogan Songs had been terminated. In both Marie's and Lena's Kinaaldá, several men, women, and children went to sleep during the all-night singing. In Marie's, the ideal woman was replaced after the first day, since the one originally chosen refused to return and be involved in a ceremony which included whites with cameras.

Informants also commented on the increase in drinking which accompanies present-day Kinaaldá. Formerly this would not have been allowed. "There were no drunks before .... You know, in those early days, I didn't even know what a drunkard was. Everything was so nice at my Kinaaldá; we didn't have any drunkards or anything .... But nowadays, when one of them comes in feeling good, it just ruins the whole thing" (Aug.S). Drinking has been present at the Kinaaldá and other ceremonies the author has witnessed. It has become common procedure for the family giving a ceremony to request police surveillance, to have a "panel"[3] arrive during the night, and even to have one or two intoxicated people forcibly removed from the premises during the singing.

According to available data, individual reactions to certain features of the Kinaaldá have remained stable for at least three generations. Representatives from three age groups (ten to twenty-five years old, ten informants; twenty-five to fifty years old, four informants; and fifty years and above, three informants) agreed on specific requirements that they found unpleasant and/or annoying. Of those listed below, "the heavy jewelries," the "hot and heavy clothes," and the "hard work" were most frequently cited.

	Age Group		
Feature Disliked	_10−25-_ _year-olds_	_25−50_ _year-olds_	_50-year-_ _olds and_ _above_
Work	X	X	
Racing	X		

---

[3]English-speaking Navaho use this term to designate a patrol wagon.

| | Age Group | | |
| | 10−25- year-olds | 25−50 year-olds | 50-year-olds and above |
Feature Disliked			
Grinding	X		
Hot clothes	X	X	X
Heavy clothes	X	X	X
Heavy jewelry	X	X	X
Staying up all night	X		
Sitting with straight back	X		
Pointless trouble		X	
Kinaaldá in winter so wet hair became icicles	X	X	

Not every informant found aspects of the Kinaaldá unpleasant; some even verbalized very positive attitudes toward the ceremony as a whole. For example, Jane Marianito found it "fun," and Sally Carson said, "it was good to do it."[4]

| | Age Group | | |
| | 10−25- year-olds | 25−50 year-olds | 50-year-olds and above |
Attitude			
NEGATIVE			
Did not like being stared at	X		
Felt ashamed	X	X	
Felt scared	X	X	
POSITIVE			
Not scared	X		
Fun	X	X	
Good to do it	X	X	X
Liked it	X		X

In each generation there were women who refused to undergo the ceremony. The Kinaaldá has also been affected by school attendance. In regions when it is mandatory that it be performed at the time of pubescence, three girls of the ten to twenty-five year-old age group were unable to have the ceremony because they were in school. In other regions, in both the ten to twenty-five and twenty-five to fifty year-old age groups, there was ample evidence of adjusting the ceremony to correspond with restrictions imposed on the girls by their school attendance.

---

[4] Anne Keith, Field Notes, August 16, 1963.

Originally, the ceremony began whenever a girl said she had it. It was a custom to fix her hair up before nightfall. Now it is changed; she might be in school. There might be a delay (FM).[5]

Now you can't always do Kinaaldá within a few days because the girls are away at school. So you can do it in the summertime. We are like the Apaches here because they save them all up for the Fourth of July and do all the girls in a group then. This is another way the two groups are getting similar in this ceremony (CS).

No differences were evident among the three generations in their attitude toward the ceremonial taboos. Augusta Sandoval (a member of the twenty-five to fifty year-old group), in answer to a question about whether the former taboos are still enforced, said:

They try to tell them about those things, but they don't listen, so I guess that they just give up. In my day, I really did believe in everything that they told me because, well, we weren't as modernized as we are now. I just went along with the folks. I really did believe in some of the things they told me. But now, if they told me the same things, I don't think I would go for it.

Geneva Kee, Marie Shirley, and Lena Shirley (members of the ten to twenty-five year-old group) and Augusta Sandoval did not believe that eating their own 'alkaan would have detrimental consequences. All ate part of their own corncakes during their puberty ceremonies. Rose Mitchell (a member of the fifty year-old and above group) questioned the efficacy of food taboos because even though she had adhered to the restrictions, her teeth were highly defective.

However, these same informants and others also supported restrictions found in Kinaaldá: "And during the time that I was a kinaaldá, I wasn't supposed to eat any sweet stuff of any kind. I just didn't believe them and I ate cookies by the boxes and I even ate some of my own cake. Now when I get toothaches, I think of that"(Aug.S).

Rosalyn Dean said that she applied the white clay to herself in the belief it would increase her height. However, she applied it in a downward rather than an upward direction and has been short in stature ever since.[6]

---

[5]David McAllester, Field Notes, July 19–20, 1961, p. 7a.
[6]Keith, Field Notes, July 23, 1963 (supra, p. 367).

Some of the material Anne Keith collected suggests that the ceremony, at least in the final night of singing, is losing meaning for the girls involved. Several informants stated they could not understand the songs.

> They sang twelve special songs [Hogan Songs]. I couldn't understand the words: they're hard words (ES).[7]

> The songs are really pretty songs but I couldn't really understand the words. (RD).[8]

> The medicine man sings all night, but I don't know what the songs are about. I don't listen to them (SC).[9]

> Even if it was my father singing the songs, I didn't listen to him. I fell asleep. My mother and father kept shaking me.
> I've forgotten what the songs are about. I don't know anything about the Holy People you pray to for Kinaaldá. If you really pay attention to the medicine man, I guess you would. I wasn't interested in anything that time because I was sick. If not, I could be really interested and stay up all night. I wanted to but I couldn't.
> I don't know how it started or who had it first. My father would probably know, but I don't. He never has time to tell us anything. He is too busy. When he is home, he is always sleeping.
> I guess 'Esdzáánádleehé is the one that started these things. When my father is going to do a singing, he always gives a speech and says where those things came from. He just mentioned those names, but I never could get it into my head (Ja.M).[10]

Other informants in the Pinedale region as well as at Chinle did, however, understand the songs and myths.

During Marie Shirley's Kinaaldá, Augusta Sandoval said she was not going to have the ceremony for her daughters when they reached puberty. Later in the summer, she was asked about this. She replied:

> Oh, yes, by all means I want them to do it. I want them to satisfy my father and mother because I want them to know that I really do think a lot of all that they did for me. I want them to know and appreciate it. I don't want them to think that just because I understand English and my kids understand English, I don't want to have anything to do with Kinaaldá. I don't want them to think that way.

---

[7]*Ibid.*, July 19, 1963.
[8]*Ibid.*, July 23, 1963.
[9]*Ibid.*, July 2, 1963.
[10]*Ibid.*, July 9, 1963. (Ja.M's father is a practitioner.)

I told Cecilia that I'm going to go all the way with it and that she is going to do the 'alkaan. I told her, "when you become a kinaaldá, you're going to do just what Mama did when she became a kinaaldá." And I told her that her grandparents won't be with us all the time; one of these days they are going to leave us. I told her that you should do that just to please them. If you turn them down and you don't want to do it, it will be disappointing to them and it will hurt me because after all, we are just going to do it for them. But even then, even if they weren't living, I would go ahead and have it because I do have a real strong belief in my father's Hózhǫ́ǫ́ji'. I have told her right along that she is going to make an 'alkaan. She is happy about it.

Culture change is in the evidence on the reservation, for with the spread of the white man's ways the Navaho of the present generation are caught between the two cultures.

The People are in a transitional stage. They are torn between their own ancient standards and those which are urged upon them by teachers, missionaries and other whites. An appreciable number of Navahos are so confused by the conflicting precepts of their elders and their white models that they tend, in effect, to reject the whole problem of morality (in the widest sense) as meaningless or insoluble. For longer or shorter periods in their lives their only guide is the expediency of the immediate situation....

...A stable social structure prevails only so long as the majority of individuals in the society find enough satisfaction both in the goals socially approved and in the institutionalized means of attainment to compensate them for the constraints which ordered social life inevitably imposes upon uninhibited response to impulse. The incipient breakdown of any culture brings a loss of predictability and hence of dependability in personal relations. The absence of generally accepted standards of behavior among individuals constitutes in fact, a definition of social disorganization.[11]

In contrast with rapid changes in certain areas, in religion, both myth and ritual tend to "preserve and to carry forward ancient Navaho tradition."[12]

The People themselves are aware of this stabilizing force of their religious beliefs. Consciously or unconsciously, they act accordingly. The revival of almost forgotten rites and the renewed zeal with which others are being used today are a form of what has

---

[11]Kluckhohn and Leighton, p. 217. (The second paragraph of the quotation has been reordered.)

[12]Ibid., p. 168.

been called "antagonistic acculturation." In other words, The People symbolically affirm their resistance to white men's efforts to change their way of life by giving even more importance and attention to their own ceremonials.[13]

In predicting the future of the Kinaaldá, perhaps no statement can be made until the effects of off-reservation living on ceremonialism can be fully determined. At present, some people return to the reservation for ceremonies; others are inducing singers to leave the reservation and perform shorter, week-end versions in off-reservation settlements. The amount of ceremonial training given to the present generation of men living on the reservation should also be determined. Currently many of the major singers are seventy or eighty years old. Their pupils should be identified before a prediction about future ceremonialism can be made.

Nevertheless, it can be foreseen that the future of Kinaaldá is assured for some time to come. The basic format of the ceremony, the underlying belief in its necessity and importance, and the frequency with which it is held have not changed for several generations. Certain alterations have occurred, as mentioned above, but these are minor ones. In the future, revisions will undoubtedly continue. But it appears likely that the innovations will be procedural, rather than functional. The basic Kinaaldá will continue until that time when Changing Woman, Talking God, White Shell Woman, and other deities cease to have meaning for the Navaho and some other principle replaces the concept of harmony obtained through orderly human effort—the concept which has been and still is the foundation of Navaho religion.

---

[13]*Ibid.*

APPENDIX A

Informants[1]

Initials	Informant	Area of Residence	Field Worker
B	Baańzizba	Red Rock, Arizona	D. McAllester
A B	Archie Begay	Lukachukai, Arizona	C. Johnson
C B	Carla Begay	Pinedale, New Mexico	A. Keith
D B	Diné łbáhí (Gray Man)	Valley Store, Arizona	C. Johnson
J B	John Bull	Lukachukai, Arizona	C. Johnson
M B	Mary Bunnell	Fort Wingate, New Mexico	A. Keith
Mrs. B	Mrs. Bedaga	Ramah, New Mexico	F. Bailey
C C	Charley Cojo	Ramah, New Mexico	C. Kluckhohn
J C	Judy Carson	Iyanbito, New Mexico	A. Keith
S C	Sally Carson	Iyanbito, New Mexico	A. Keith
L D	Linda Dickson	Pinedale, New Mexico	A. Keith
R D	Rosalyn Dean	Pinedale, New Mexico	A. Keith
W D	Walter Davis	Chinle, Arizona	C. Johnson
J F	Janice Fernandez	Iyanbito, New Mexico	A. Keith
J H	Janie Henio	Ramah, New Mexico	J. Chappat
J I	Jackie Izzie	Chinle, Arizona	C. Johnson
L J	Lisa Jones	Tohatchi Mountain, New Mexico	A. Keith
G K	Geneva Kee	Chinle, Arizona	C. Johnson
B L	Bertha Lorenzo	Ramah, New Mexico	F. Bailey / C. Kluckhohn
A M	Anna Marianito	Pinedale, New Mexico	A. Keith

[1]Keith's informants have been given pseudonyms in this work. Their identity may be ascertained by contacting Anne Keith.

Initials	Informant	Area of Residence	Field Worker
BM	Blue Mule (Dzaa nééz dootł'izhi)	Lukachukai, Arizona	C. Johnson
DM	Dick Morton	Church Rock, New Mexico	A. Keith
FM	Frank Mitchell	Chinle, Arizona	D. McAllester C. Johnson
IsM	Isabelle Mitchell	Chinle, Arizona	C. Johnson
JM	Jane Marianito	Pinedale, New Mexico	A. Keith
Ja.M	Jeannette Marianito	Pinedale, New Mexico	A. Keith
KCM	Kay Chee Martin	Ramah, New Mexico	R. Rapoport
RM	Rose Mitchell	Chinle, Arizona	C. Johnson
SM	Seya Mitchell	Cottonwood School, near Black Mountain, Arizona	C. Johnson
Sa.M	Sam Martinez	Ramah, New Mexico	E. Vogt
TM	Totsoni Mark	Lukachukai, Arizona	C. Johnson
WM	Willie Marianito	Pinedale, New Mexico	A. Keith
N	Natansito	Ramah, New Mexico	A. Leighton D. Leighton
DP	Dick Pino	Ramah, New Mexico	C. Kluckhohn
FP	Frank Pino	Ramah, New Mexico	C. Kluckhohn
Mrs. FSP	Mrs. Frank Sam Pino	Ramah, New Mexico	A. Leighton D. Leighton
Mrs. JP	Mrs. Jose Pino	Ramah, New Mexico	F. Bailey
RP	Robert Pinto	Ramah, New Mexico	C. Kluckhohn
Aug.S	Augusta Sandoval	Chinle, Arizona	C. Johnson
CS	Albert G. (Chic) Sandoval ('Éé'neishoodii yázhí—Small Priest)	Lukachukai, Arizona	D. McAllester C. Johnson
Ce.S	Cecilia Sandoval	Chinle, Arizona	C. Johnson
DS	Dave Skeet	Two Wells, New Mexico	F. Bailey C. Kluckhohn A. Leighton D. Leighton
ES	Edna Sterns	Pinedale, New Mexico	A. Keith
HS	Happy Skeet	Two Wells, New Mexico	A. Leighton D. Leighton
LS	Lena Shirley	Chinle, Arizona	C. Johnson
MS	Marie Shirley	Chinle, Arizona	C. Johnson
MCS	Mrs. Albert G. Sandoval	Lukachukai, Arizona	C. Johnson
TS	Tessie Skeet	Two Wells, New Mexico	D. Leighton

Appendix A

Initials	Informant	Area of Residence	Field Worker
T	Tł'aáh (Left-Handed One)	Nava, New Mexico	M. Wheelwright
BT	Ben Thomas	Ramah, New Mexico	A. Leighton D. Leighton
DT	Diné tsósí (Slim Man)	Lukachukai, Arizona	D. McAllester C. Johnson
BW	Billie Wilson	Iyanbito, New Mexico	A. Keith
Bd.W.	Bird Woman	Chinle, Arizona	C. Johnson
CW	Charlie Watchman	Chinle, Arizona	C. Johnson
VW	Virginia Wilson	Iyanbito, New Mexico	A. Keith
IY	Inez Yazzie	Pinedale, New Mexico	A. Keith
WY	Wilson Yazzie	Chinle, Arizona	C. Johnson

APPENDIX B

Kinaaldá Myths

A. References for the nine[1] previously available versions of the Kinaaldá
Origin Myth.

Curtis, Edward. *The North American Indian.* Vol. I. *Apache, Jicarillas,
Navaho.* Cambridge, Mass.: The University Press, 1907, Pp. 94-95, 98.

Franciscan Fathers, *An Ethnologic Dictionary of the Navaho Language.*
St. Michaels, Ariz.: St. Michaels Press, 1910. Pp. 355, 359.

Goddard, Pliny. "Navaho Texts,"*Anthropological Papers of the American
Museum of Natural History,* XXXIV, Part I (1933), pp. 62-67, 150-153.

Haile, Father Berard. "Blessingway" Versions I, II, and III, with introductions, notes, appendices, and supplementary songs; MSS, Special
Collections Division, University of Arizona Library, Tucson, Arizona.
Version I: Informant: Slim Curly (1932); 604 pp. and 44 pp. of appendices. Version II: Informant: Frank Mitchell (1932); 644 pp. and 10 pp.
of songs from "Who dragged a warrior out of" (no date). Version III:
Informant: Curley Parallel Streams (no date); 456 pp. (228 pp. of text
and 228 pp. of translation) and 61 pp. of notes.

———, "Origin Legend of the Navaho Enemy Way," *Yale University Publications in Anthropology,* XVII (1938), 84-91 and notes on p. 251.

Matthews, Washington. "Navaho Legends," *Memoirs of the American
Folklore Society,* V (1897), 111, 133-134, 238.

Reichard, Gladys. *Navaho Religion.* 2 vols. Bollingen Series XVIII. New
York: Phantheon Books, 1950. II, 409.

Wheelwright, Mary. *Navajo Creation Myth.* Navajo Religion Series, Vol. I.
Santa Fe, N. Mex.: Museum of Navajo Ceremonial Art, 1942. Pp. 76-77,
152-153.

---

[1]There is another version available in Frances Gillmor and Louisa Wade Wetherill, *Traders to the Navajos* (Albuquerque; University of New Mexico Press, 1965 reprint), pp. 242-251. This
version was omitted from this study because of reservations about its source.

Wyman, Leland, and Bailey, Flora. "Navaho Girl's Puberty Rite," *New Mexico Anthropologist*, XXV, No. 1 (January-March, 1943), pp. 3-4.

B. Previously unavailable Kinaaldá myths.

1. **Alexander Leighton**, Field Notes for May 13, 1940. Files of the Laboratory of Anthropology, Santa Fe, New Mexico. (Informant: DS.)

    The beginning came about at *Hachinsib'dahi*; that means the place where the people first came on the earth. This is when my cousin says these Holy People started the Blessing Way sings. This is when these Holy People were trying to get the Blessing Way straightened out. At another place, they worked on all the different kinds of Ways and the songs. These include the Ghost Way, Holy Way, and every other Way. This Blessing Way is not only of one kind; one of the Blessing Ways is called *Hashjiltikehlohozozi* and the other one *Na'ye'ehozozi*. This *Naye'e* is used at the time when a man comes back from a war or goes to war. The same thing is done when girls and boys go away to start attending school. Another type of Blessing Way is the Eagle Way Blessing Way. They use that when they are catching eagles. That is all I heard about it. There is another one called *Naatahozozi*. That is used for a girl when she has the first bleed. That is supposed to be the right order for the girl. But they have mixed it all up there now.

2. **Dorothea Leighton**, Field Notes for March 4, 1940. Files of the Laboratory of Anthropology. Santa Fe, New Mexico. (Informant: TS.)

    My mother's mother, my grandmother, used to tell me the story of the puberty cake. *Yidlkad* is the name for this cake; it means, "it is sweetened." Some people say *yidlkadbijeeh*; that's the name for the whole cake. *Bijeeh* means the heart, the round part in the center. Grandmother says that the Navaho Indians started to make this a long time ago. I do not know how many years ago and she did not know either. The Holy People alone were on the earth at that time. They were just the same as human beings; they used to have men and women. My grandmother says that this woman's name was *Ascaa nadlehe*; this means "woman changing." The woman gets old and young; she is young one time and then she gets old. Then she comes back to being young again. One time Changing Woman was a girl about fourteen or fifteen years old. About that time, she had the first bleed. They had the moon then, it was just about that time. At the same time she was having the first bleed, the moon was in its first quarter. These Holy People decided what they were going to do about it. They said they were going to have a Sing for the girl. They cut up strips of great long buckskin to tie her hair. When they had tied her hair, they told her to run a race every morning. Supposing that we had a girl right here; we would tie her hair tonight; for three mornings she would have to run a race. For three nights she would not do anything; on the fourth night, they would have the Sing.

The first time this happened, it took place in a hogan. The hogan was made in the shape of a sweat bath, only bigger. *Aalchii'd eezah* means the three poles that lean against each other in this house. The rest of the women figured that they would grind white corn during this time. On the last day, they started to mix up the corn meal, just like you saw them do here the other day. My grandmother says it was just the same way. She says the fire had to be there just one night because the ground was dry. These people chose which one was to be the singer for that last night. They got that all straightened out and notified the man two days before the Sing. And they decided that instead of giving something to the singer like money, cattle, or horses, instead of that, the singer was to get the center piece of the cake. So that is what they call *yidlkad bijeeh*. They still do this, but sometimes they do not have any corn. Then they do not make a cake. Instead, they give the singer something worth about two dollars. They said that the singer does not have to get very much, just a little bit. The reason they have Kinaaldá is that they sure are interested that this girl had the bleed. So the last day, they poured this meal in the pit and covered it up, just the way we did here. The girl is not to take any corn pollen at the Sing, to eat any salt or any of the cake; she has to let all of these things alone.

Changing Woman was told she was to mind what the people told her. If she did, her teeth would last long. On the last night, after twelve, they started to sing over Changing Woman. In this kind of Sing, they do not bathe the patient, but they do wash her hair after the songs end in the morning. They sing all night what they call the First Song, the Hogan Songs. There are twelve of these songs. The singer sings those and then a few more besides. After that, he just turns it over to the people and everybody sings his own songs. Those include Horse songs and Sheep songs; just the good hope songs can be sung. In the morning, they turn the singing back to the singer and he finishes. The last songs will be the racing ones. Changing Woman ran the race four different times, first toward the east, then to the south, west, and north. After she had run four times, they cut up some of that cake and made the girl stand up back (west inside) in the hogan with a basket of that cake. Then they took her outside, just next to the door. These people piled up blankets, deerskins, and mountain lion skins and made her lie down on the top. One of the women shaped her; she shaped her legs, back, arms, and every place all over her body. Then Changing Woman had to get up and pass these things back to all of the people who owned them. Everybody there had put something in that pile.

That was the end of it. When she had the second menstruation, they had a Sing just like this again. The only difference between them is that white corn is used for the first and yellow corn for the second. Everything else is the same. My grandmother said that the Holy People did this first. They figured out a way so that the bleed would bring babies. So they sang over the first woman who had it. Those Holy People already knew what is going to happen in the future. They knew that the Navaho people were going to be the next people on the earth, that the earth was going to be turned over to the Navaho people. That has happened; the Navaho people were the next people to come on the earth; it has already been turned over to us.

My grandmother said that the basket they used was called *yoł-goicha* which means "white shell basket." She said that according to the old people, the Navaho did not have any baskets in those early days. They only had baskets of white shell, abalone, black shell, and blue shell, and they had to use those. The songs that they sang—the Horse, Sheep, Bead, and the other songs—tell about those things that the Navaho started growing. The Holy People said that Changing Woman was the only girl who had to run her race in the four directions. From then on, girls would only have to run to the east once.

They told us that the Holy People did Kinaaldá that way in that place, and we believe it. Therefore, we have Kinaaldá when a girl first has the bleed....

3. **Anne Keith**, Field Notes for July, 1963. The notes are in Anne Keith's possession. (Quoted from "The Origin Myth," as told by Informant AM.)

First Man and First Woman were praying so that they could have a lot of people. For four days it was foggy, and then on the fourth night they heard a baby crying on the top of a mountain. She was to be called *Esdzą́ą́nádleehé*. First Man went over there and brought the baby back.

The baby was lying on cedar branches that were specially fixed when he found her. The baby could only eat cedar food, and the cradle had to be made out of cedar. It took her four days to crawl and four days to stand. Everything that a baby learns, she learned in four days. After fifteen days, when she was about fifteen years old, she got her period. Then she did her Kinaaldá. First Man and First Woman said for her to do it, and they did the singing. She did everything that we do today, such as the running and making the corncake. At that time, instead of cornhusks, they used a different kind of plant to line the baking pit.

4. **David McAllester**, Field Notes for July 19-20, 1961. Files of the Department of Anthropology, Wesleyan University, Middletown, Connecticut. (Informant: FM.)

The *Hózhǫ́ǫ́jí* is the main ceremony. The Kinaaldá was originated by Changing Woman when she became of age. She said, "Hereafter, all Earth People will have to go according to this."
. . . .
According to our legend, when Changing Woman had her first period, they prepared her by using the dews of various plants. They put that into her body to enable her to produce offspring for the human race. On that account, today we believe that when a girl has her first period, there is nothing wrong with that. It is something sacred to us.
. . . .

Of course, the beginning of the Kinaaldá was with Changing Woman when she had her first menstruation. At that time, there were no
human beings on earth; it was just the supernatural people who congre-
gated there for that occasion. It was decided to do that from then on, in
order to revive the holiness of that time.... At the first Kinaaldá, they
sang, of course, all night until about daybreak. Then the singing was
terminated and the whole thing was turned back to the leader.
· ·

According to our story, "Changing Woman" is the name given to
her a long time after the name of "White Shell Woman." The first
"White Shell Woman" was Salt Woman who was on earth long before any
humans. After the one she had named White Shell Woman went to her
home in the west, two small children were kidnaped and taken there supernaturally. When they arrived, White Shell Woman was old and feeble;
she could barely get up. While they watched, she slowly moved to the
east and back, then to the south and back, and the west and back. By the
time she had completed a circle and returned from the north, she was
a young woman again. She told the two children how things were created and put on the earth for the use of human beings. When the children
returned and told of their experience, the name of Changing Woman was
adopted for this woman. That is why the songs usually mention White
Shell Woman first.

5. **Charlotte Johnson**, Field Notes for August 20, 1964. Files of the Department of Anthropology, Wesleyan University, Middletown, Connecticut, and in the author's possession. (Informant: FM.)

Changing Woman was created to bring good life to the people on
the earth. There was nothing bad or wicked about her. She caused all the
Holy People who were here to help the Earth People.

The Kinaaldá ceremony, which comes from the Blessing Way,
originated for Changing Woman, but her ceremony was not like a real
Kinaaldá today. The ceremony with the *biji* was just to be done for the
human race so that girls would have their first and second periods, and so
they could have children. Changing Woman never really had that period;
she just imitated it. She just was there to represent the present day Kinaaldá.

This is what happened at the ceremony of Changing Woman. She
was given clothes and various jewels for her garments. Of course, she already had these things from the time when she had been picked up by Talking God and brought home. It is not known what she did with those things
during the night. Today they dress the girl that way because it was done
for Changing Woman. The things they use do not always belong to the
girl or her family. They can be borrowed from neighbors and other people. The girl wears these things so she will acquire wealth.

When this was done, she was molded by Salt Woman. Monster
Slayer was also rebuilt that way, but Changing Woman was the first to be

molded. Now, anyone can do that molding for the girl; they do not get a special name for this.

After she was molded, Changing Woman ran for the first time just a short distance from the hogan. She ran for four days, each time stretching the distance further than before. She was the first one to run. The Racing Songs were not started then. They had been sung when Changing Woman ran races in the early morning when she was growing up. Changing Woman instructed the two boys she kidnaped to the west that hereafter the people were to use those Racing Songs just for the running of the Kinaaldá.

No corncake was baked, no *biji̱* was held, and no Twelve Word Song or Dawn Songs were sung for her ceremony. All these things were started by the two boys after they had been instructed in the west concerning the ceremonies to be done on earth.

Holy People gathered on the fourth day and contributed songs belonging to them. They did not sing them in the manner we are doing it now. The *biji̱* did not start until Changing Woman gave the two boys the rules about the ceremonies to be done on the earth. It was probably night when the singing was done, but of course we do not know how they figured night and day at that time. What they classed as night may have been the winter months, and day, the summer months. I do not know which of the Holy People were there at that time besides Talking God. The only songs that I am certain were used were the twelve Hogan Songs of Talking God. These blessed the hogan. The Vegetation People were also there; because of this we now have the corncake baked in the pit.

I am not sure if Changing Woman's hair was brushed or if her face was painted on the last morning. If these things happened, Salt Woman was in charge of them.

I have told you what I was taught about the ceremony. I am not going to tell anything that I did not learn from my instructor.

6. **Charlotte Johnson**, Field Notes for August 10, 1964. Files of the Department of Anthropology, Wesleyan University, Middletown, Connecticut, and in the author's possession. (Informant: TM.)

    The Kinaaldá was first given for Changing Woman. She had two ceremonies; these were to help with the production of future generations. The Chief Hogan songs were used for the first ceremony and those of Talking God for the second Kinaaldá. Both sets of songs helped bless the hogan where the ceremony was taking place. Regarding the original Hogan songs, those were created at the rim of the Emergence Place. There is no connection between their creation and Changing Woman's periods. The Talking God Hogan Songs are recent, later than the original. There are fourteen songs in the Chief Hogan Song set and twelve in Talking God's group.

    Songs were used for everything that happened, such as when they dressed her up, molded her, and when she raced on the first day. It is hard to say just how many songs there were. I think about ten were used there for brushing her hair. When I do it today, of course I do not use all these songs; I just pick some from the group.

When she ran on that first day, they used several songs. The main word in the first one was *sidits'ą́ą́'*, "the sound is going off." The next one is *'asolts'ą́ą́'*, "the sound is traveling along"; then, *naselts'ą́ą́'*, "the sound has reached its furthest distance." Then, *nasists'ą́ą́'*, "the sound is returning"; *daselts'ą́ą́'*, "the sound is right next door"; and finally, *naselts'ą́ą́'*, "the sound has returned."

During the fourth night, everyone contributed songs. The leader took over again in the morning to do the Dawn Songs while her hair was being washed. When she started to run again, they used songs that were different from those used for the race on the first morning.

The songs for the last morning race are songs that pertain to the *Haskiin deskahí* and *Ádéstíní*. The *Haskiin deskahí bighiin* and *Ádéstíní bighiin* are used for her morning race on the last morning. They come from the story of the two heroes. These heroes were sent to invite medicine men to the first Corral Dance that was ever held. One went to the White Mountain Apache; the other went to the Jicarilla Apache. They both came back. The one that went to the Jicarilla brought back a roasted corn ear. The other brought back a yucca fruit to show that he had been to the White Mountain Apache. While they were gone, their grandmother sang these songs. These songs were used because they were fleet-footed; they had been practicing for a long time. I do not know how many songs their grandmother sang for them.

That is all that I can tell you about these various things. I appreciate your asking about these things because I know that this will be preserved for generations to come. Even after you die of old age, it will still be in use.

The Frank Mitchell Family

As of 1964

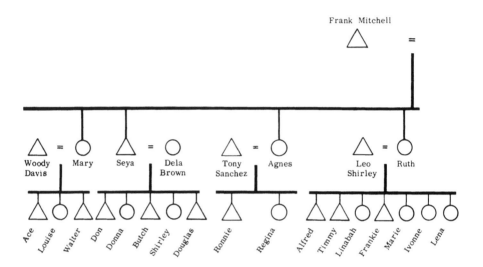

Ages are shown from left to right, with the oldest child at the left.

Rose Delaghoshi

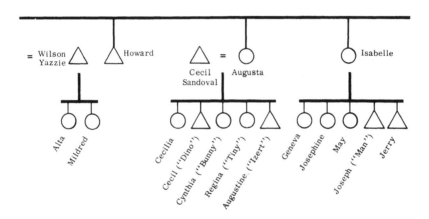

Navaho Terminology
Used in Kinaaldá

THE words below have been collected from the following sources:

Bailey, Flora. "Navaho Foods and Cooking Methods," *American Anthropologist*, N.S., XLII, No. 2, Part 1 (April-June, 1940), pp. 274, 281.
———. Field Notes for 1938 (on file at the Laboratory of Anthropology in Santa Fe, New Mexico).

Curtis, Edward. *The North American Indian*. Vol. I. *Apache, Jicarillas, Navaho*. Cambridge, Mass.: The University Press, 1907. P. 124.

Franciscan Fathers. *An Ethnologic Dictionary of the Navaho Language*. St. Michaels, Ariz.: St. Michaels Press, 1910. P. 412.

Gifford, Edward. "Apache-Pueblo," *University of California Anthropological Records*, IV, No. 1, Culture Element Distributions: XII (1940), pp. 161-163.

Johnson, Charlotte. Field Notes for summers of 1963 and 1964 (on file at the Department of Anthropology, Wesleyan University, Middletown, Connecticut).

Keith, Anne. Field Notes for the summer, 1963 (in Anne Keith's possession).

Kluckhohn, Clyde. Field Notes for 1937 and 1941 (on file at the Laboratory of Anthropology in Santa Fe, New Mexico).

Leighton, Alexander. Field Notes for May 13, 1940. Informant: DS. (The notes are on file at the Laboratory of Anthropology in Santa Fe, New Mexico.)

Leighton, Dorothea. Field Notes for March 4, 1940. Informant: TS. (The notes are on file at the Laboratory of Anthropology in Santa Fe, New Mexico.)

Leighton, Dorothea and Alexander. Field Notes for February 2-3, 1940 (on file at the Laboratory of Anthropology in Santa Fe, New Mexico.)

McAllester, David. Field Notes for July 19-20, 1961 (on file in the Department of Anthropology, Wesleyan University, Middletown, Connecticut).

Rapoport, Robert. Autobiography of Kay Chee Martin, 1948 (on file at the Laboratory of Anthropology in Santa Fe, New Mexico).

Reichard, Gladys. *Social Life of the Navajo Indians.* Columbia University Contributions to Anthropology, VII. New York: Columbia University Press, 1928. P. 138.

Wyman, Leland, and **Bailey, Flora.** "Navaho Girl's Puberty Rite," *New Mexico Anthropologist*, XXV, No. 1. (January-March 1943), pp. 3-12.

The Navaho word, its English meaning, and the source of its definition (including the informant, when possible) will be given for each term. When the word "general" is used instead of a specific source, the term may be considered to be well known to Navaho scholars and frequent in most of the literature available for Navaho studies.

'aadii cósi—small bleeding. Wyman and Bailey.

'aalchii'd eezah—the three poles which lean against each other in the construction of the original type of hogan. (TS.) D. Leighton.

'aalkaan—puberty cake. Bailey (1940).

'ałką́ą́ k'e hahógyééd—dig it out; earth over. (FM.) McAllester.

'ałkąął—corncake. (FM.) McAllester.

'alkaan—corncake. (FM.) Johnson.

'Alkena 'asli bighiin—Corn Songs. (FM.) McAllester.

'Anłt'ánii bighiin—Corn Beetle Songs. (FM.) Johnson.

'Asdzą́ą́ bighiin—Women's Songs. (FM.) Johnson.

'Asdzą́ą́ nidii yáalgii—Songs of the Picking Up of Changing Woman. (FM.) Johnson.

'ashi bizhi—salt voice. Kluckhohn (1941).

'ask'as—straightening of the limbs. Franciscan Fathers.

'atsi be'etł'oh—hair tied up in a pony tail. (FM.) McAllester.

Bee'echííh—Red Ocher Song. (FM.) Johnson.

Bee'edleesh—White Clay Song. (FM.) Johnson.

béé'ejhó—grass brush. Bailey (1941).

béé'ézhó—brush. (FM.) Johnson.

bee'iłchin da'yaa'igi—Songs Pertaining to the Pairs. (FM.) Johnson.

beeldléé—blanket. (FM.) Johnson.

Be'eshde'elné—fixing something up; Soft Goods Songs. Wyman and Bailey.

belagáana—American, non-Navaho, white person. General.

bigagiswu—subsequent menses. Gifford.

bijeeh—heart; round part of the center of the cake. (TS.) D. Leighton.

bijį—special day; day of the all-night singing. (FM.) Johnson.

chííh—red ocher. General.

chííh dokǫ́ǫ́zh—red, salty substance. Keith.

chiih dókǫǫzh—sour red-ocher medicine. Wyman and Bailey.
ch'il dahtoo'—plant dew; menstrual blood. (FM.) McAllester.
Ch'óol'į'í—Gobernador Knob, New Mexico. General.
cih dokoz—mixture of red clay, etc. Kluckhohn (1941). (See Haile: *University of Chicago Publications in Anthropology*, 1943, p. 39.)
cooghiin—menstrual blood; arthritis. Wyman and Bailey.

Dá'ák'ehjigishí—"Where one gazes on a cornfield" (Name of a cornfield belonging to Changing Woman). (FM.) Johnson.
daascah—I am sick (term for menstruation). Wyman and Bailey.
Dibéńtsah—La Plata Mountains, Colorado. General.
diné—the People; the Navahos' name for themselves. General.
dinésą—green wheat. Bailey (1940).
dleesh—white clay. General.
Dleesh bighiin—Song for clay application. Wyman and Bailey.
dok'aak'éé'éh—unwounded buckskin. (CS.) Johnson.
dókózhii—chamiso. Bailey.
doobahacidi—"something is in my way" (term for menstruation). Wyman and Bailey.
Dook'o'ostííd—San Francisco Peak, Arizona. General.
dóghózhii—greasewood. (FM.) Johnson
dsiłgacda—"He stays awake all night" (Name for the singer in Kinaaldá). Reichard.

'ádístsiin—stirring sticks. (FM.) Johnson.
'éédésciin—corn-stirring sticks, made of chamiso. Bailey.
'Esdzą́ą́nádleehé—Changing Woman. General.

Haashch'éhooghan—Hogan God (Some feel the term cannot be translated). General.
Hachinsib'dahi—Place where the first people first came upon the earth. (DS.) A. Leighton.
Hashtł'ishni—Mud Clan. General.
Hastl'elt biyiin—Mountain Songs. Bailey (1938).
hooghan ("hogan" in English)—house, dwelling place. General.
Hooghan bighiin—Hogan Songs. General.
Hózhǫ́ǫ́ji—Blessing Way. General.

'ida'īsts'ód—pressing the limbs. Franciscan Fathers.

Jaadesin—Running Songs. (FM.) McAllester.
Jááh deesin—Legs Song. Wyman and Bailey.
Jaashzhini—Black ears, ghouls. (FM.; CS.) Johnson.
       These people, those building the fires at Squaw Dances, and the fire dancers who carry torches in the Mountain Chant cannot come near the fire pit or help with the digging. If they do, the cake may not cook; it may stay all mushy (CS).

Jaashzhini, the fire-eaters, and the clown of the *Yeibichai* dance are forbidden to dig that hole. They are considered to be people who go wild all the time and who do not observe rules (FM).

Jaashzhini, the fire dancers, and the corral dancers cannot be around the cooking fire when cornmeal cakes are being cooked. They can treat children's burns by chewing and spitting a mixture of coals onto the burns.

I do not know much about *jaashzhini* in connection with not digging the *'alkaan* pit at a Kinaaldá. I don't think the word really means "black ears"; I think it means something more like "ghouls." There is a myth of a woman bringing seven boys to where Monster Slayer was. He chased them and then reconsidered when the woman warned him to do so. The boys got into a cornfield and stole some corn. They were always doing something foolish. These seven are the seven Pleiades (CS).

k'ad ni—it is finished; that's all; I'm finished. (FM.) Johnson

k'eet'ą́ą́ń—prayer sticks. General.

kehasdon—straight, level. (WY.) Johnson.

kenasta—first menses. Gifford.

Kiiya'áani—Tall House Clan. General.

kin—house. General.

Kinaaldá—first menses. (FM.) McAllester.

Kinaaldá bé'ézhóó'igíí bighiin—Songs for hair-brushing. (FM.) McAllester.

Kinaaldá beidleesh—Songs for applying clay. (FM.) McAllester.

Kinalda biki biiji—a sing over a girl who has just started to bleed. A. Leighton and D. Leighton.

kinalta—first blood. Rapoport.

kinsista—I have done my period. Keith.

kin ya shidáh—Navaho form of what originally was *sidá*, sitting alone. (CS.) Johnson.

Lajisin—One Day Song. (FM.) Johnson.

Łii bighiin—Horse Songs. (FM.) Johnson.

Naaghéé neezghání—Monster Slayer. General.

naakits'áada doo'igíí—Twelve Word Song. Johnson.

naałdá—to sit. General.

Naalyéhí bighiin—Soft Goods Song; Wyman and Bailey. Songs for dressing up the Girl. Bailey (1938).

na'e'dołisi—special woman; one who presses with the foot. (FM.) McAllester.

na'é'el'es—to mold a body; to press with the feet. (FM.) McAllester.

náneeskaadí—tortilla-type Navaho bread. General.

nashditso—mountain lion. (CS.) Johnson.

Nasilá—source for sacred clay. (FM.) McAllester.

násolsįį—the sound is returning. (FM.) Johnson.

Nat'aa hooghan bighiin—the Chief Hogan Songs. (FM.) McAllester.

natsíltsą—the sound has returned to its starting point. (FM.) Johnson.

Nohosdzáán bighiin—Placing the Earth Song. (FM.) Johnson. Also: Songs concerning Planting Things on Earth and the Soul of the Pairs.

ntł'izh bidahtoo'—jewels, their dew; male jewels; part of conception; semen. (FM.) McAllester.

ntł'iz iltas'éi—all kinds of hard goods; a collective term for jewel stones. General.

Są̨'ą naghei bighiin—Songs of Old Age. (FM.) Johnson.

sidá—sitting alone. (CS from E. Sapir.) McAllester.

sideskla—the race before sunrise. Gifford.

sis lá chii—the Kinaaldá sash. (FM.) Johnson.

Sisnaajini—Blanca Peak, Colorado. General.

tádídíín—corn pollen. General.

tanááníil—cake batter. Wyman and Bailey.

Tó'áháni—Short Distance to Water Clan. General.

Tó bájíshchíní—Born for Water. General.

Tó dichiini—Bitter Water Clan. General.

tsê bee názhó—grindstone broom; "rock with brush." (FM.) McAllester.

tsê daashjéé—metate. General.

tsê daashjiń—mano. General.

tsiklólh—deerskin strings. Curtis.

Tsódził—Mount Taylor, New Mexico. General.

txá bastiin—otter skin. (CS.) Johnson.

yidlkad—"it is sweetened" (Name for the cake). (TS.) D. Leighton.

yidlkadbijeeh—a name for the whole cake. (TS.) D. Leighton.

yiilkaad bijeeh—cake's lungs. Wyman and Bailey.

Yikai yiin—Dawn Songs. (FM.) McAllester.

Yikai yischį yisin—Birth of Dawn Songs. (FM.) Johnson.

yilkąąd—the Kinaaldá cake. Kluckhohn (1937).

yódi'iltas'ei—all kinds of soft goods; a collective term for fabrics. General.

yołgoicha—white shell basket. (TS.) D. Leighton.

Yołkááł bighiin—Dawn Songs. (FM.) Johnson.

APPENDIX E

Recipe for 'Alkaan:

Priscilla Becenti,[1] Crownpoint

TO one-half pail of boiling water, add six handfuls of corn flour. Stir this with corn-stirring sticks. Then add one cup of sprouted wheat flour and continue stirring. This wheat is *dinésá*—green wheat which has been placed in a sack and put underground to sprout, then dried and ground on a metate. Remove the mush or batter from the fire and cool it for ten or fifteen minutes. Then rub and squeeze it between the palms, as if you were washing your hands. Continue doing this until all the lumps are removed. It will take about thirty minutes. Then add as many raisins as desired.

Moisten dry cornhusks and make half-inch tears in the ends in five or six places. Make a cross of husks—two on the bottom and one on the top, pinning the pieces firmly in place with a short piece of grass broom-straw. Join the tips of the east and south arms of the cross with two more husks. In the same way, close the other three quadrants, working sunwise. Add other husks to make a mat.

Rake the coals of the pit in which the fire has been burning for about a day. The pit should be about eighteen by six inches. Brush the bottom with juniper branches and place the cornhusk mat on it. Lay more husks around the sides, tucking these under the mat.

Pour the mush into the pit and smooth it out. Sprinkle cornmeal on the surface from the east to the west, south to the north, and all round, moving sunwise. Meal is always sprinkled on this kind of cake "to make it holy." Cover the cake with cornhusks. Then add layers of dirt and hot coals and build a fire on the top. Bake the cake overnight.

In the morning, remove the dirt and ashes, using a juniper branch and grass broom. The first piece should be cut from the center and di-

---

[1]Bicenti (mimeographed), n.d. Crown Point School, Arizona.

vided into four parts. Sometimes, though, it is cut from the northwest corner. When the cake is hot, it is quite mushy; when it cools, it hardens.
When this cake is made for the Kinaaldá, there must be at least four large
pieces, one for the main singer and the others who helped with the songs.
Guests also are given portions of the cake.

APPENDIX F

Points of Interest on the Navaho Reservation

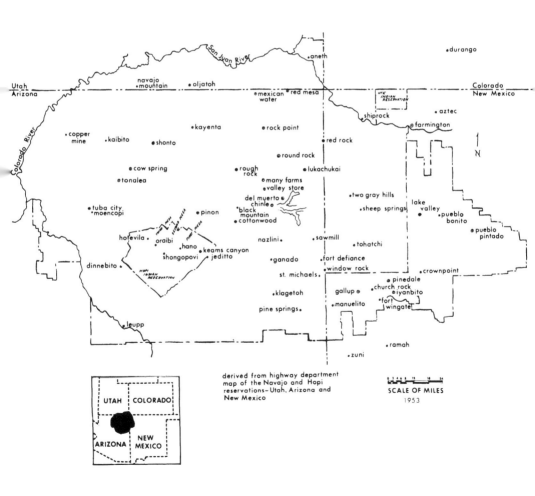

derived from highway department
map of the Navajo and Hopi
reservations—Utah, Arizona and
New Mexico

SCALE OF MILES
1953

APPENDIX G

Kinaaldá Material
in Mary Wheelwright's <u>Creation Chants</u>

Burden of the Song	Type of Song	Number
She moves	Unidentified	4[1]
She stands up	Unidentified	4
She stands	Unidentified	4
She dances	Unidentified	4
She jingles	Unidentified	4
Her ornaments push upon her again and again	Unidentified	4
She stands up with them	Unidentified	4
She has stopped moving	Unidentified	4
She runs out	Racing	*1[2]
She runs back	Racing	*1
They run out shouting	Racing	*1
They run back shouting	Racing	*1
They have smeared her with white clay	Painting—White Clay	*1
They have smeared her with old clay	Painting—White Clay(?)	*1
They have smeared her with red clay	Painting—Red Ocher	*1

---

[1]Songs in groups of four use the same texts, but move through different sacred jewels, which are always ordered: white shell, turquoise, abalone, and black jewels (jet).

The texts of the first two of four songs which have the burden "she moves" have been published; they appear on pp. 152-153 of Mary Wheelwright, *Navajo Creation Myth*, Navajo Religion Series, Vol. 1 (Santa Fe, N. Mex.: Museum of Navajo Ceremonial Art, 1942). Navaho and English texts of these and the other songs are on file at Wesleyan University in the Laboratory of Ethnomusicology.

[2]The * is used to mark songs which, being comparable to others presently available, are included in the discussions in this publication.

The music of the Racing Song which has the burden "She runs out" has been transcribed from the Wheelwright cylinders by Dr. George Herzog and is given on pp. 288-289.

Key to Symbols Used in

Transcriptions and Analyses

---

glissando (a slide in pitch from the tone of the first note to that of the second).

a glissando on the final tone of the song, in which the down-ward slide is done in a retarded manner, and the final tone, indicated by the point on the staff at which the double lines end, is held.

an upward glissando.

a slur.

grace notes.

a tone of indefinite pitch.

fermata.

staccato.

stress.

stressed stacatto.

a tremoloed tone; in Frank's songs only the slower, more emphasized tremolos are indicated, due to his tendency to tremolo consistently.

( )   part of the song sung in the original recording, but later de-
             signated as a "mistake" by the singer. FM wanted these
             "mistakes" removed from the tape altogether.

[ ]   part of the song omitted in the original recording, but later
             added by the singer as a correction which was necessary
             in order to make the original version "correct."

x introductory phrase.

a, b small phrases within verses.

a, a^1, a^2, a^3 closely related phrases.

$a/$ the "a" phrase approximately halved.

$a/1$ The "a" phrase approximately halved and slightly varied.

$a^{1/3}$ approximately one-third of the original "a" phrase.

a^+ the "a" phrase extended.

   an illustration of the tonal system of a particu-
             lar song. The metrical values assigned to
             the tones indicate their relative frequency
             of usage; the horizontal brackets show the
             intervals of skips.

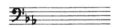   the key signatures of many of these songs do
             not resemble those found in Western Euro-
             pean music. While Navaho songs do have a
             tonality, they are not sung in any "key" in
             our sense; hence, the signatures contain
             only those accidentals which are used in
             each song.

All the transcriptions are done at the original pitch.

Bibliography

Astrov, Margot. "The Concept of Motion as the Psychological Leitmotif of Navaho Life and Literature," *Journal of American Folklore*, LXIII,No. 247 (January-March, 1950), pp. 45-56.

Bailey, Flora. Field Notes for 1938 (on file at the Laboratory of Anthropology in Santa Fe, New Mexico).

———. "Navaho Foods and Cooking Methods," *American Anthropologist*, N.S. XLII, No. 2, Part I (April–June, 1940), pp. 270-290.

———. "Some Sex Beliefs and Practices in a Navaho Community," *Papers of the Peabody Museum of American Archaeology and Ethnology, Harvard University*, Vol. XL, No. 2 (Reports of the Ramah Project, Report No. 2). Cambridge, Mass.: Peabody Museum, 1950.

Brown, Anne. "The Navaho Girls' Puberty Ceremony: Function and Meaning for the Adolescent." Unpublished senior honors thesis for the Harvard-Radcliffe Department of Social Relations, 1964.

Brown, Judith. "A Cross-Cultural Study of Female Initiation Rites," *American Anthropologist*, LXV, No. 4 (August, 1963), pp. 837-853.

Cancian, Francis. "A Photo-Ethnography of the White Mountain Apaches." Unpublished thesis for a Bachelor of Arts Degree with Distinction in Anthropology, Wesleyan University, Middletown, Connecticut. 1956.

Chappat, Janine. Field Notes for 1945 and 1946 (on file at the Laboratory of Anthropology in Santa Fe, New Mexico).

Charles, Lucile. "Growing Up Through Drama," *Journal of American Folklore*, LIX, No. 233 (July-September, 1946), pp. 247-262.

Coolidge, Dane and **Mary.** *The Navajo Indians*. New York: Houghton, Mifflin, 1930.

Curtis, Edward. *The North American Indian*. Vol. I. *Apache, Jicarillas, Navaho*. Cambridge, Mass.: The University Press, 1907.

Curtis, Natalie. *The Indians' Book*. New York: Harper, 1907.

Driver, Harold. "Girls' Puberty Rites in Western North America," *Uni-*

versity of California Anthropological Records, VI, No. 2, Culture Element Distributions: XVI (1941), pp. 21-90.

Dyk, Walter. *Son of Old Man Hat*. New York: Harcourt, Brace, 1938.

Elson, Louis. *Elson's Pocket Music Dictionary*. Philadelphia, Penna.: Oliver Ditson, 1909.

Franciscan Fathers. *An Ethnologic Dictionary of the Navaho Language*. St. Michaels, Ariz.: St. Michaels Press, 1910.

Gifford, Edward. "Apache-Pueblo," *University of California Anthropological Records*, IV, No. 1, Culture Element Distributions: XII (1940), pp. 1-207.

Gillmor, Frances, and Wetherill, Louisa Wade. *Traders to the Navajos*. Albuquerque: University of New Mexico Press, 1953. (Reprint edition, 1965).

Goddard, Pliny. "Navaho Texts," *Anthropological Papers of the American Museum of Natural History*, XXXIV, Part I (1933).

Grove's Dictionary of Music and Musicians, H. C. Colles, ed. Third Edtion. New York: Macmillan, 1927.

Haile, Father Berard. "Blessingway" Versions I, II, and III, with introductions, notes, appendices, and supplementary songs; MSS, Special Collections Division, University of Arizona Library, Tucson, Arizona. (To be published 1967, by the University of Arizona Press with introduction and notes by Leland C. Wyman.)

———. "Creation and Emergence Myth of the Navajo" (MS on file at the Museum of Navajo Ceremonial Art, Santa Fe, New Mexico).

———. "Origin Legend of the Navaho Enemy Way," *Yale University Publications in Anthropology*, XVII (1938).

———. "Origin Legend of the Navaho Flintway," *University of Chicago Publications in Anthropology*. Linguistic Series. Chicago: University of Chicago Press, 1943.

———. *A Stem Vocabulary of the Navaho Language*. Vol. I: *Navaho-English*. Vol. II: *English-Navaho*. St. Michaels, Ariz.: St. Michaels Press, 1950, 1951.

Herzog, George. Transcription of Kinaaldá Racing Song from Wheelwright cylinders (on file at the Museum of Navajo Ceremonial Art in Santa Fe, New Mexico).

Hill, W. W. "The Agricultural and Hunting Methods of the Navaho Indians," *Yale University Publications in Anthropology*, XVIII (1938).

———. Field Notes, Quoted by Wyman and Bailey (see their entry below).

Johnson, Charlotte. Field Notes for the summers of 1963 and 1964 (on file at the Department of Anthropology, Wesleyan University, Middletown, Connecticut).

———. Field Tapes of Kinaaldá music collected in 1963 and 1964 (copies of all tapes are on file at the Laboratory of Ethnomusicology, Wesleyan University, Middletown, Connecticut, and at The Fine Arts Library, University of New Mexico, Albuquerque, N.M.)

———. Kodak colored slides of Kinaaldá held during the summer of 1963 (in the author's possession).

———. "Navaho Corn Grinding Songs," *Journal of the Society for Ethnomusicology*, VIII, No. 2 (May, 1964), pp. 101-120.

———. "Talking God's Hogan Songs," MS, 1963 (on file at the Laboratory of Ethnomusicology at Wesleyan University in Middletown, Connecticut).

Keith, Anne (Brown). Field Notes for the summer of 1963 (in Anne Keith's possession).

———. Field Tapes from final night's singing at a Kinaaldá in Pinedale (a copy of these tapes is on file at the Laboratory of Ethnomusicology at Wesleyan University in Middletown, Connecticut).

———. "The Navajo Girls' Puberty Ceremony: Function and Meaning for the Adolescent," *El Palacio*, Vol. 71/1. (Spring, 1964), pp. 27-36.

———. Personal communication.

———. Taped Interviews for July, 1963 (in Anne Keith's possession).

Kluckhohn, Clyde. Field Notes for 1936, 1937, 1940, 1941, 1942, and 1947 (on file at the Laboratory of Anthropology in Santa Fe, New Mexico).

———. "Navaho Women's Knowledge of Their Song Ceremonials," **Richard Kluckhohn** (ed.), *Culture and Behavior. The Collected Essays of Clyde Kluckhohn*. New York: The Free Press of Glencoe, 1962, pp. 92-96.

Kluckhohn, Clyde, and Leighton, Dorothea. *The Navaho*. Cambridge, Mass.: Harvard University Press, 1948.

Kluckhohn, Clyde, and Wyman, Leland. "An Introduction to Navaho Chant Practice," *Memoirs of the American Anthropological Association*, LIII (1940).

Kluckhohn, Richard (ed.). *Culture and Behavior. The Collected Essays of Clyde Kluckhohn*. New York: The Free Press of Glencoe, 1962.

Ladd, John. *The Structure of a Moral Code*. Cambridge, Mass.: Harvard University Press, 1957.

Leighton, Alexander. Field Notes for May 13, 1940 (on file at the Laboratory of Anthropology in Santa Fe, New Mexico).

Leighton, Dorothea. Field Notes for March 4, 1940 (on file at the Laboratory of Anthropology in Santa Fe, New Mexico).

Leighton, Dorothea, and Kluckhohn, Clyde. *Children of the People*. Cambridge, Mass.: Harvard University Press, 1947.

Leighton, Dorothea and Alexander. Field Notes for 1940, April 1, 1940, April 6, 1940 and May 13, 1940 (on file at the Laboratory of Anthropology in Santa Fe, New Mexico).

———. "Psychotherapy and Navaho Religion," *Psychiatry*, IV, No. 4 (November, 1941), pp. 515-523.

———. *The Navaho Door*. Cambridge, Mass.: Harvard University Press, 1944.

Lord, Albert. *The Singer of Tales*. Harvard Studies in Comparative Literature, No. 24. Cambridge, Mass.: Harvard University Press, 1960.

Matthews, Washington. "Navaho Legends," *Memoirs of the American Folklore Society*, V (1897).

————. "The Night Chant, a Navaho Ceremony," *Memoirs of the American Museum of Natural History*, VI (May, 1902).

————. "Songs of Sequence of the Navajos," *Journal of American Folklore*, VII, No. 26 (July–September, 1894), pp. 185–194.

McAllester, David. "Enemy Way Music," *Papers of the Peabody Museum of American Archaeology and Ethnology, Harvard University*, Vol. XLI, No. 3 (1954).

————. Field Notes for July 19–20, 1961 (on file in the Department of Anthropology, Wesleyan University, Middletown, Connecticut).

————. Field Tapes of Blessing Way as sung by Frank Mitchell and Gray Eyes in 1957 (on file in the Laboratory of Ethnomusicology, Wesleyan University, Middletown, Connecticut).

————. "The Form of Navajo Ceremonial Music," In Mary Wheelwright, *Texts of the Navajo Creation Chants*. Cambridge, Mass.: Peabody Museum of Harvard University, n.d., pp. 35–38.

————. Personal communication.

McCombe, L., Vogt, E., and Kluckhohn, C. *Navaho Means People*. Cambridge, Mass.: Harvard University Press, 1951.

Mills, George. *Navaho Art and Culture*. Colorado Springs, Colo.: The Taylor Museum, 1959.

Newcomb, Franc, and Reichard, Gladys. *Sandpaintings of the Navajo Shooting Chant*. New York: J. J. Augustin, Inc., 1937.

Opler, Morris. *An Apache Life Way*. Chicago, Ill.: University of Chicago Press, 1941.

Rapoport, Robert. "Autobiography of Kay Chee Martin," 1948. Unpublished field notes (on file at the Laboratory of Anthropology, Santa Fe, New Mexico).

Reichard, Gladys. *Dezba: Woman of the Desert*. New York: J. J. Augustin Inc., 1939.

————. *Navaho Religion*. 2 Vols. Bollingen Series XVIII. New York: Pantheon Books, 1950.

————. *Prayer: The Compulsive Word*. Monographs of the American Ethnological Society, VII. New York: J. J. Augustin Inc., 1944.

————. *Social Life of the Navajo Indians*. Columbia University Contributions to Anthropology, VII. New York: Columbia University Press, 1928.

————. *Spider Woman*. New York: Macmillan, 1934.

Richards, Audrey. *Chisungu*. New York: Grove Press, 1956; London: Faber and Faber, 1956.

Sapir, Edward, and Hoijer, Harry. *Navaho Texts*. Iowa City: Linguistic Society of America, 1942.

Underhill, Ruth. *Here Come the Navaho!* Lawrence, Kans.: Haskell Institute, 1953.

————. *The Navajos*. Norman, Okla.: University of Oklahoma Press, 1956.

————. *Red Man's America*. Chicago, Ill:: University of Chicago Press, 1953.

Villaseñor, David. *Tapestries in Sand.* Healdsburgh, Calif.: Naturegraph Company, 1963.

Vogt, Evon. Field Notes for August 7, 1947 (on file at the Laboratory of Anthropology, Santa Fe, New Mexico).

Wall, Leon, and **Morgan, William.** *Navajo-English Dictionary.* Window Rock, Ariz.: Navajo Agency, 1958.

Webster's Collegiate Dictionary. Fifth Edition. Springfield, Mass.: G. and C. Merriam Co., Publishers, 1937.

Wheelwright, Mary. Navaho and English Texts to the Songs of the Creation Chants (MS on file at the Laboratory of Ethnomusicology, Wesleyan University, Middletown, Connecticut). Some of these texts have been published in Wheelwright's *Navajo Creation Myth* and *Texts of the Navajo Creation Chants*.

———. *Navajo Creation Myth.* Navajo Religion Series, Vol. I. Santa Fe, N. Mex.: Museum of Navajo Ceremonial Art, 1942.

———. *Texts of the Navajo Creation Chants.* Cambridge, Mass.: Peabody Museum of Harvard University, n.d.

Wyman, Leland, and **Bailey, Flora.** "Navaho Girl's Puberty Rite," *New Mexico Anthropologist,* XXV, No. 1 (January-March, 1943), pp. 3-12.

Wyman, Leland, and **Kluckhohn, Clyde.** "Navaho Classification of Their Song Ceremonials," *Memoirs of the American Anthropological Association,* Vol. L (1938).

Young, Robert. "The Navaho Language," *The Navaho Yearbook,* Report VI, Fiscal Year 1957. Window Rock, Ariz.: Navajo Agency, 1957, pp. 153-184.

———. *The Navaho Yearbook.* Nos. VI, VII, VIII. Window Rock, Ariz.: Navaho Agency, 1957, 1958, 1961.

Young, Robert, and **Morgan, William.** *The Navaho Language.* Salt Lake City, Utah: Deseret Book Company, 1958.

Index